Dedication......*to my fabulous sisters, Angela and Rosemary,
who are always there for me.*

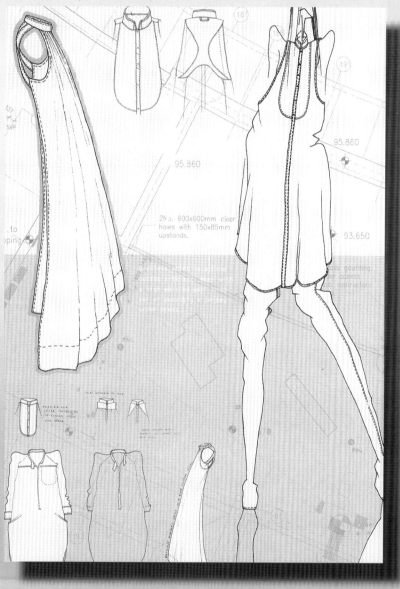

Above: Design Development by Fashion Designer Entrepreneur Jessica Whitehead

Opposite: Fashion Design Entrepreneur: Hannah Marshall

Photographer: Victor de Mello

content

FASHION ENTREPRENEUR
Starting your own fashion business

SANDRA BURKE

www.burkepublishing.com, www.fashionbooks.info

Fashion Entrepreneur - Starting Your Own Fashion Business

Burke, Sandra

ISBN (10): 0-9582 733-0-8

ISBN (13): 978-0-9582733-0-5

First Published: 2008

Copyright ©:   Burke Publishing

Email: sandra@burkepublishing.com

Website: www.fashionbooks.info

Website: www.burkepublishing.com

Distributors: **UK:** Marston Book Services Limited, email: trade.orders@marston.co.uk

USA: Partners Book Distributing, email: saraspeigel@partners-east.com

South Africa: Blue Weaver Marketing, email: orders@blueweaver.co.za

Australia: Thames and Hudson, email: orders@thaust.com.au

Hong Kong: Publishers Associates Ltd (PAL), email: pal@netvigator.com

DTP: Sandra Burke
Cover: Simon Larkin
Back Image: Hannah Marshall and Victor de Mello
Printed: Everbest, China

Production Notes: Pages Size: 210x297mm (A4)

ISBN (10): 0-9582 733-0-8
ISBN (13): 978-0-9582733-0-5

Authors Note

During my lecture tours to universities around the world, I am constantly impressed by the number of students I meet who are bursting with innovative ideas and creative designs, and eager to start their own fashion businesses. But, the questions are, *'Can they translate these creative designs into marketable products?'* and, further, *'How can they sell their products?'*

To bridge the gap between design fantasy and commercial reality, they need entrepreneurial vision to identify opportunities and small business management skills to develop, plan and control their businesses.

It is encouraging to see that there are an increasing number of fashion schools and universities starting to offer modules and papers in fashion enterprise which outline the basic business skills - how to produce a business plan and how to start a business.

Fashion Entrepreneur - *Starting Your Own Fashion Business* aims to support these courses with the theory and practical application of fashion entrepreneurship and small business management, together with case studies of successful fashion entrepreneurs. As a text book and self-learning guide, this book progressively takes you through the key steps required to start and develop your own business.

The fashion and creative industries are challenging and competitive, so it is essential to be well equipped with a 'portfolio of entrepreneurial skills'. I hope this book will inspire you to develop your creative and innovative talents into marketable products, to develop a successful business and direct you on the 'fast track' to riches. You will need to be totally dedicated, believe in your own judgement, and have a great deal of chutzpah! I wish you every success in the world of fashion.

Sandra Burke
M.Des RCA
(Master of Design, Royal College of Art)

Emerging fashion design entrepreneurs often aspire to fashion innovators, such as, Vivienne Westwood, John Galliano and Julien Macdonald, with images of stunning models strutting down the catwalks at the London, Paris, Milan and New York fashion shows in the most amazing creations. But how do they bridge the gap between fantasy and reality and start their own business? **Fashion Entrepreneur** - Starting Your Own Fashion Business *will demystify the whole process.*

Foreword

Sandra Burke is the ideal person to write a book on fashion entrepreneurship. Her diverse background in the fashion industry along with her global contacts translate into someone who does indeed have her pulse on the various aspects of how to be a fashion entrepreneur.

Fashion students graduate today with stronger skills in design but often are forced to rely upon trial and error to learn how to gain business experience. Few design schools can find the time in their curriculum to teach their students how to be entrepreneurs.

The process of how to integrate their design ideas into today's marketplace is something that is often only learned by years of experience in the field. Our global economy today demands prospective entrepreneurs be more knowledgeable and flexible to meet the ever-changing demands of fashion. This book will help potential entrepreneurs gain that knowledge much more quickly and easily.

Professor Karen Scheetz, *is an* Assistant Chair in Fashion Design at FIT (Fashion Institute of Technology, New York). *She has been an educator for the past 15 years in Fashion Design. Prior to that she worked for diverse fashion clients doing design, fashion illustration and art direction. She has also taught at* Parsons School of Design *her 'alma mater'.*

Fashion Institute of Technology

Successful fashion businesses of the future will not just be those that produce the best fashion. The new capital in a progressively unstable global economy will be information, business acumen and innovation. These are fast becoming the key assets for those wishing to accomplish something of value in fashion design, manufacture and retail. Fashion professionals now need to anticipate the future needs of consumers, recognise new business opportunities, and create something new and of value as innovative responses to changing needs – **in short to embrace the spirit of entrepreneurship**.

The word entrepreneur has a wide variety of meanings and myths surrounding entrepreneurship still persist. Sandra Burke's book unpacks the myths to provide insights into a dynamic process that balances creativity with business skills, risk with opportunity and challenge with reward to make the notion of entrepreneurship accessible and achievable.

Drawing on a wealth of personal experience and a network of designers, creatives and entrepreneurs within the global fashion industry Sandra takes a down to earth approach presenting entrepreneurship as both a discipline that can be learnt and a way of thinking.

Sandra's understanding of working with creative people, her knowledge of the fashion industry and the necessary survival strategies for innovative businesses, means that **Fashion Entrepreneur** will be an invaluable tool for students, managers and for anyone who wants to be entrepreneurial.

Ursula Hudson, Director of Fashion Business Resource Studio, London College of Fashion. *Ursula has developed and established the studio concept, building it to become a recognised model of best practice for industry and education. She has also enjoyed a secondment to the British Council's Creative Industries unit, and led the curriculum development for the first Fashion Retail Academy London. Prior to this she was Course Director for BA Product Design and Development. Under her leadership the course won the Graduate Fashion Week Marketing award for 6 years running. Her international fashion-marketing specialist background includes strategic design and marketing consultancy for many of the leading fashion retail, sport and lifestyle global brands.*

University of the Arts London
London College of Fashion

Acknowledgements

The research for **Fashion Entrepreneur** - *Starting Your Own Fashion Business* has taken me to some of the most influential fashion companies and fashion schools around the world and further established the link between the fashion and textile industry and education.

I wish to thank all those who contributed to the content of this book. The sharing of ideas, encouragement and support from the fashion industry, lecturers, colleagues and friends from around the world has been absolutely incredible. I would never have been able to write this book without them. My sincere thanks to you all.

Fashion Industry

Abigail Bisogno, Managing Director Foschini, Cape Town

Ash, Sales/Creative Manager, Nike, London

Barry and Adel Laden, Laden, Brick Lane, London

Dave Edgar, Bureaux, London

Ellen Brookes, Abercrombie and Fitch, London

Ewa Liddington, Womenswear Buyer, Auckland

Frances Howie, Central Saint Martins (CSM) and Lanvin, Paris

Hannah Marshall, Fashion Designer, London

Laura, Manager, @work, Brick Lane, London

Lock Leong, Visual Merchandiser, New York

Maria Leeke, Womenswear Buyer, London

Melanie Casper, Munko, Kidswear Designer, Cape Town

Mike Scroope, Catalyst, International

Dan Pinch, Total Media, Nokia Fashion Week (NCTFW)

Peter Flowers, Director Foschini, Cape Town

Ricki and Aviva Wolman, Citron, Los Angeles

Sally Moinet, Fashion Designer, Cape Town

Sarah Beetson, IllustrationWeb, International

Tim Rathbone, Fashion Retail Consultant, London

Victor de Mello, Photographer, London

Universities and Fashion Schools

Alison Rapsey, Birmingham City University (BCU)

Andy Penaluna, Swansea Institute

Ann Marie Kirkbride, Cleveland College of Art and Design

Ann Muirhead, Coventry University

Bashir Aswat, University of Salford

Brian Ericksson, Linea Academy

Caroline Darke, Royal College of Art (RCA)

Christine Mee, Manchester Metropolitan University (MMU)

David Backhouse, University of Leeds

Eric Hagen, University of Technology Sydney (UTS)

Gill Rowe, Northumbria University

Jan Hamon, Dr., Auckland University of Technology (AUT)

Jane Mills, University College Northampton

Jane Sarkar, Birmingham City University (BCU)

John Dodgin, University of Plymouth Colleges Somerset

Jonathan Farmer, Academy of Arts University, San Francisco

John Hopkins, The Arts Institute at Bournemouth

Laura Krusemark, The Arts Institute of California San Diego

Lee Harding, Birmingham City University (BCU)

Lesley Ford, Thurrock and Basildon College

Lisa Mann, Southampton Solent University

Lucy Jones, University of East London (UEL)

Lyle Reilly, Auckland University of Technology (AUT

Lynnette Murphy, Central Saint Martins (CSM)

Pammi Sinha, Dr., University of Manchester (UMIST)

Paul Rider, Anglia Ruskin University

Samantha Lovell, Stafford College

Sandy Barnett, Tafe NSW, Sydney Ultimo

Simon Zakka, Sydney Institute

Tim Gunn, Parsons, New York

Val Jacobs, Colchester

Wendy Dagworthy, Royal College of Art (RCA)

Designers and Illustrators

Abdul Yusufu, Illustrator

Aina Hussain, Fashion Designer

Alissa Stytsenko, Creative Director/Textile/Fashion Designer

Amy Lappin, Fashion Designer

Aoife Ni Chofaigh, Fashion Designer and Accessories Designer

Avne Patel, Fashion Marketing and PR

Bob Shilling, Creative Director

Buddy Mendis, Illustrator

Camilla Ramirez, Fashion Designer, Manager Laden Showroom

Casey Rogers, Jewellery Designer

Cherona Blacksell, Fashion Designer

Chi Chi, Fashion Designer

Ella Tjader, Illustrator

Emily Crump, Fashion Designer

Eric Hagen, Fashion Illustrator

Frances Howie, Fashion Designer, Lanvin, Paris

Frances Shilling, Knitwear Designer

Gavin Rajah, Fashion Designer

Hannah Hoyle, Fashion Designer

Hannah Marshall, Fashion Designer

Jessica Haley, Fashion Illustrator

Jessica Whitehead, Fashion Designer

Joanne Hill, Marketing & PR Assistant

Justin Smith, Fashion Designer and Milliner

Katie Ruensumran, Fashion Designer

Kerry Hobbs, Fashion Design and Marketing

Klûk & CGdT, Malcolm Klûk, Fashion Designer

Klûk & CGdT, Christiaan Gabriel du Toit, Designer

Kyle Farmer, Fashion Illustrator

Lesley Ford, Fashion Stylist and Textile Designer

Lidwine Grosbois, Fashion Illustrator

Linda Logan, Fashion Designer

Lucy Laucht, Fashion Stylist and Illustrator

Lynnette Murphy, Fashion Illustrator, Fashion Designer

Maria Cardelli, Illustrator

Marlies Ball, Fashion Designer

Montana Forbes, Illustrator

Mr Wobbles, Super Model

Naomi Austin, Fashion Illustrator

Nicholas Huxley, Fashion Illustrator

Nigel Fairhead, Footwear Designer

Nikki Burns, Pink Nik, Fashion Designer

Poppy Beckwith, Fashion Designer

Rhonda Khulman, Jewellery Designer

Richard Thorner, Fashion Designer

Robert Stapleton, Graphic Designer

Samantha Payne, Fashion and Textiles Designer

Sarah Beetson, Illustrator

Satya James, Fashion Designer

Scott O'Byrne, Illustrator, Graphic Designer, Any Broken Nerd

Tina Fong, Fashion Designer

Yelena Smirnova, Fashion Designer

Zoe Birnie, Fashion Designer

Desk Top Publishing

Writing this book was one challenge, but having to become a complete technocrat and setting it up in colour using InDesign was another. Particular thanks for guiding me through the hurdles; Alan Taylor, Brian Farley, Bert Parsons, and especially Simon Larkin who also produced the cover.

Illustrator: Ella Tjader

Proof Readers

A big thank you to my proof reading team; Dr Jan Hamon, Ewa Liddington (Womenswear Buyer), Kath Archibald (Accountant), Maria Leeke (Womenswear Buyer), and Mike Scroope (Marketing Consultant).

And my husband, Rory Burke for project managing me through the whole book writing process.

Foreword

I particularly wish to thank Karen Scheetz, *Assistant Chair in Fashion Design at FIT (Fashion Institute of Technology, New York)*, and Ursula Hudson, *Director of the Fashion Business Resource Studio, London College of Fashion,* for their inspirational forewords.

1

Fashion Entrepreneurs' Runway to Success

With your head buzzing with innovative and creative ideas welcome to the **Fashion Entrepreneurs'** world of glamour, style and wealth. From concept to creation, from the fashion catwalk to the street, fashion entrepreneurs are continually looking for marketable opportunities to exploit and start a new business venture.

Who Is This Book For?

Fashion Entrepreneur - *Starting Your Own Fashion Business* is aimed at emerging fashion entrepreneurs; students, graduates and those already in industry who have a keen interest in fashion and want to set up their own fashion businesses. They might be from the creative industries; fashion designers, fashion illustrators, fashion marketing; or the commercial sector, but will have the passion and determination to drive them forward to achieve success.

Fashion Entrepreneur is the third book in this *Fashion Design Series*. It focuses on the business opportunities for emerging fashion entrepreneurs and explains how to identify, manage and develop new products, new ideas and new services. It looks at the innovative, creative and entrepreneurial skills fashion entrepreneurs need to start their own fashion businesses and enter new markets - businesses and ventures that will grow and shape the future of the fashion industry.

There is an increasing recognition by the fashion industry that entrepreneurial and small business management skills are an essential component of the fashion entrepreneurs' portfolio of management skills, together with leadership, team building, communication and networking. This book will set out these key skills and traits and show how they relate to the fashion entrepreneurs' portfolio of skills. *Fashion Entrepreneur* aims to achieve three main objectives:

- Support the Fashion Enterprise and Small Business syllabus.
- Nurture and guide emerging fashion entrepreneurs to start up, survive and grow their own businesses.
- Demonstrate how fashion graduates can use entrepreneurial skills to explore work opportunities within the fashion industry.

Emerging fashion entrepreneurs need passion and determination to drive them forward to achieve business success.

Illustrator: Maria Cardelli

'It's not enough to have a talented designer, the management must be inspired too. The creative process is very disorganized; the production process has to be very rational.' Bernard Arnault, chairman and CEO of LVMH (Louis Vuitton Moët Hennessy luxury goods company).

Nike's pet pooch sits on the sales counter wearing his Nike trainers!

Fashion design does not only include womenswear, menswear and childrenswear but fashion and accessories for 'man's best friend'! Why not?!

What Is An Entrepreneur?

'Entrepreneur' is a French word dating back to the 1700s. Since then it has evolved to mean someone who undertakes a venture, particularly starting a new business, and this is central to the understanding of the word *'entrepreneur'* in the English language. Apparently the French prefer to use *'créateur d'enterprise'* (creator of an enterprise).

DEFINITION: An **Entrepreneur** may be defined as, *a person who identifies an opportunity or new idea and develops it into a new venture or project.*

The fashion entrepreneur is the key, innovative person managing the entrepreneurial process. This will usually involve planning, organizing, directing and controlling the input of suppliers, contractors and the design team members, together with accepting the associated business risks. The key words from these explanations are; innovation, opportunity, new venture, enterprise, management and risk.

Fashion Entrepreneur: Entrepreneurs are acknowledged as being the driving force behind innovative change in our society and the fashion and textile industry is no exception. Using the above definition, a fashion entrepreneur can, therefore, be defined as someone who sets up a new fashion venture, or starts a new fashion label. To achieve this, the fashion entrepreneur needs to be able to spot commercial opportunities and determine customer needs by co-ordinating resources to design, manufacture and supply fashion products or provide a service.

Fashion Design Entrepreneurs: According to US Government statistics, fashion designers are **five times** more likely than any other profession to start their own businesses. This is partly due to; a low barrier to entry (starting with a sewing machine at home); the fashion industry's acceptance of fresh, creative ideas; and that fashion designers are able to offer a product or service (fashion collection, fashion illustration, fashion design, pattern and garment making).

Employment: Gone are the days when an excellent CV was all that was needed to find a job in the fashion industry - you now need entrepreneurial skills as well. In Britain, the government reported that 25% of all graduates were doing a job that did not require a university qualification. To overcome this weak link in the education process, fashion entrepreneurs need to develop their entrepreneurial skills to help them establish a network of useful contacts and to help them identify career path opportunities. This includes, not only starting their own businesses, but finding a job within the fashion industry as an **intrapreneur**.

Fashion Intrapreneur: Large companies are increasingly recognising that they need entrepreneurial spirit from their employees to keep their company at the leading edge of technology and prevent their organization becoming overloaded with head office bureaucracy. Hence, many fashion intrapreneurs work within a fashion company using their entrepreneurial skills before leaving to start their own fashion ventures.

Work Experience: Emerging fashion entrepreneurs will benefit hugely from the experience of working within the fashion industry before they start their own businesses. Apart from the 'hands on experience', the potential for establishing a network of contacts will be invaluable. Even as a student, work experience is essential and students can achieve this through the fashion internships (industrial placements) that many fashion designers and fashion companies offer.

Young Rich List: A recent *Business Review Young Rich List* revealed that 37% of the top 100 young millionaires made their fortunes in the creative industries, the fashion industry being one of them. This is encouraging for all fashion entrepreneurs as it shows there is a 'pot of gold' at the end of a successful business.

Entrepreneurs Throughout History: There have been endless accounts of fashion entrepreneurs starting successful fashion ventures; in the 60s Carnaby Street, a small back street off London's then highly fashionable Regent and Oxford Streets, became the epicentre of the *World of Fashion* due to many young, innovative design entrepreneurs starting their own fashion businesses and making it the 'hippest' street in London.

Fashion Entrepreneurs' Portfolio Of Skills

Fashion entrepreneurship has been the driving force in developing the fashion industry but, as a profession and an academic syllabus, it is still relatively new and has yet to formally establish a defined *Portfolio of Skills* (*Body of Knowledge - syllabus*).

   The *Fashion Entrepreneurs' Portfolio of Skills* is an inclusive term used to describe the sum of the knowledge of the industry; the skills, traits, tools and techniques within the fashion profession.

In the early 1900s, Coco Chanel (Gabrielle Bonheur Chanel), acquired experience in sewing and millinery before she opened her own hat shop in Paris. She was to become one of the world's most influential fashion designers. Long after her death in 1971, Coco Chanel's signature pieces, the Channel suit, gilt bag and string of pearls, are regularly being revamped, copied and reintroduced into fashion collections as the 'must have' of the season.

Fashion Entrepreneur			
Fashion Industry	**Entrepreneur Traits**	**Starting Your Own Business**	**Small Business Management**
Technical Skills	Creativity, Innovation, etc.	Business Plans	Sources of Finance
Opportunities	Spot Opportunities	Registration	Accounts
Design and Manufacturing	Networking Skills	Market Research, Trend Research	Small Business Management Skills
Retail and Distribution	Risk Management	Marketing and Branding	Project Management
Supply Chain Management		Sales and Negotiation	Leadership and Teamwork

Figure 1.1: Fashion Entrepreneurs' Portfolio of Skills – shows a structured subdivision of the key fashion entrepreneurship topics subdivided into their component parts.

Entrepreneur Traits: To become a successful fashion entrepreneur you need innovation to be able to identify opportunities in a climate of ambiguity and chaos, together with passion and enthusiasm for your products to encourage you to constantly improve your products' features. You also need determination and persistence to drive your ideas through the many obstacles and challenges you come up against. In a competitive market, it is not sufficient to only be creative, you also need to be entrepreneurial with small business and project management skills and to be able to build a network of useful contacts.

Technical Skills: The technical skills refer to the technical knowledge you need to design and make your products. Every profession has its unique range of technical and trade skills and, as a fashion apprentice, you will need to learn your trade to be able to produce professional products so that your venture and products are commercially viable. Training courses will help you *'fast track'* up the learning curve (university/college, fashion schools, short courses).

'When we started we never thought about making money; a lot of creative people don't. We wanted to create beautiful things,' Sarah-Jane Clarke, made it to the Business Review Young Rich List as co-founder of the fashion label Sass & Bide.

Successful fashion entrepreneur Hannah Marshall *advises, ' Do all your groundwork prior to starting a business.'*

Fashion Designer: Hannah Marshall

Photographer: Victor de Mello

'Life is an adventure, so I make clothes to have adventures in.'
Vivienne Westwood

What Is In This Book?

The chapters are set out in a logical learning sequence to present the entrepreneurial and small business management skills you will need to run a creative company on a day-to-day basis. It is enriched with case studies, illustrations, photographs, graphics and exercises.

Chapter 2: *Opportunities in the Fashion and Creative Industries* - Statistically 80% of entrepreneurs start their first ventures in their field of expertise. It is therefore essential that, as an emerging fashion entrepreneur, you have a clear understanding of the extent of the fashion industry and where you can find fashion business opportunities. This chapter uses the **fashion supply chain** to subdivide the fashion industry into its component parts and identify these business opportunities.

Chapter 3: *Fashion Entrepreneurs' Traits* – Would you be able to recognize an entrepreneur if you met one in the street? According to research by the BBC, if you know what to look for, the entrepreneur's actions, behaviours and traits could give them away. So by identifying these people, and their traits, you can use them as role models. This chapter will outline the traits you can use to spot innovative opportunities, 'make them happen' and take 'calculated' risks.

Chapter 4: *Networking* - Networking skills are one of the most important entrepreneurial traits that enable you to develop a network of useful business contacts. This chapter will explain how to identify and analyse your key stakeholders' needs and expectations, together with the benefits of working within a fashion cluster and working with a mentor.

Chapter 5: *Competitive Advantage* – Competitive advantage goes right to the heart of fashion entrepreneurship – this is the underlying reason why someone would buy your garments in preference to another brand. This chapter will outline how you can achieve competitive advantage, particularly how you address barriers to entry, niche markets, outsourcing and the SWOT analysis.

Chapter 6: *Business Plan* - As creative ideas and opportunities evolve into marketable products, at some point, you need to develop a coherent business plan to outline where you want your business to go and how you plan to get there. This chapter will explain how to develop a business plan using seven key subheadings; *Executive Summary, Product/Service Plan, Organization Plan, Sales and Marketing Plan, Production and Distribution Plan, Financial Plan,* and *Risk Management Plan.*

Chapter 7: *Starting Your Own Business* – Before rushing out to start a new business you should be aware of the benefits and problems associated with starting a new venture. This chapter will discuss the advantages and disadvantages of starting your own business and the steps you need to take to get started, including; company registration, intellectual property, budgets, setting up your premises, buying equipment, the design and production cycle, and the triggers that encourage you to start your own business.

Chapter 8: *Market Research* - Behind every successful fashion story is an innovative product, and behind every successful product is market research. This chapter discusses how to conduct market research to determine your target market and includes; trend research, competition and pricing strategy.

Chapter 9: *Marketing and Branding* - Creating the 'right' image has become a key factor when producing a marketable product. This particularly applies to the fashion and creative industries as consumers have become much more conscious of brands, and their perceived status and reputation. This chapter will discuss how to develop and implement a marketing and branding strategy to advise your potential and existing customers of your products and 'create an interest'.

Chapter 10: *Sales and Negotiation* - Generating sales is the reality test of your business. Convincing your potential customers that your business and your products will satisfy their needs and are better than the competitions' is the key to your success. This chapter will discuss the sales function; where to sell, how to present your products to the potential customer, and how to close the sale.

Chapter 11: *Design and Production Cycle* - Whether you produce one fashion collection every year, every season, or every month, you will go though a design and production cycle. This chapter will outline the key topics in this cycle; the design and production brief, the production plan, research and sourcing, design development, selling your collection, pre-production, production, distribution and shipping.

Chapter 12: *Sources of Finance* - Ready cash and seed money are the life-blood for starting your own business. Without sufficient funds your new venture's success will be self-limited because there simply will not be sufficient resources available to produce your products. This chapter will demystify the financial requirements needed to run your fashion business.

Chapter 13: *Small Business Accounts* – If your business is to become successful and expand, you will need more than a 'shoebox' accounting system. Accounting terms guide you in your choice of accounting system and demystify some common reports. This chapter will explain how to produce and manage; the cash book accounting method, the profit and loss statement, the cash flow statement, the breakeven analysis and the balance sheet.

Chapter 14: *Project Management Skills* - Project management is recognised as a key skill within the fashion entrepreneurs' portfolio of technical and small business management skills. This is because fashion tasks and events have all the characteristics of a project; starting your own business, designing new products, putting on a fashion show. This chapter will show how you can use a range of special project management techniques to plan and control your projects so they are produced and delivered on time, within budget, and meet your clients' goals and objectives. It will also discuss small business growth phases and how you need to develop leadership and team building skills.

Case Studies/Interviews: To support the text and present examples from different sectors of the fashion industry there are case study interviews with fashion entrepreneurs who have developed their own successful fashion businesses .

The *Appendices* contain useful fashion industry documents; the *Glossary* helps you learn the language of fashion entrepreneurship and small business management; *Internet Resources, Further Reading* and the *Index* include useful websites, company names, trade publications, text books and key words.

Top: *Many emerging fashion entrepreneurs enter fashion competitions/contests which help them gain exposure to the fashion industry. If they win they generally receive a substantial monetary prize and/or an internship to help them 'kick-start' their fashion entrepreneurial careers!*

Hannah Hoyle awarded 'Young Designer of the Year'.

Above: *Image, glamour, lights - your fashion runway to success!*

Exercises:

1. Define entrepreneurship in your own words.
2. Give examples of entrepreneurs in the fashion industry.
3. Discuss your entrepreneurial career path.

The Fashion and Textiles Calendar: Lists some of the key trade shows in the International Fashion and Textile calendar and their typical dates. The four main centres for fashion have been; Paris, London, Milan and New York, but events are held all over the world.

The twice yearly ready-to-wear (womenswear) fashion show schedule for buyers traditionally takes place over a four week period. For example, Spring/Summer Designer Collections usually start in the middle of September after the stores have received their Autumn/Winter (Fall) lines that would have been shown the previous February/March.

As an emerging fashion entrepreneur, you need to be aware of the industry holidays as this will influence your design and production scheduling. For example, European mills usually close for the month of August, and mills and factories in China close during Chinese New Year.

This calendar is a guide and dates do change. You also need to be aware of new trade fairs that emerge as part of the fashion and textiles calendar, such as, Bread and Butter, Barcelona. Fashion weeks are held all over the world, such as, Australia Fashion Week, Cape Town Fashion Week, Hong Kong Fashion Week. You can check all current data on the Internet (see *Internet Resources* at the end of the book).

A/W = Autumn/Winter

S/S = Spring/Summer

FASHION and TEXTILES CALENDAR	
Jan	Milan Menswear Collections A/W
	Paris Womenswear Collections S/S, and Menswear for A/W
	Florence Pitti Filati Yarn Show (Knitwear)
Feb	Frankfurt Interstoff Fabric Show
	London Womenswear Designer Collections and Ready-to-Wear A/W
	Madrid Menswear and Womenswear Collections A/W
	New York Fashion Week and Menswear Collections A/W
	Milan Womenswear Designer Collections - Milano Collezioni Donna
	Paris Première Vision Fabric Show and Paris Expofil (Colour Trends and Yarn)
Mar	New York Womenswear Market Week Fall 1
	Paris Womenswear Designer Collections and Prêt à Porter Paris Exhibition A/W
Apr	
May	Midseason/Transeason Shows
	New York Womenswear Market Week Fall 2
Jun	London Graduate Fashion Week (Student Catwalk Shows)
Jul	Florence Pitti Filati Yarn Show (Knitwear)
	Milan Menswear Designer Collections S/S
	Paris Womenswear Couture Collections A/W
	Paris Menswear Collections S/S
Aug	Las Vegas Magic Show (Fashion Accessories and Sourcing)
	New York Menswear Collections S/S
Sept	London Womenswear Designer Collections and Ready-to-Wear S/S
	Madrid Menswear and Womenswear Collections S/S
	Milan Womenswear Designer Collections and Moda Pronta Exhibition S/S
	New York Fashion Week
	Paris Première Vision Fabric Show and Paris Expofil (Colour Trends and Yarn)
	Paris Womenswear Designer Collections and Prêt à Porter Paris Exhibition S/S
Oct	Midseason/Transeason Shows
	New York Womenswear Market Week S/S

Opposite Page: Design Development example - *As an emerging fashion design entrepeneur you will typically be researching new trends and sourcing fabrics and trims internationally as you develop your designs and products. This book will guide you in all these aspects.*

Fashion Designer: Amy Lappin

"COLLAR HIGHER AT THE BACK"

GOLD PIPING?

detail repeated?

EXPERIMENTING WITH COAT IDEAS — PANELS OF JACQUARD, "AD OF LUXURY"

NEED TO FIND A BALANCE OF REGAL INFLUENCE AND CONTEMPORARY/PERSONAL DESIGN —
HOW MODERN CAN I PUSH IT?

"PLEATING" TO CREATE FEMININE CURVES? MOULDED TO THE BODY?

INTRODUCING MY CREST/EMBLEM IDEA
- PLACEMENT ON COATS?
- BLOWING UP TO CREATE AN ILLUSTRATION
  • T-SHIRT PRINT?
- USING IT OBVIOUSLY — THE SHAPE OF A CREST AS TO INFLUENCE MY DESIGNS

THIS IDEA REMINDS ME A BIT OF ARMOUR — WITH THE SHAPE COMING OUT OF THE SHOULDER, PLEATING OUT OF THE BACK.

TOO LONG.

Fashion and Music - Rock On!

Illustrator: Montana Forbes

2

Opportunities in the Fashion and Creative Industries

The fashion industry is a key player within the creative industries which, in turn, is a key sector within most economies. The fashion industry primarily includes the designing, manufacturing, promoting, advertising and retailing of 'fashionable' clothing, but also includes a range of supporting professions and boundary industries.

Statistically 80% of entrepreneurs start their first venture in their field of expertise. This means that emerging entrepreneurs with skills in fashion (particularly fashion graduates) are more likely to identify an opportunity within the fashion industry. Therefore, it is essential that entrepreneurs understand the full extent of the fashion industry and where they might find potential business opportunities.

This chapter will use two different methods to subdivide the fashion industry to help you to identify opportunities and new markets where you can apply your skills and start your own fashion business:

- **Fashion and Textiles Supply Chain or Value Chain** (Figure 2.1 - explores vertical, horizontal and 'Z' growth opportunities).
- **Fashion and Textiles Industry Breakdown** (Figure 2.3 - explores niche market opportunities).

Despite the challenges of cheap labour posed by countries such as China and India, where the bulk of the world's clothes are now made, the fashion industry in the West is still thriving with plenty of opportunities for innovative fashion entrepreneurs. For example, Zara and H&M, two major fashion retailers, have gained competitive advantage by developing new design and manufacturing methods to produce *'fast fashion'*, where their latest styles are delivered into the shops within a few weeks of the designers spotting new styles and trends, rather than the industry average of nine months.

In parallel, the more unique, creative, technical skills and craftsmanship of individual designers are becoming more sought after by the more affluent consumers; for example, in luxury, high-end womenswear design, bespoke tailoring, hand knitting, corsetry (lingerie). Intuitive, fashion entrepreneurs are instinctively seeking out these opportunities and gaps in the market and exploiting them by using their expert skills to start their own businesses.

Intimate apparel - the skills of corsetry and lingerie have become sought after skills of late, creating an opportunity for entrepreneurs within this niche market.

Fashion Designer: Cherona Blacksell

Fashion and Textile Industry Supply Chain

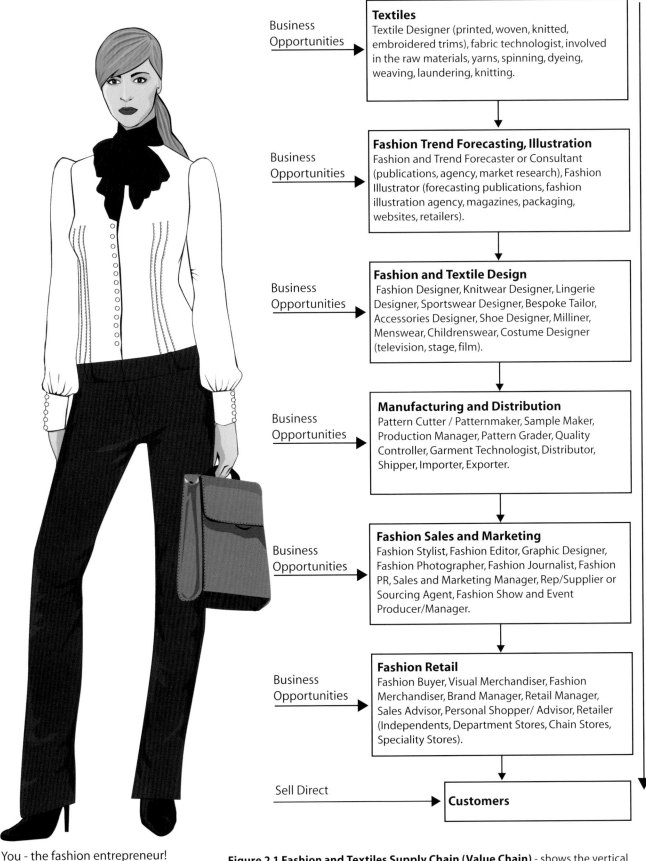

Business Opportunities →

Textiles
Textile Designer (printed, woven, knitted, embroidered trims), fabric technologist, involved in the raw materials, yarns, spinning, dyeing, weaving, laundering, knitting.

Business Opportunities →

Fashion Trend Forecasting, Illustration
Fashion and Trend Forecaster or Consultant (publications, agency, market research), Fashion Illustrator (forecasting publications, fashion illustration agency, magazines, packaging, websites, retailers).

Business Opportunities →

Fashion and Textile Design
Fashion Designer, Knitwear Designer, Lingerie Designer, Sportswear Designer, Bespoke Tailor, Accessories Designer, Shoe Designer, Milliner, Menswear, Childrenswear, Costume Designer (television, stage, film).

Business Opportunities →

Manufacturing and Distribution
Pattern Cutter / Patternmaker, Sample Maker, Production Manager, Pattern Grader, Quality Controller, Garment Technologist, Distributor, Shipper, Importer, Exporter.

Business Opportunities →

Fashion Sales and Marketing
Fashion Stylist, Fashion Editor, Graphic Designer, Fashion Photographer, Fashion Journalist, Fashion PR, Sales and Marketing Manager, Rep/Supplier or Sourcing Agent, Fashion Show and Event Producer/Manager.

Business Opportunities →

Fashion Retail
Fashion Buyer, Visual Merchandiser, Fashion Merchandiser, Brand Manager, Retail Manager, Sales Advisor, Personal Shopper/ Advisor, Retailer (Independents, Department Stores, Chain Stores, Speciality Stores).

Sell Direct →

Customers

You - the fashion entrepreneur!

Fashion Illustrator: Naomi Austin

Figure 2.1 Fashion and Textiles Supply Chain (Value Chain) - shows the vertical integration of the key links in the supply chain from textiles to retail (sales to the customer). At each point on the supply chain there are potential business opportunities for the fashion entrepreneur.

Supply Chain Opportunities

Figure 2.1 shows the supply chain for the fashion and textile industry as a *vertical* flow chart, but there are also *horizontal* and 'Z' components to consider. Horizontal integration refers to the number of products for sale (catalogue / list of products) and 'Z' refers to the number of customers (sales and marketing).

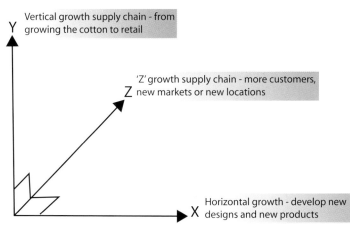

Figure 2.2 Supply Chain (three dimensional) - shows the components of the supply chain; vertical growth, horizontal growth and 'Z' growth.

Vertical Growth is achieved by expanding your business activities up and down the product's supply chain - from raw materials to manufacture, from distribution to retailing. The parts of the supply chain that you can expand into obviously depend on where your products are positioned in the supply chain. A fashion design entrepreneur could:

• Move up the supply chain by designing and printing fabric.
• Move down the supply chain by becoming involved in manufacturing, distribution and retail.

Zara is an excellent example of a company that has achieved nearly full vertical integration. Its success is due to the fact that it has control of the business from design, to factory to the shop floor. Zara designs all its own clothes, makes most of them locally in Spain, and supplies them through its own distribution channels to its own retail stores.

   Expanding your business up or down the supply chain will not necessarily increase the number of products you sell, but it will certainly increase your percentage of the income from each sale.

Horizontal growth is achieved by selling more types of products or services. This can be achieved in a number of ways:

• Design new products for your customer base, widen your product range by offering, perhaps, lingerie or accessories to complement your womenswear.
• Provide more services - offer a pattern making service as well as fashion design; offer a web design service as well as fashion illustration.

Z growth is achieved by generating more customers. This can be achieved by increasing your sales and marketing effort:

• Attract new customers locally and nationally - contact potential customers directly, local advertising, offer special deals, lower prices.
• Export to new geographical areas.
• Sell globally through the Internet.
• Find other companies prepared to pay for the privilege of using your creative ideas and selling your product - franchising, licensing, rights and royalties.

In practice, sustained growth is usually achieved by a combination of vertical, horizontal and Z expansion.

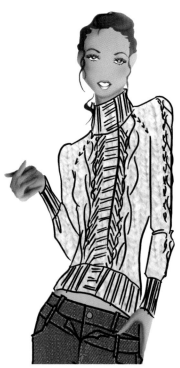

Knitwear and jeanswear design.
Fashion Designer: Tina Fong

Case Study Niche Market Specialization: John Smedley, *a long established, UK based company, in the last few years has successfully overcome the challenges of mass production in China. The key to the company's survival has been the decision to operate in a low-volume, niche market, concentrating on quality rather than price. The business is thriving, manufacturing luxury knitwear favoured by celebrities including* Victoria Beckham, Tom Cruise and Madonna.

1. Fashion and Textile Design	2. Manufacturing and Distribution	3. Fashion Sales and Marketing
Trend Forecasting	Manufacturing (Clothing and Textiles)	Fashion Styling
Textile Design	CMT (Cut, Make and Trim)	Fashion Media (Magazines, Periodicals,
Fashion Design	Production Management	Television, Music Industry)
Knitwear Design, Bespoke Tailoring	Pattern Grading	Fashion Promotion, Advertising
Fashion Accessories, Footwear	Quality Control (QC)	Fashion Photography, Journalism
Design, Millinery	Distribution (Warehousing, Shipping and	Public Relations (PR)
Fashion Illustration	Transport)	Sales (Representatives, Agency, Suppliers,
Pattern Cutting/Patternmaking	Importing and Exporting	Sourcing Agent - Design, Illustration, Clothing,
Sample Making		Textiles, Trims)

Figure 2.3 Fashion and Textiles Industry Breakdown – shows the industry subdivided into six key areas listing the specialisms where fashion entrepreneurs might find business opportunities. This list is a guide and by no means the total extent of the fashion and textiles industry.

Fashion professionals tend to specialise in a particular area, a niche market. The image above shows designs for sportswear (equestrian) and, in contrast, an independent designer label.

Illustrator: Montana Forbes

1. Fashion and Textile Design

Figure 2.3; starting on the left, trend forecasting, textile design fashion design and fashion illustration lead the fashion cycle. This is where market research comes together to produce the latest textile and fashion designs. Trend forecasting identifies the newest trends and fads which includes; the latest fabrics, colours, themes, silhouettes and styling.

Business Opportunity: To use design and technical skills to become a Fashion/Trend Forecaster or Consultant, Textile Designer, Fashion Designer, Knitwear Designer, Bespoke Tailor, Accessories Designer, Footwear/Shoe Designer, Millinery Designer, Fashion Illustrator, Pattern Cutter / Patternmaker, Sample Maker.

2. Manufacturing and Distribution

Manufacturing and distribution is at the production heart of the fashion industry where the garments are made, warehoused and delivered to retailers. Production focuses on making the product efficiently and achieving the desired quality. Distribution focuses on stock control and shipping the goods to retailers to meet the agreed deadlines.

Business Opportunity: To use garment manufacturing skills to become a Production Manager, Pattern Grader, Quality Controller, and use business skills to become a Distributor, Shipper, Importer, Exporter.

3. Fashion Sales and Marketing

'Sales' involves the selling of products and services to companies in the fashion industry (retailers, suppliers) and to the end consumer. Marketing is the promotion and advertising of fashion merchandise and services to inform the customers about the products and services, and generate an interest. Without effective marketing no-one would know about the products and without effective sales there would be no business.

Business Opportunity: To use sales and marketing skills and/or promotion and advertising skills to become a Fashion Stylist, Fashion Editor, Graphic Designer, Fashion Photographer, Fashion Journalist, Fashion PR, Sales and Marketing Manager, Representative/Agent/Supplier or Sourcing Agent (Fashion Design, Textile Design, Fashion Illustration, Recruitment, Apparel, Textiles Trims).

4. Fashion Retail	5. Fashion Industry Pathways	6. Fashion Industry Boundaries
Fashion Buying	Costume Design	Beauty, Hair and Make-up Artists
Visual Merchandising	Fashion Shows and Events	Model, Model Agency
Fashion Merchandising	Fashion Consulting, Fashion Services	Jewellery Design, Fancy Dress (adults/
Brand Management	Fashion Education, Fashion Publishing	children), Petswear, Homeware
Retail Management	Fabric Technology, Garment Technology	Fashion Franchise
Sales Advice, Personal Shopping		Fashion Software, Fashion Web Design
		Suppliers, Wholesalers and Merchants

4. Fashion Retail

Fashion retail is the *'shop window'* of fashion and the last link in the supply chain. The fashion retail business involves the buying, selling, and display of fashion merchandise. It is essentially the link between the product, the manufacturer and the customer. The *'shop window'* could be a retail store, design studio, market stall, catalogue (mail order) or web site. The aim of fashion retailers is to know their market, and persuade and entice customers to buy their merchandise.

Business Opportunity: To use retail and buying skills to become a Fashion Buyer, Visual Merchandiser, Fashion Merchandiser, Brand Manager, Retail Manager, Sales Advisor, Personal Shopper/ Advisor, Retailer (Department Store, Speciality Store, Chain Store, Discounter, Supermarket, Mail-Order, E-commerce, Direct Seller).

5. Fashion Industry Pathways

The fashion industry reaches out to include a wide range of other professions which are extensions of fashion and textile design courses and careers - these professions are fashion pathways.

Business Opportunity: To build on fashion and specialist skills to become a Costume Designer, Fashion Show and Event Producer/Manager, Fashion Consultant (Wardrobe, Image, Makeover, Appearance, Personal Branding), Fashion Educator / Professor / Lecturer, Fashion Publisher, Fashion Author, Fabric Technologist, Garment Technologist.

6. Fashion Industry Boundaries

The boundaries of the fashion industry include a wide scope of opportunities where fashion entrepreneurs can apply their entrepreneurial talents and start new ventures.

Business Opportunity: To use specialist skills to become a Beauty/Hair and Make-up Artist, Model, Model Agent, Jewellery Designer, Fancy Dress Designer, Designer (pets), Fashion Franchisee, Fashion Software Programmer, Web designer (fashion), Fashion Supplier/Wholesaler/Merchant.

Top: *Fashion boundaries - make-up artists create for fashion shows, fashion shoots, theatre, television and film.*

Illustrator: Montana Forbes

Above: *Shoe design is a specialised field within the fashion industry.*

Illustrator: Maria Cardelli

Niche markets for the fashion entrepreneur - bridal wear and maternity wear.

Illustrator: Ella Tjader

Figure 2.4 Fashion Levels and Clothing Categories - shows the fashion industry subdivided into various levels, and clothing categories. Fashion entrepreneurs might spot opportunities to use their expert skills in any one or more of these areas.

© Fashion Entrepreneur - Sandra Burke

1. Fashion and Textile Design Professions

Fashion/Trend Forecasters (coolhunters) research and collate information on the latest, global, fashion trends and fads. This information is used to enable them to predict the colours, yarns, fabrics, silhouettes and styles for a particular season which is typically 18 months ahead of the current fashion season. The information is published as visual trend reports which are purchased primarily by the textile and fashion industry. Fashion businesses (designers, buyers, merchandisers etc.) use these reports as a guide to design and produce marketable products and develop their brands.

Fashion Forecasting Consultants work directly with their clients to help them develop their individual brands. Brand development might include not only developing the clothing, but also, the complete process from the brand logos through to store design and layout.

Textile Designers work closely with fabric manufacturers but might also work with fabric technologists, textile suppliers, fashion designers and retailers. Their scope of work could involve the design of printed, woven, knitted and embroidered fabrics and trims for clothing and accessories, and might also extend to; homeware, interiors and even the aeronautical, marine and automotive industries.

Fashion Designers are at the hub of the fashion industry and typically specialise in designing collections for particular areas of fashion (see Figure 2.4). They work with the support of the fashion design team which includes textile designers, illustrators, pattern cutters, sample machinists and manufacturers. They might also work with other professions in the supply chain, from stylists, public relations, photographers, sales agents, merchandisers, journalists, fashion show producers to fashion models. Fashion Knitwear, Accessory, Footwear and Millinery Designers, and Bespoke Tailors often start their training as fashion designers but divert to become specialists in their particular field of interest.

Fashion Illustrators give a signature style to fashion designs through their creativity, expert hand drawing and computer skills. Fashion illustrations are used for; fashion design presentations, advertisements, marketing and editorial (magazines and books). Fashion illustrators work with client briefs to produce fashion illustrations of clothing, fashion collections and fashion products and could include textiles, homeware and lifestyle.

Fashion Levels	Genre	Garment Types	Speciality
Haute Couture	Womenswear	Casualwear	Petites
Ready-to-Wear	Menswear	Jeanswear	Plus Sizes
Luxury Brands	Childrenswear	Sportswear / Activewear	Tall/Short Sizes
Mid-Level Brands	Teens	Swimwear	Bridalwear
Independent Designer Labels		Clubwear	Maternity
Casualwear and Sportswear Brands		Lingerie/Intimate Apparel, Sleepwear	Corporate
Highstreet		Eveningwear	Accessories
Supermarket (Budget)		Tailoring	Footwear
Discounters		Knitwear	Special Needs
		Showpieces	

Pattern Cutters/Patternmakers make the patterns according to fashion designers' garment specifications. Patterns are made manually and/or by computer (CAD - Gerber, Lectra). **Sample Machinists** sew the samples for fashion designers and work with all types of fabric and designs They are specialists in their field compared to the machinists on the manufacturers' production lines who sew only sections of garments. Pattern cutters and sample machinists are particularly sought after in the West as many fashion designers still prefer to work with local specialists to make their collections and their short production runs (many of these skills have been lost to the East). For the fashion entrepreneur this could be the opportunity to set up a viable business by offering a service to potential fashion industry clients.

2. Fashion Manufacturing and Distribution Professions

Fashion Manufacturers and CMTs work on the production side of the fashion business and all the processes required to make the garments.

Production Managers are responsible for the smooth operation of the manufacturing of the products to meet the required design specifications, quality requirements and production deadlines.

Pattern Graders are responsible for grading (sizing) the approved patterns for the garments that go into production.

Distribution Managers and the **Distribution Team** are responsible for the warehousing, shipping and transportation of the products, along with the administrative work that goes with it, which includes importing and exporting. This involves all the jobs associated with moving the garments/products from the manufacturing plant to the warehouse. Once the products are in the warehouse and the orders are complete, the orders must then be distributed to the relevant retail stores or online services etc.

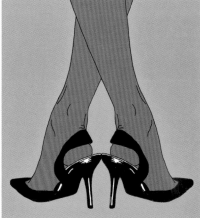

Niche markets for the fashion entrepreneur - millinery and footwear.
Illustrator (top): Maria Cardelli
Illustrator (above): Montana Forbes

3. Fashion Sales and Marketing Professions

Fashion Editors are responsible for heading up their publishing teams to report the latest fashion and trend news for their publications while working to strict publishing deadlines. With their team, they cover the seasonal designer fashion shows in the major cities; London, Paris, Milan, New York etc., together with relevant articles to satisfy their readers.

Fashion Stylists select clothing and accessories to put together specific 'looks' to create 'styles' or 'themes' for the fashion and creative industries, private clients and celebrities. This includes; the media, film, fashion shows, fashion shoots, advertising, retail and music. Stylists are like 'cultural sponges', constantly aware of not only the fashion scene, but also what is happening in the arts, sport, history, even politics etc.

Fashion Promoters, Graphic Designers, Fashion Photographers, Fashion Journalists work with fashion and textile publications, advertising agencies, marketing and promotion and are responsible for capturing the latest fashion and trend news.

Sales Representatives, Agents, Suppliers, Sourcing Agents (Fashion Design, Textile Design, Fashion Illustration, Recruitment, Textiles, Trims, Fashion Products) specialise in supplying professional services, industry professionals, the latest fabrics and trims to the textile and fashion industry.

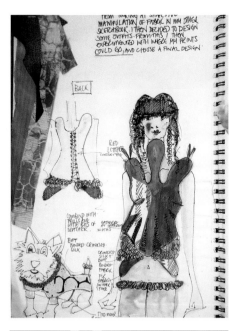

Fashion boundary - design for pet pooches!

Top: *Sketchbook - clothing ideas for a womenswear and petswear collection.*

Above: *Garden tea party.*

Fashion Designer: Zoe Birnie
Stylist and Photographer: Lesley Ford
Model: Mr Wobbles

4. Fashion Retail Professions

This includes all those involved in fashion retail; Department Stores, Chain Stores, Speciality Stores, Supermarkets, Mail-Order, E-commerce, Direct Sales. They need to understand their company's brand and who their target market and customers are, to enable them to persuade their customers to buy their latest merchandise.

Fashion Retail Buyers follow their range plans to select and buy merchandise for their stores to sell to their target market/customers. Buyers typically place orders five or six months ahead of the season with their manufacturers and with fashion designers for the styles they believe their customers will want.

Visual Merchandisers are responsible for planning, co-ordinating and producing effective window and store displays with the aim of generating interest in the merchandise and maximising sales.

Fashion Merchandisers co-ordinate and liaise with their buying team and suppliers to ensure; their product ranges (range plans) are planned according to their budgets, that the buyers have selected the right type of merchandise according to the range plan, and that the supplier will deliver the merchandise to the stores to meet the required deadlines.

Retail Managers and Brand Managers are responsible for maximising the sales and profits of their retail stores and brands. They do this by; managing and leading their teams, ensuring the merchandise is displayed and presented correctly, and maintaining a professional standard of customer service.

Sales Advisers (personal advisers, personal shoppers) advise their customers and clients of the latest fashion looks to suit and enhance their personal style, and advise them as to what items they should purchase. Personal shoppers often select and purchase the clothing on behalf of their clients to allow their clients to try them on at home before making their final selection.

5. Fashion Industry Pathways Professions

Fabric Technologists ensure the fabric samples and production fabrics achieve the required quality standards determined by the fashion and textile industry.

Garment Technologists ensure that the production samples and production garments achieve the required quality standards determined by the fashion and textile industry.

Fashion Show and Event Organisers, with their teams, produce seasonal fashion shows and exhibitions for the fashion and textile industry - for retailers and charity events etc.

Fashion Educators lecture in universities and fashion schools. They generally come from the fashion and textile industry, having gained valuable skills and product knowledge through working in their field of expertise.

Fashion Publishers/Editors work with their publishing teams, fashion authors and numerous fashion experts to produce fashion text books and coffee-table type glossy books for education, the fashion industry and the general market.

Costume Designers may have completed a degree in costume design as their specialist subject area but fashion and textile designers often find themselves involved in designing for theatre, film and television. These designers include; Zandra Rhodes, Giorgio Armani, John Paul Gaultier.

The Wee Small Hour

Textile design for Moontide.

Fashion entrepreneur, Alissa Stytsenko designed this print using her fashion textile, design, illustration and computer skills. Alissa has her own textile design company.

Fashion and Textile Designer: Alissa Stytsenko

6. Fashion Industry Boundary Professions

The boundary of the fashion industry offers many more business opportunities for fashion entrepreneurs to apply their skills.

Beauty, Hair and Make-up Artists are responsible for enhancing or creating a particular *'style'* or *'look'* for models, actors, musicians, etc. and often work alongside fashion designers, fashion stylists and fashion photographers.

Models and Model Agents work with all the key players in the fashion industry when putting on fashion shows, events and working on fashion shoots - fashion designers, stylists, photographers, the media and events managers. Models strutting down the runway are the fashion designers' vehicles for displaying their latest, seasonal collections.

Costume, Fashion and Textile Designers often find spin-off work opportunities in jewellery design, fancy dress design and even designing clothing and accessories for pets, designs for interiors, soft furnishings and homeware.

Fashion Software Designers, Web Designers (fashion) traditionally come from information technology (IT) but many fashion designers have also become experts in this field as they have the computer and fashion design skills to help them understand the application. All the top fashion designers and brands have a presence on the net - this is the new market place, along with the expectation that fashion sites must reflect the spirit or zeitgeist of the company and its brand.

Exercises:

1. Discuss where you sit or where you would like to sit on the fashion supply chain.
2. Discuss how you could move one step up and down the supply chain.
3. Identify business opportunities for yourself in each of the six fashion areas.

Illustrator: Jessica Haley

3

Fashion Entrepreneurs' Traits

Would you be able to recognize a fashion entrepreneur if you met one in the street? According to research by the BBC, if you know what to look for, the entrepreneur's actions, behaviours and traits could give him/her away. By identifying these traits, emerging entrepreneurs can use them as role models.

Fashion entrepreneurs' traits can be defined as distinguishing features or characteristics of their personality which are their:

- Natural and intrinsic ways of doing things.
- Intuitive, streetwise approaches to solving problems.
- Enthusiastic, passionate and instinctive ways of always searching for innovative and creative ideas, and opportunities.
- Keenness to make decisions and accept the associated responsibilities and risks.
- Ability to communicate and network to make useful circles of contacts (see *Networking* chapter).
- Ability to co-ordinate their resources, implement their business plans, along with their determination and persistence to 'make it happen'.

By looking at the entrepreneur's traits in Figure 3.1 you can build up a picture, an '*identikit*', of an entrepreneur's likely characteristics, behaviour and skills.

Would you be able to recognize a fashion entrepreneur if you met one in the street?

Illustrator: Montana Forbes

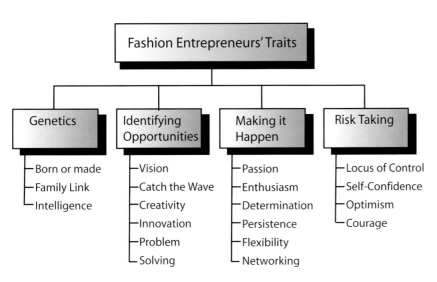

Figure 3.1 Fashion Entrepreneurs' Traits Matrix - shows *an identikit of the fashion entrepreneurs' traits.*

Top: *The Beatles - famously rejected by Decca records!*
Illustrator: Buddy Mendis

Above: *Fashion entrepreneurs have a reputation for having vision and being able to spot an opportunity.*
Illustrator: Maria Cardelli

Case Study (family link): *Did* Stella McCartney's *parents help her become a top fashion designer? Although they were not fashion designers they were certainly creative and had many entrepreneurial traits themselves. Indirectly,* Paul McCartney *had a big influence on fashion in the 60s (Beatle suits, Beatle boots, Beatle hair-cuts). Stella's family would have instinctively encouraged her by giving her a good education (Central Saint Martins), and expected her to become a high achiever, introduced her to the right connections (networking), and supported her (attending her fashion shows).*

1. Genetics

Are Fashion Entrepreneurs Born or Made?: There is evidence to suggest that genetics can contribute to peoples' personality but, what appears to be more important, is how young peoples' genetic make-up is cultivated - how their development is encouraged or discouraged in their early years.

Family Link: Researchers have found a link between entrepreneurs and their family. If the parents are entrepreneurs then their children are more likely to follow in their footsteps and become entrepreneurs themselves.

Intelligence: Entrepreneurs who generate lots of innovative and creative ideas are thought of as being something special - and special equals intelligence. Intelligence is usually measured with an IQ test. The findings from Stanford University suggest that a certain level of IQ is necessary to be innovative but, interestingly, scores above 120 do not imply greater creativity.

People with a high IQ tend to be good at focusing on a problem and coming up with the solution very quickly, whereas creative people, and this includes fashion designers, tend to come up with a variety of solutions simultaneously. It has been suggested that people with a high IQ use a small area of their brain very efficiently, whereas creative people co-ordinate several regions of their brain to produce a flood of creative ideas.

2. Identifying Opportunities

Ultimately, fashion business success is achieved by those who understand how to identify opportunities and exploit them to convert them into a profitable reality. Spotting changes in the marketplace means not only detecting fashion trends but, also, interpreting the impact these changes have on consumer spending. Fashion entrepreneurs are proactive rather than reactive and will actively go looking for opportunities rather than sit back and wait for luck to come to them.

Entrepreneurs have a reputation for being able to spot opportunities other people miss although the same information is there for all to see. They appear to thrive in a climate of ambiguity and chaos - they can sift through large amounts of information, piecing together snippets of seemingly unrelated information until they come up with potential opportunities. Entrepreneurs can sense by instinct what clues are worth pursuing.

A good idea for a new venture or small business does not need to be earth-shatteringly complicated or high tech. Fashion entrepreneurs know the secret is to find a simple way of providing something that is perceived to be more fashionable, less expensive, better quality or more efficient than the competition.

Vision: Successful entrepreneurs have the vision to predict what their market will look like in the future and what products will be popular. Steve Jobs (Apple computers) had the vision of seeing a computer on every desk. No market research at that time would have given the Apple computer the slightest chance of success. And, without Steve Jobs, we would not have the latest, *must have*, fashion accessories and status symbols– the iPod, the iPhone and the MacBook Air!

In the 60s, if Mary Quant, John Bates and André Courrèges, had not had the vision that women would accept such a radical change in dress, they may never have designed and popularized the **mini skirt**. Think of how many times the mini has been revived to become the newest fashion trend - where would fashion be without it?

Catching the Wave: Successful fashion entrepreneurs intuitively know when and how to catch the next big wave of opportunity - the next big fashion trend or fashion cycle, or the next new fashion business opportunity. Just like a surfer riding a wave, if fashion entrepreneurs get on the wave at the right time they can ride it, make the most of it, then, as the wave starts to decline, catch the next fashion wave. Being able to anticipate and identify the next fashion wave of new trends gives fashion entrepreneurs time to prepare and position themselves to gain maximum exposure and not be caught with outdated products.

Creativity and Innovation: Our minds work in mysterious ways – one minute we think logically and rationally, the next minute we think intuitively and laterally. It is the entrepreneurs' ability to vary the ways they think that enables them to come up with many of their creative ideas and innovative products.

Creativity is the generation of ideas, the use of ingenuity and imagination to create a novel approach or a unique solution to a problem. Creative ideas come any time, anywhere - in the car, in the shower, in the garden, at the gym, waiting for a plane, relaxing on a beach - in fact the last place most of us find inspiration is at our office desk! This is because we get our best ideas when our normal everyday conscious thinking is side lined. This allows our subconscious mind to spontaneously bring creative ideas to the surface.

For every thousand great ideas we have unfortunately only a few filter through to form the basis of a successful business enterprise. Some ideas will be impractical and some ideas too obscure but, the important thing is to keep them coming and make sure they are written down as soon as possible. Research has shown that if we have a problem we cannot solve we should consider sleeping on it to let our subconscious mind do the work undisturbed. This subconscious problem solving state is called active imagination or *Hypnagogia* (see Burke R., *Entrepreneurs Toolkit*, 2006).

Innovation is the process of converting new ideas into innovative products or ventures. Innovation is more than a flash of inspiration; it is the systematic development and implementation of a creative idea. It is what helps entrepreneurs decide on their unique selling point (USP). Innovation is all about change to develop a new product or improve the product in the eyes of the consumer. Innovation could be:

- Tailoring the product for a particular need or application - swimwear for Olympic swimmers.
- Finding a new type of fabric to substitute for the original, which could be technically superior or less expensive.
- Improving the manufacturing method to reduce production costs (Just-In-Time - JIT).
- Streamlining the administration costs to reduce overheads – join up with a friend or partner.
- Opening a new market - an export market, through the Internet.
- A way to improve customer service to encourage repeat business - offer personal fashion styling advice *(What to wear and what not to wear!)*.

Fashion entrepreneurs are good at adapting and combining existing technology to produce new products to exploit a marketable opportunity. In the fashion context, creativity and innovation is not just about designing fashionable garments but ensuring there is a market and supply chain to manufacture, distribute and sell the products.

Top: *Creative ideas come any time, anywhere even when gardening!*
Illustrator: Ella Tjader

Above: *Hypnagogia - when we sleep on a problem we often come up with our best and most creative ideas.*
Illustrator: Maria Cardelli

Problem Solving and Decision-Making: Entrepreneurs are natural problem solvers. They use their creative and innovative skills to overcome problems and obstacles that would put many people off. They also have an intrinsic ability to turn problems into marketable opportunities. Fashion entrepreneurs willingly accept the challenge, and are always looking for innovative solutions. Anita Roddick (Body Shop) encouragingly said, '*If you sense a problem - you have just found another opportunity.*'

Problem solving and decision-making are often confused as being one and the same process but, in fact, they are very different. (see Figure 3.2). **Problem solving** is the process of generating a number of design or technical solutions to solve a problem, whereas, **decision-making** is the process of focusing on gaining collective support from the team, shareholders and stakeholders, to accept one or more solutions and to commit the resources of the businesses to implement them - financial resources, personnel and equipment) .

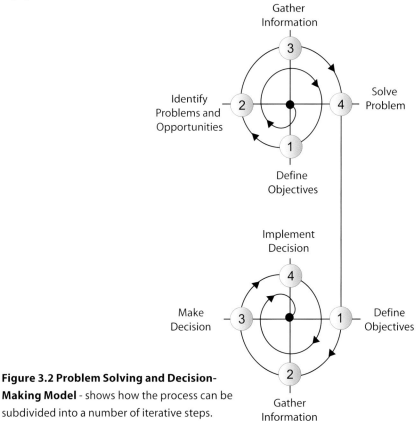

Figure 3.2 Problem Solving and Decision-Making Model - shows how the process can be subdivided into a number of iterative steps.

Fashion design entrepreneurs use their creative and innovative skills to overcome problems and obstacles when designing their unique products.

Top and Middle: *Bespoke milliner, and fashion entrepreneur,* Justin Smith, Royal College of Art *graduate, creates and sells ladies' and gentlemen's hats and caps - work in progress.*

Above: *An inspiring selection of millinery trims encourages the designer's innovative and creative design process.*

Brainstorming: This is a popular problem solving technique used to generate ideas and solutions to problems. Consider using the following steps to encourage brainstorming:

1. Assemble the design or project team, brief them on the purpose of the session, then present them with the problem and encourage them to spontaneously contribute ideas for solutions to the problem.
2. Write all the suggestions on a white board or flip chart - there should be no evaluation of the comments as this could kill the flow of further ideas.
3. Encourage a flood of suggestions, the more innovative and extreme the better, as this will stimulate a cross-flow of ideas.
4. The session should run for about 20 minutes and produce about 30 or more suggestions from the team.
5. Finally, group the suggestions and evaluate them, selecting the best options for the decision-making process.

3. Make It Happen

A great idea is not an end in itself, it takes the co-ordination of resources and the implementation of plans to facilitate change and start new ventures. Opportunities, new ideas and solutions do not come neatly packed, fully complete and ready to go – there are always plenty of hurdles and challenges to contend with. This is when fashion entrepreneurs needs passion, enthusiasm, determination and persistence, together with effective project management skills to make it happen.

Fashion entrepreneurs are driven by a strong inner urge to get things done and succeed - they are not procrastinators. Starting a new venture can be a lonely affair, without outside motivation and encouragement. Fashion entrepreneurs can forget working nine to five, they will have to work long hours to succeed, sometimes with little reward! It is at these times that they will need to be highly motivated to continue.

Passion and Enthusiasm: These traits are two extremely powerful inner forces which totally consume the entrepreneurs' thinking. When designing new products or implementing new ventures they are constantly looking for ways to make improvements and enhancements. It is these traits which drives them on until their products are right for the market.

Determination and Persistence: With their business goals and objectives in sight, the traits of determination and persistence motivate entrepreneurs to achieve their targets. These are the traits that keep them working through their problems and rejections, giving them the resilience to bounce back - it is as if they refuse to accept failure. This desire to succeed shapes their winning attitude and gives them the energy and tenacity to tackle problems head on – diplomacy is not one of their strong points!

Implementation, Co-ordination and Expediting: Successful fashion entrepreneurs have the project management traits and skills required to plan, implement and control their projects and resources. They naturally become the team leader, co-ordinating and integrating their resources as they manage their projects. They are natural 'progress chasers' and expeditors, checking on their projects' performance and quality, and searching for problems (and opportunities) before they happen.

Flexibility and Response Speed: When the circumstances demand, fashion entrepreneurs are astute enough to be flexible and adjust their planning to suit the situation. They make quick decisions when the circumstances demand a fast response to get their products to market before the competitions'.

Networking: See the *Networking* chapter.

Top: *Creativity and innovation are two of the key traits fashion entrepreneurs use to design new, marketable products - stylish iPods versus MP3s - current fashion accessories.*
Illustrator: Sarah Beetson

Above: *Leather and feather trim shoe.*
Illustrator: Maria Cardelli

Case Study (passion, enthusiasm, determination and persistence): *Fashion entrepreneur and shoe designer,* Nigel Fairhead, *started his very successful footwear business making basic leather sandals, selling them from a street stall. As his business steadily grew, he opened first one, then another shoe store and, eventually, his own footwear factory. When creating a new style he would design the shoe himself, make the prototype, and was so passionate about the design he would not let it out of his sight until it was perfect. He would take it home, sit with it on the table when he was eating his meals, put it on his bedside table when he slept, and dream about it, and when he awoke in the morning he would have some new ideas about the shoe, helping him converge on his optimum design....another winner!*

Innovative and creative design - it takes courage to change the status quo!

Fashion Illustrator: Kyle Farmer

Case Study(entrepreneurial traits - confidence, determination, passion, enthusiasm, dedication, and hard work): Paul Smith (Sir), *opened his first boutique in Nottingham in 1970 selling fashionable clothes he made himself, and also other designers' clothes. He showed his first menswear collection in Paris in 1976. His passion, determination and vision led him to own and run retail outlets in London, and currently has 200 stores in Japan.*

4. Risk Taking

Entrepreneurs are often considered to be foolhardy risk takers almost by definition. They certainly do take risks but it is more accurate to say that they are calculated risk takers from a position of self-confidence and control.

For the purpose of this section a risk can be defined as any situation or problem which prevents entrepreneurs achieving their objectives.

Figure 3.3 shows that fashion entrepreneurs who are knowledgeable and self-confident about their work may perceive a problem as being quite manageable (A), whereas someone who is not as self-confident would perceive the problem as a major risk (C). In each case they will respond rationally to their perception. This means the risk averse person (C) would feel the fashion entrepreneur (A) is a risk taker.

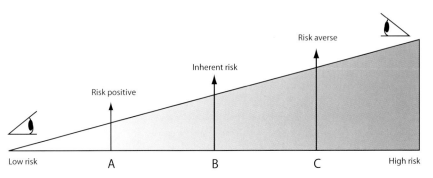

Figure 3.3 Risk Perception Continuum - shows how the fashion entrepreneurs' traits influence how they respond to risks.

Internal Locus of Control: Fashion entrepreneurs who have a strong internal locus of control believe their lives, their destiny and their successes are determined by their own actions and not by the actions of others. By analysing their own actions and addressing their shortcomings, entrepreneurs know they will be successful next time round. It follows that if entrepreneurs feel they are in control of their lives they also feel in control of their risks - if they have a problem they will fix it.

In contrast, **external locus of control** applies to people who believe their lives, their destiny and their successes are determined by the actions of others. They expect other people to make decisions for them and, if there is a problem, they expect other people to fix it - entrepreneurship is not for them!

Self-Confidence: Fashion entrepreneurs believe in themselves. They are self-confident and know they can do the job. This is reflected in their **decision-making.** Research shows that entrepreneurs are statistically more confident of their decisions than other managers, even though their decisions may be no better and, in many cases, they make the wrong decisions.

When entrepreneurs are decisive it makes other people believe they are right which, in turn, helps to make the decision right! In many cases the ability to make a quick decision between two similar products, A or B, is better than a protracted lengthy debate to select the best option. A quick decision enables entrepreneurs to take advantage of opportunities rather than wait for the outcome of lengthy detailed feasibility studies - opportunities do not last forever.

Optimism: Entrepreneurs are born optimists who have strong expectations that, despite setbacks and frustrations, things will turn out right in the end - their glass is always half full! Couple internal locus of control and self-confidence with a healthy dose of optimism, and you start to see why entrepreneurs are prepared to take risks. Not only do they believe they can

Creativity enables fashion illustration entrepreneurs to come up with innovative ideas, and persistence and determination helps them complete their projects.
Protect the environment - sustainable and eco fashion.
Fashion Illustrator: Jessica Haley

do the job in the first place, and fix any problems that may occur, but they also have a positive attitude and believe everything will work out for the best. They see failure and rejection as being due to something that can be changed so that they can succeed next time round. By contrast, pessimists take the blame for their failures, ascribing them to some lasting personal characteristic they are helpless to change.

These differing explanations have profound implications on how people respond to rejection and failure. For example, in reaction to a disappointment such as being refused an appointment with the fashion editor of Vogue, optimists will respond actively and positively, by formulating a plan of action - seeking out help and advice. They see the rejection as a short term setback, and something that can be put right.

Courage: Even if all the problem solving calculations and feedback are positive, it still takes courage for entrepreneurs to take the plunge and commit their money and resources to starting a new business.

Businesses that change the status quo will always encounter problems and resistance to change. Confronting problems takes courage - it is always easier to go with the flow. Ironically doing nothing might well make situations worse! If businesses are not developing new products it means they will be clinging on to obsolete technology. It takes courage for entrepreneurs to stand and fight for their ideas and products but, by doing so, they will be catching the latest fashion waves and selling the latest fashion products.

Exercises:

1. Discuss how your upbringing, family life and schooling has influenced and encouraged you to become a fashion entrepreneur.

2. Discuss what entrepreneurial traits you have to start a new venture.

3. Discuss how you relate your self-confidence to your risk taking.

4. Discuss how you are able to identify opportunities.

5. Discuss how you intuitively are able to co-ordinate and organise resources to implement opportunities.

Social functions present an ideal opportunity for fashion entrepreneurs to network.

Illustrator: Maria Cardelli

4

Networking

Networking skills are one of the most important entrepreneurial traits that you can use to help you start and develop your own business because people, naturally, prefer to do business with people they know and like.

The ability to develop a network of useful contacts will enhance your work experience and help you to apply your fashion portfolio of academic degrees and certificates. The phrase, *'It's not what you know, but who you know,'* will never have been more applicable than now! Although, to some degree, what you know usually influences who you know in the first place!

Your network of useful contacts could be other designers, companies, people at work, family and friends. You could meet them through work, friends of friends, university/fashion school, fashion shows and trade fairs, even through chance meetings with someone at a social event.

> **DEFINITION: Networking** may be defined as, *the ability to connect with a broad range of contacts for the purpose of sharing useful information and resources. The relationship is usually mutually advantageous and collaborative (win-win).*

Barneys New York *is a chain of luxury department stores. Amongst their high end, global brands they have an unerring eye for emerging talent, upcoming designers. 'Barneys New York is a mecca for discerning fashionistas and clothing connoisseurs since 1923'.*

Through your network of relevant contacts, you can use the back door to borrow, gain access to new ideas and information, and utilize resources to develop your products. For example, if you have a garment manufacturing problem, you can ask your contacts for advice, or perhaps borrow their machinery and resources. This is the classic entrepreneurial networking approach to getting started – to learn from the experts and gain free access to useful facilities, keeping costs as low as possible and reduce your financial risks.

Successful entrepreneurs are often said to be **'lucky'**. There are times when this might be true, such as, being in the right place at the right time. For example, if you were on a flight and upgraded to a first class seat beside the womenswear buyer for Barneys of New York, this could be considered lucky. But the successful pursuit of a lucky opportunity relies entirely on proactive **networking** skills - so what happens next is not luck. Constructive networking would be to engage the buyer in conversation and, by the end of the trip, you have made an appointment to present your latest fashion collection to the buyer.

This chapter will discuss how to develop a network of useful contacts to help you start and grow your new business using the following headings;

- Working with Stakeholders
- Fashion Clusters
- Fashion Incubators
- Mentors
- Internet - Social Networking

Top: *Fashion entrepreneurs often meet their relevant contacts at social functions.*
Illustrator: Montana Forbes.

Above: *Informal networking in a social environment.*
Illustrator: Maria Cardelli.

1. Working with Stakeholders (Network of Contacts)

Entrepreneurs do not operate in a vacuum; they work within a company, within an industry and within a particular market sector. Networking is the entrepreneur's lifeblood - it is really too important a skill to leave to chance. Successful entrepreneurs will almost certainly have proactively developed their networks of relevant professional contacts.

This section will show how you can use a stakeholder analysis approach to identify your key stakeholders, including:

- Those **actively** involved in your business; business partners, pattern makers, sample room staff, manufacturers, suppliers, accountants, buyers, retailers, administrators, clients/customers.
- Those who could have an **impact** on your business; bank manager, venture capitalist, business angel, the Animal Protection Society (against using fur and animal testing), the Child Protection Society (against using child labour).

Cultivating your business and useful social contacts (stakeholders) is like nurturing a tree to grow - done successfully, the branches will grow into other branches, so that, ultimately, you will have access to someone who knows, or someone who knows someone who knows (Figure 4.1).

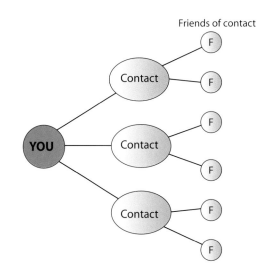

Figure 4.1 Network of Contacts - shows how your relevant professional network of contacts progressively grows as your contacts introduce you to their contacts and friends.

Network Control Data Base: With the enormous effort you have put into establishing a comprehensive network of contacts it is essential to maintain them, and to nurture your client/customer list. As the list grows you will need to formalise your network list onto a data base, so that it can be developed into a 'contact plan'. The frequency of making contact obviously depends on the type of business you have, but once or twice a year should be a minimum - it does not go down well to only contact someone when you need something!!!

Network Control Data Base						
Company	**Name**	**Tel**	**Email**	**Address**	**Date Contacted**	**Notes**

Figure 4.2 Network Control Data Base - shows the headers for your network of contacts formalised on to a data base spread sheet created in Excel.

Stakeholder Types: Consider the following list of stakeholders, people, organisations, internal and external who could have an impact on your business:

STAKEHOLDER		NEEDS	EXPECTATIONS
Originator	The originator is the person who suggested the innovative idea or spotted the opportunity in the first place – the designer (fashion, textiles, accessories, graphics), stylist, event organiser (fashion shows).		
Owner	The owner is the person (fashion entrepreneur), department or company whose strategic plan created the need for the venture.		
Sponsor	The sponsor is the company or client who will authorise expenditure for the venture - this could be family or friends.		
Contractors and Manufacturers	The contractors, manufacturers or people who design and make the products, or supply a service - CMT, pattern-cutters, pattern graders.		
Buyers	Retail outlets - chain stores, department stores, independent stores.		
Potential Customers	The consumers who buy and use your fashion products.		
Boss	The fashion entrepreneur's boss who plays an important role in establishing the fashion entrepreneur's working environment, the support received and career prospects within the organisation.		
Colleagues	Although work colleagues or team members might not be working on the same venture, indirectly they can supply useful background information and peer support.		
Administrators	The company's administration sets up the business processes and keeps the wheels of information turning.		
Suppliers	The suppliers of materials and consumables have a wealth of knowledge and experience about their products – fabrics, trims, machinery, computers, software.		
Equipment Hire Firms	The suppliers of hire and lease equipment have a wealth of knowledge and experience about their products- sewing machines, overlockers, specialist machines for print, knit, laser cut, embroidery.		
Distributors (Warehousing)	Those who are involved in delivering and storing the products - distributors, shippers, importers, exporters.		
Financiers	The sources of finance - family, friends, bank manager, venture capitalists, business angels, grants.		
Support Companies	Suppliers of services - telephone, mail service, couriers, service provider (Internet), gas, electricity, water, waste collection, insurance.		
Government Officials	Those who deal with rules and regulations, Health & Safety, taxes, imports and exports, customs, quality standards, .		
External Companies	Trade Unions, Green Lobby, Animal Rights.		
Fashion Organisations	Trade shows (Fashion and Textiles), Fashion Council (British, US, Canadian etc.), Textile Society, Costume Society.		

Figure 4.3 Stakeholder Types - shows how to identify all your stakeholders to determine their needs and expectations so they can be integrated with your venture's objectives. You should aim to create an environment where the stakeholders are encouraged to contribute their skills and knowledge as this will be useful to the success of your venture. This is your most proactive way of gaining power and influence to develop a business.

London's fashion cluster includes many outlets where emerging fashion design entrepreneurs can sell their creations.

Top: *The Laden Showroom – based in the über-cool Brick Lane, houses some of the UK's hippest young designer talent.*

Above: *Fashion design entrepreneur, Chi Chi, Spitalfields Market.*

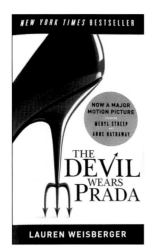

Case Study: *In 'The Devil Wears Prada,' costume designer,* Patricia Field, *had to use her extensive network of useful fashion industry contacts to procure the incredible amount of garments and accessories she required to portray the fashion opulence of the movie. If she had purchased every item it would have far exceeded her 'healthy' costume budget.*

2. Fashion Clusters

A fashion cluster is formed when a number of companies working in the fashion industry set up in close proximity and form a critical mass providing; sufficient work for freelancers and contractors to be fully employed in their specialist fields; a pool of fashion industry talent; and a fertile environment encouraging innovation, creativity and competition. This would include most of the supporting industries and services; fashion designers, pattern makers, marketing agencies, publishing, retailers, and educational establishments that teach the fashion skills. These clusters form a potential environment for emerging fashion entrepreneurs to start up their new fashion ventures. Numerous cities have established fashion clusters - some of the most well known are in; London, Paris, Milan, Barcelona, New York, Los Angeles.

London's Fashion Cluster: London is one of the top fashion centres, its cluster includes:

- Fabric and trims wholesalers and agents, fashion design studios, fashion publications, forecasting agencies, fashion recruitment, fashion mentors, bookshops, modelling agencies.
- Retailers; Department stores - Liberties, Selfridges, Harvey Nichols; the high end, fashion brands in Bond Street; the mainstream retailers in Oxford Street; numerous independent stores spread throughout London - Marylebone High Street, Kings Road; and emerging, young designers in Brick Lane, Spitalfields market and Camden.
- Fashion events - London Fashion Week, Graduate Fashion Week.
- Fashion education - Royal College of Art, London College of Fashion, Central Saint Martins, University of East London, etc., including private schools.

New York's Fashion Cluster: Includes its *Garment District* and its vast retail sector, and all the related industries previously mentioned plus:

- Retailers; Department stores - Barneys, Bergdorf Goodman, Saks Fifth Avenue; high end fashion brands - Armani, Chanel, Versace; independent stores in Greenwich Village and Soho; and the fashion markets.
- Fashion events - New York Fashion Week, Trade shows.
- Fashion education - the Fashion Institute of Technology, Parsons, etc.

Collaboration: Clusters encourage the development of strategic alliances with other companies specialising in different aspects of fashion, making it easier to network and find useful industry contacts to share ideas with and solve problems. This gives companies sufficient work to enable them to focus on what they do best, encouraging them to invest in equipment and systems so that they can produce their products quicker, improve their services, reduce unit costs and ultimately grow faster.

Film Cluster: This is a specialist area within the fashion and creative industries with plenty of opportunities for costume designers, fashion designers and stylists etc. There are many national film industries producing blockbuster movies - the big two are *Hollywood* and *Bollywood*. Hollywood is THE place for actors, producers, directors, writers and agents to network - to see and be seen. Hollywood is also the place where film makers arrange finance and distribution contracts. Smaller clusters and areas to network would be the *Cannes Film Festival,* the *Sundance Film Festival.*

3. Fashion Incubators (Mentoring Groups, Sponsorship Programs)

Fashion incubators are a development of the science park concept (Silicon Valley) which are set-up to offer support to small business entrepreneurs, helping them to develop a market, overcome many of the problems they encounter during the start up phase, and attain sustainable growth. Incubators provide; hands-on management assistance, shared office services, access to equipment, a resource pool, flexible leases, and access to finance, together with formal government-sponsored hand-holding to help get entrepreneurs started.

Emerging fashion entrepreneurs are encouraged to speak with other entrepreneurs and mentors who have already gone through the process of setting up their own businesses, and have a wealth of start up experiences. Incubators provide a stimulating, networking, environment for new entrepreneurs to test out their creative ideas and receive immediate feedback.

The time spent in the incubator is usually limited, typically two years. The objective is to get the fledgling businesses off the ground, and up and running profitably, so the entrepreneurs can leave the nest and prosper.

4. Mentors

Mentors are usually experienced business people (often previously fashion entrepreneurs themselves) who have a wealth of experience in the business environment and offer their advice to start up fashion entrepreneurs to help guide them through the pitfalls and minefields of starting a business.

Poor small business management practices have derailed many start up companies, compounded by entrepreneurs who are reluctant to ask for help until it is too late. To overcome this problem small businesses are encouraged to network with mentors. Lending institutions often link their loans to entrepreneurs who have mentor support as they prefer to see that there is a safe pair of hands guiding entrepreneurs' through the business start up phase.

Mentors usually offer their advice free to the small business entrepreneur as this is their way of putting something back into society. Their reward is seeing the business get started, seeing it survive the initial phases and grow into a prosperous company.

5. Internet (Social Networking)

The enormous growth of the Internet has fuelled the demand for online social networks which means fashion entrepreneurs meet not only at fashion shows, trade fairs, after show parties and clubs; they can now meet in chat rooms and social networks through Facebook, MySpace, YouTube etc. Search engines have made it even easier to find industry related companies and make important connections to help entrepreneurs develop their new ventures.

Exercises:

1. Discuss a 'lucky' experience you have had and how you used your networking skills to increase your network of relevant professional contacts.
2. Identify your key stakeholders and subdivide them into a number of distinct categories and establish their needs.
3. Discuss a business relationship you have where there is a collaborative two way transfer of ideas and information.
4. Identify the cluster you work in, and discuss how it influences and benefits your business.

Top: *Hannah Hoyle is interviewed by the press after being awarded* Young Designer of the Year *at the Clothes Show Live.*

Above: *Hannah's winning printed, satin dress, inspired by Hollywood icon, Marilyn Monroe and pop art creator Andy Warhol, is modelled on the Maybelline New York Image Catwalk. The bosses of Europe's top fashion houses judged her design to be the 'cream of the crop' and, as a result, she was awarded an internship with a leading designer - a great way to kick-start her career as a young fashion design entrepreneur.*

BEADED BODICE

Illustrator: Sarah Beetson

5

Competitive Advantage

Entrepreneurs thrive in a changeable environment where there are plenty of opportunities to supply new products and services to gain competitive advantage over their rivals. And, there can be no more changeable environment than the fashion industry! Fashion by definition means a succession of ever changing trends, fads and concepts.

> **DEFINITION: Competitive Advantage may be defined as,** *the strategies, skills, knowledge, resources and competencies that differentiate a business from its competitors - this may be by offering a product which customers find is more attractive than the competitors'.*
>
> A **Competitor may be defined as,** *a business that provides the same or similar products and operates in the same market or location.*

Although competitive advantage may sound like management speak, in practice the concept of competitive advantage goes right to the heart of fashion entrepreneurship and small business management. One of the key traits determining fashion entrepreneurs' successes is their ability to identify marketable opportunities, to exploit and commercialise them to gain competitive advantage.

This chapter will discuss competitive advantage and show how it applies to fashion entrepreneurs by using the following headings:

- Competitive Advantage
- Barrier to Entry
- Niche Market (product or service)
- Outsourcing and Contracting
- SWOT Analysis

Fashion Entrepreneurs do well working in a niche market - this could be specializing in designing and making shirts for mens.

Illustrator: Sarah Beetson

1. Competitive Advantage

Once you intuitively understand the concept of competitive advantage, this principle will become your reality check and the driving force to help you select winners from a bag of possible business opportunities.

The following table presents ways in which fashion entrepreneurs and small fashion businesses can create a 'unique selling point' (USP), or 'point of difference' (POD) to gain competitive advantage over their competitors in general, or larger more established competitors in particular. They do this by:

Pioneering Designs	Pioneering new designs, new fabrics, and incorporating new technology to make new products, create a distinctive style, and develop innovative designs. With short production runs this means they can test the market.
Experts	Being expert in a particular field - this could be a skill or offering a service in; fashion design, textile design, fashion illustration, pattern making etc.
Niche market	Working in a niche market, and becoming an expert in that field means that entrepreneurs become more efficient (doing the same job repetitively). For example, made-to-measure (bespoke clothing) is a niche market appealing to customers who want exclusivity and quality garments custom made and fitted for their specific body shape.
Quick Decision-Making	With a small business there are fewer people and there is less internal bureaucracy. This means entrepreneurs can make quick business decisions because they do not have to consult or refer to other managers for approval, or need to compromise their preferred decisions. Being intuitive decision-makers, they make fast decisions and do not get bogged down in the analysis of forecast sales figures and cash flows, by which time the opportunity might have gone.
Flexibility	A small business should be more flexible than larger companies because they are proficient with short production runs where their workforce multi-task. This means they can quickly change from job to job and adapt their designs and products to suit the market, (custom make their products) as the work demands. They are not shackled by conservatism - they can quickly modify their processes and respond faster while larger, more established companies tend to be inflexible with bigger production lines with greater inertia taking longer to gear up.
Speed to Market	Being first to market with new ideas and the latest trends means they stand to capture the *'lion's share'*. Fast fashion retailer, Zara takes just three weeks to get its designs from the note pad to the shop floor (the industry average is nine months). Fashion entrepreneurs who can spot new trends, make quick decisions and get their new products to market before the competition can also capture some of this sector - independent stores, designer markets.
Costs	Larger companies, with larger production runs can reduce the unit costs, but small business entrepreneurs can also be competitive by: • Lowering their overheads by working from home, or sharing offices - this reduces their rent, telephone and electricity costs. • Lowering material costs - using ends of lines of materials and markdown fabrics. • Networking to find cheaper ways of producing their products (beg, borrow and befriend).

Pioneering designs for niche markets - designers work in progress.

Opposite: Fashion Accessories Designer, Aoife Ni Chofaigh, Royal College of Art, *utilises her design and hand crafting skills in creating luxury handbags for her latest collection. Traditional bag and luggage shapes are reinvented, the focus is on surface embellishment, fabric manipulation, digital print and embroidery.*

Top right: Fashion Designer, Richard Thorner *draping on the mannequin - 'nips and tucks' as he creates his haute couture evening gown.*

Below right: Fashion Designer, Poppy Beckwith *has found her niche market - creative machine embroidered textiles.*

Location	Large companies usually position themselves in the high street to capture the passing traffic. To compete, small businesses need to position themselves in a trendy part of town or as part of a fashion cluster - shopping malls, shopping lanes, fashion markets, designer markets, designer emporiums (see *Networking* chapter).
Branding	Large companies have large marketing and advertising budgets to spend on establishing their brands. To compete, small businesses must identify a niche market where their customers prefer their more unique, individual style and personal service. To develop their *brand identity*, fashion entrepreneurs must link their products with their market to communicate their identifiable signature and work closely with their customers to achieve *brand loyalty* (see *Marketing and Branding* chapter).
Customer Service	Large companies have customer service departments to formally respond to customer enquiries. To compete, small businesses have to adopt a more personal relationship with their customers to satisfy their customers' needs and wants. This way they can offer a more personal customer and after sales service and, as a result, increase customer loyalty and sales.
Lifecycle Costing	Lifecycle costing considers the cost of the products over a number of years and includes the initial purchase price, the maintenance and longevity. This means a cheap product which is expensive to maintain may be more expensive overall. Small businesses typically gain competitive advantage by making quality products for a niche market. In clothing, this means using quality fabrics that hold their shape, do not fade or pill, are easy to maintain, (wash, dry clean), fabrics that withstand abuse (sportswear - ski wear, gym gear, swimwear, rugby shirts), and fabrics that withstand constant wear (corporate clothing and uniforms). *Quality products are only expensive once.*

Competition: Competitive advantage is all about comparing performance against competitors. The line graph below presents this as a competition matrix which lists key performance indicators on the left and quantifies performance as a line graph. For example, the graph shows that although your speed to market is more competitive, the competitors are situated in a better location.

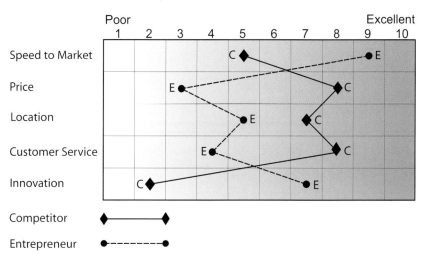

Figure 5.1 Competitor Comparison (Matrix) - shows how you can visually compare your key performance indicators with your competitors.

Niche products in a niche market.

Top: Rhonda Khulman *uses Americana pop art images and religious icons and recycles 1930s to the 1970s vintage bottle caps to create her funky jewellery.*

Middle: Casey Rogers' *collection of quirky dog and cat brooches and key rings are screen printed on funky textiles.*

Above: The @work, *Brick Lane store stocks a mixture of talented, innovative and creative designers' work - this includes jewellery designers* Rhonda *and* Casey.

2. Barrier to Entry

Barrier to entry is a business term used to imply how easy or difficult it is to set up a new business in a particular industry in a particular location. For example, a clothing business setting up as CMT factory with the latest CAD/CAM machines, sewing machines, storage and tracking distribution systems etc. would be expensive to set up, require detailed planning approvals that would take a considerable amount of time to process and, therefore, be considered to have a high barrier to entry. Whereas, a young fashion designer setting up at home in a spare room, with a sewing machine and overlocker, and operating as a sole trader would be considered to have a very low barrier to entry (see *Starting Your Own Business* chapter).

Barriers to entry usually favour the large established companies who are able to achieve economy of scale. By having substantial production runs and buying fabric and trims in bulk they are able to offer lower unit costs. To compete, fashion entrepreneurs need to identify niche markets where a different set of economic criteria apply. Low barriers to entry focus on; small production runs, flexible working conditions and personal contact with customers (see the previous table).

Many sectors of the fashion industry have been dominated by large companies (LVMH, Gucci, Gap, Marks and Spencer) where it used to be the *big eat the small*. But all is not lost for the fashion entrepreneur as these large companies are under threat from small businesses with flexibility, quick decision-making and speed of response to market - it is now a case of the *fast eat the slow!*

3. Niche Market

One of the main ways fashion entrepreneurs can gain competitive advantage is to identify a niche market where they can specialize and develop a unique selling point (UPS), a unique product or service to capture market share.

A niche market may be defined as a portion (or subset) of a market sector, where a narrowly defined group of potential customers have a need for a special product or service that is not being supplied by the mainstream providers. For large companies these market segments are often too small to cover their high operating costs, and the numbers too small to enable them to gain an economy of scale.

Niche Products: These can be found in all sectors of the fashion and creative industries. Some of the specific areas where fashion entrepreneurs have found they can offer their unique designs and made-to-measure or hand crafted products have focussed on; high end luxury fashion, clothing for special occasions (weddings, christenings, 'red carpet' or 'black tie' type events), lingerie, bespoke tailoring, hand knitted garments, millinery, accessories and jewellery.

Niche Service: By specializing in one area, fashion entrepreneurs are able to gain a greater depth of technical ability, product knowledge and experience as much of the process is repetitive (fashion illustration, fashion design, pattern making, grading) and, further, they can warrant the investment in special equipment and systems enabling them to offer a higher quality and more efficient service.

4. Outsourcing and Contracting

Where fashion companies and manufacturers used to produce everything in-house, they are increasingly more likely to outsource part of their non-core work to gain competitive advantage. Although there are obvious financial benefits for outsourcing, there are also a number of disadvantages and these need to be considered, particularly when outsourcing offshore.

> **DEFINITION: Outsourcing** may be defined as, *the process of contracting work to another company which specialises in that particular field - this could be local or offshore.*

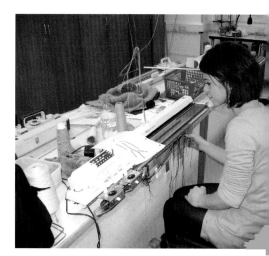

Outsourcing Advantages: The benefits of outsourcing work are:
- To lower manufacturing costs - this particularly applies to offshore companies where the labour rate is significantly lower.
- To reduce internal capital expenditure on non-core equipment and systems.
- To lower internal training and supervision costs.
- To reduce the size of the work force, which means less supervision, less admin, and smaller premises which results in lowering the overhead costs.

Outsourcing Disadvantages: The disadvantages of outsourcing, and this particularly applies to outsourcing offshore, are:
- Manufacturers prefer large production runs to achieve an economy of scale - there is a trade-off here with shipping, storage and investment costs.
- Manufacturing in China, for instance, increases the product turnaround time - if you are in a fast changing market such as 'street fashion', you may not be able to respond quickly enough to beat your competition.
- Products may need to be redesigned to simplify the manufacturing, tooling and setting up.
- Managing quality in your own company is hard enough, but trying to control quality in a foreign company, in a foreign language, halfway around the world is even more difficult - this reinforces the need to simplify the manufacturing process and the importance of clear specifications and documentation.
- Lines of communication between your business (in the West) and the manufacturer (offshore) make you totally reliant on telecommunication facilities. Any interruptions or downtime could have a negative impact on your business.

Outsourcing work to other small businesses specialising in a particular niche market can save on capital expenditure on specialist equipment and systems. For example, working with a knitwear designer or tailor to produce specialist samples for your collection.

Knitwear Designer: Northumbria University

Savile Row Bespoke: Tailor Raj Mirpuri

 Outsourcing Locally: Companies that outsource (contract) their work locally are able to employ contractors when they need them and, therefore, are not involved with hiring and laying-off employees as the work load changes. They can employ specialist freelancers (small businesses entrepreneurs) on a part time basis for a set period. For example, a fashion designer, pattern maker or sample machinist may only be required twice or four times a year, for a few weeks at a time, to design, produce the sample patterns and make the garments for the company's latest collection.

Although the hourly rate of contractors will be more than employees, companies need to balance this with their employees' rights to sick leave, holidays, pensions and redundancy packages. As specialists in their field, contractors (small businesses entrepreneurs) should be more flexible and quicker at their job, and when evaluated overall, they can be less expensive.

Small Business Outsourcing: Conversely, small businesses fashion entrepreneurs may outsource some of their work to other small businesses specialising in a particular niche market. This enables them to expand their product range under their brand name without having to incur capital expenditure for equipment and systems.

Savile Row, London - traditional home of bespoke tailoring. Bespoke tailoring has seen a huge revival of late due to a growing number of business people and upcoming professionals who desire top quality design, fabric and fit in their tailored suits.

5. SWOT Analysis

SWOT is an acronym for **S**trengths, **W**eaknesses, **O**pportunities and **T**hreats. The SWOT analysis will enable you to develop strategies that will match your strengths with business opportunities, while limiting the impact of your weaknesses and external threats.

Strengths: These are identifiable attributes that will enable you to perform certain tasks well, which will give you competitive advantage and help you to achieve your objectives.

Weaknesses: These are identifiable attributes which will limit your ability to perform certain tasks well. They could hold you back, and may prevent you from achieving your objectives.

Opportunities: These are the future possibilities for new products (goods or services) within your field of work.

Threats: These are the external conditions, circumstances, barriers and blocks that could have a negative impact on your business (new venture) and prevent you from achieving your long term objectives.

SWOT Analysis Matrix: The SWOT analysis can be shown as a matrix format for ease of presentation, plotting positive and negative attributes against now and future situations.

5.1 SWOT Analysis – Starting Your Own Business

Consider a SWOT analysis for starting a business as a fashion designer providing a bespoke service for a niche market:

SWOT	Positive	Negative
Now	**Strengths**	**Weaknesses**
	Trend Awareness.	Lacking business skills.
	Creative design concepts, fresh ideas.	Limited fashion and business contacts.
	Dynamic illustration skills.	Lack of finance, cash flow - limited funds available.
	Creative design skills.	
	Expert pattern making skills.	Lack of equipment and systems.
	Expert sewing skills.	Not 'streetwise' - need to understand the market and potential customer.
	Local competitors and designers have poor products and lack the skills.	Unknown label / brand.
Future	**Opportunities**	**Threats**
	Platform to supply another market.	Competition undercutting prices.
	Outsource manufacturing to reduce capital expenditure costs.	
	Develop new products and services.	
	Growth - increase workforce as business becomes established.	

5.2 SWOT Analysis - Fast Fashion

Fast fashion is the entrepreneurs' response to cheap garments manufactured in China. Consider a SWOT analysis for setting up a fast fashion design and manufacturing business.

SWOT	Positive	Negative
Now	**Strengths**	**Weaknesses**
	Ability to spot new fashion trends.	High set up costs - barrier to entry.
	Fast response to the latest trends.	Difficult to plan ahead - no previous sales records.
	First to market with the latest fashion before the competition.	Lack of experience in warehousing and distribution - could lead to overstocking.
Future	**Opportunities**	**Threats**
	Grow the business to include other markets and products.	Competition from other manufacturers.
	Outsource work to reduce capital expenditure.	China will move into fast fashion and air freight their garments.
	The market should grow because consumers are: • updating their wardrobe regularly with the latest fashion. • keen to buy reasonably priced fashion more frequently - more spending power.	Market tired of cheap garments that are outdated quickly and do not wash and wear well.

Sales and marketing professional, Ash, at Nike's Flagship London *store demonstrates* Nike's *new product concept where customers can design and purchase their own sports shoes online or in store.*

5.3 SWOT Analysis - Opening a Fashion Retail Shop

It is a natural desire for people who love fashion to consider opening a fashion retail store. Consider a SWOT analysis for opening an independent store.

SWOT	Positive	Negative
Now	**Strengths**	**Weaknesses**
	Location - trendy area, plenty of passing traffic.	Lack of storage - use Just-in-time (JIT).
	Buying skills - selection and price. Visual merchandising - store layout and window display.	Cashflow, start-up cash-drain.
	Ability to train staff.	Lack of retail experience, processes and systems.
Future	**Opportunity**	**Threats**
	Expand product range.	Lose market share to an online fashion retailer.
	Spot another niche market to supply.	Government introduces new rules and regulations and high compliance costs - takes time to fill in forms.
	The platform to expand into other areas.	
	Franchise brand.	

Exercises:

1. Discuss how your company could gain competitive advantage in a niche market.
2. Identify and quantify the barriers to entry for your proposed business.
3. Develop a SWOT analysis for your fashion business.

Independent

Young

Professional

Green

FABRIC BOARD
CAPSULE COLLECTION
SPRING/SUMMER
MODIFICATION

67% bamboo 28% tencel 6oz	65% hemp 35% silk charmeuse 5,2oz	100% bamboo twill 7,7oz	70% bamboo 30% silk satin	85% hemp 15% silk jacquard 4,7oz	100% cotton organdie 3,9oz

In my collection I used natural sustainable fabrics such as organic cotton, bamboo, hemp and silk blend
These fabrics have many advantages:
Breathable and dry
Absorb and disperse sweat fast
Thermal regulation
Washable
Using eco-fabric generally will not cause any allergic reactions because harmful chemicals are not used
during production.

Production points:
My collection could be produced in Belarus. This country has the following
competitive advantages for textile production:
Current technological developments in modern and innovative technologies
Skilled staff and high potential of labour resource
Availability of free production facilities allowing increase of competitive products
output with relatively low production cost

Fashion Designer: Yelena Smirnova - emerging fashion entrepreneur

6

Business Plans

As creative ideas and opportunities evolve into marketable products, at some point you need to develop a coherent business plan which outlines where you want your business to go and how you plan to get there.

Essentially, the business plan is a road map to a successful venture. It is an all-encompassing document identifying the key components of the business. Most importantly the business plan should address the proposed new venture's three main considerations, to confirm whether:

- There is a market for your products or services.
- You can make the products or they can be outsourced to someone who can.
- The new venture is feasible, will make the best use of your resources (time and money) and will make a profit.

Your business plan is an essential document when approaching a bank or private investor to raise finance, but its other uses should also be acknowledged:

- It will force you to take an objective, critical and unemotional look at the business concept and confirm that all aspects of the idea and opportunity are working together.
- It is an invaluable document outlining how you plan to continue developing, operating and growing your business.
- It establishes a business framework for your new venture and will help guide you when making decisions now and in the future.
- It will give investors confidence that you have the ability to manage the business and address the problems.
- It helps to communicate the purpose of the venture to the stakeholders (the employees and all those who have an interest in or have an impact on, or are impacted upon by the venture).

Whichever finance and market research route you take, whether the business is to be financed from personal savings or family (the most common methods), the bank, or a private investor (less likely), your business plan will help ensure that the funds are not being put into an unacceptable risk.

If you require help to develop your business plan, this is the time to consider seeking a **mentor** who can collate and present your entrepreneurial and creative ideas into a coherent document (see the *Networking* chapter).

DESIGN DEVELOPMENT
CAPSULE COLLECTION
SPRING/SUMMER

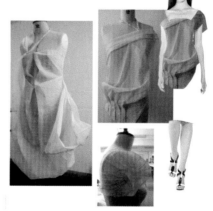

Eco friendly and sustainable, hemp and silk blend designs.

Fashion Designer: Yelena Smirnova

Many fashion entrepreneurs would probably consider that writing a business plan, just to convince the bank manager or interested parties they are worthy of a loan, as a complete waste of time. But it is important to appreciate that the business plan can be one of the most important documents fashion entrepreneurs will ever develop, ensuring feasibility and the financial success of their businesses.

© Fashion Entrepreneur - Sandra Burke

Hannah Marshall, *fashion entrepreneur has her own womenswear design business and advises, 'Do all your groundwork prior to starting a business...For my business to be successful I know it cannot solely survive with creativity, and I need to be able to back up my ideas and plans with sound business knowledge and planning.'*

Photographer: Victor de Mello

Imagine you are standing in front of the Dragons' Den, a panel of potential investors, and you only have 30 seconds to introduce your new venture and create an investment interest.

"Hello my name is Aviva, I'm a fashion designer and I have just produced a new summer range for the luxury womenswear market using the latest natural and sustainable, hemp and silk blend fabric. I have already shown my collection to five key independent luxury womenswear stores and taken orders of 500 units. I need to raise $100,000 to manufacture and distribute the garments to my retailers, and help grow my business.

Business Plan Structure

The typical business plan structure can be subdivided into seven key documents or plans that clearly outline what you intend to achieve with respect to the five Ws + H (what, why, who, where, when and how). Business plans tend to follow a standard format giving a clear overview of the new venture in a format potential investors and bank managers prefer and understand.

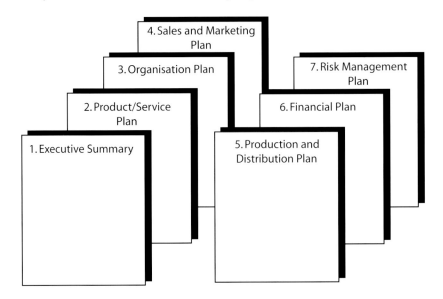

Figure 6.1 Business Plan Structure – shows the business plan presented as the integration of seven key documents.

1. Executive Summary
- Outlines the field of business and the products (goods and services).
- Outlines the type of business and its strengths.
- Identifies the market and competition.
- Outlines the who and how of manufacturing and distributing the products.
- Outlines the business potential and sales forecast.
- Estimates how much money needs to be raised and when.
- Estimates a profit forecast, calculates the return on investment (ROI) and risk.

2. Product/Service Plan
- Describes what the products or services offer, the unique features.
- Briefly outlines the competition's products.
- Explains how the products will be developed, what new products are in the pipeline, and how the business will adopt new technologies, new trends and new fashions.
- Lists what patents have been applied for, copyrights, trademarks, government approvals, product liability (insurance requirements and costs).

3. Organization Plan
- Presents an organization structure of the business and its associates (particularly important if you are a sole trader).
- Presents an organization structure (management plan) outlining lines of responsibility, authority and communication.
- Includes a CV of key team members with qualifications, special skills and business experience.
- Lists strengths and weaknesses of team members and management.
- Identifies stakeholders, particularly close beneficial links with suppliers, contractors and outsourcing arrangements.

4. Sales and Marketing Plan

- Outlines customer profiles/targeted customer - their age, gender, profession, income, where they work, where they live, their attitudes, beliefs, social status, hobbies.
- Target market size - estimates market size, potential number of customers and growth (past, present, future).
- Identifies the niche market - luxury womenswear, sportswear, design service.
- Identifies competitors - who they are, their market share, their possible responses to your products, price strategy and discounts.
- Explains how the products will be sold and distributed - Internet, direct mail, telesales, distributors, retailers, own retail store.
- Outlines the marketing strategy - promotions, advertising, sales brochures.
- Outlines the branding strategy - company name, product names, logos.
- Explains how customer service will be handled.
- Describes the location of the business - studio, factory, retail store, retail space.
- Lists retail facilities required, shop display.

Fashion Designer: Satya James - fashion label
Illustrator: Sarah Beetson

5. Production and Distribution Plan

- Lists equipment, manufacturing and retail facilities required, shop display.
- Lists suppliers of materials and equipment.
- Describes the supply chain - distribution and warehousing, stock control (JIT), shipping, transport and vehicles (see the *Fashion and Textiles Supply Chain*, page 20).
- Outlines the manufacturing sequence and the feasibility study - shows the business is viable.

6. Financial Plan

- Estimates the set up costs to get the business operational including marketing and advertising.
- Estimates the manufacturing costs – how much it will cost to manufacture the products (unit costs).
- Forecasts sales – shows the projected sales determined from market research.
- Determines the breakeven point – how many products must be sold to recover setup costs.
- Determines the payback period – the time to reach the breakeven point.
- Determines the survival period - the time to achieve an operating profit.
- Produces a cashflow statement showing income and expenditure together with funding (how much, by when and when it will be repaid).
- Estimates the return on investment (ROI)
- Identifies the sources of finance – who is supplying the funds (seed money).

7. Risk Management Plan

- Identifies possible risks, and responses.
- Discusses disaster recovery (fire, floods, lost data) and how to develop contingency plans (data backup) to be able to continue trading after a major problem has occurred.

James Caan, *investor and the head of a multi-million dollar global business, is best known for passing judgement on other people's business ideas on the* Dragons' Den. *'Every investment I make, a team arrives and each one of us has a specialist area. That's how we can increase profitability by over 100%. I'm comfortable in most sectors so I'll invest more in the* **person** *than the idea. Whoever I back has to be passionate about their market. They'll be industry experts that know far more about their sector than I ever will. I'm not interested in competing with my investments. My job is to guide, direct and mentor.'*

And:

Plans don't sell new business ideas to investors, people do. Investors invest in people, not ideas. Although business plans are the best way to present information.

Fashion stylist, illustrator, personal shopper, Lucy Laucht - *promotional image for high end, luxury fashion.*

Photographer: Petra Setvinova

Model: Lucy

1. Executive Summary

It is accepted practice to start a business plan with an executive summary to give a brief overview of the new venture. Your summary should get straight to the point focusing on the key issues and the bottom line so that the potential investor can immediately get a feel for your new venture without having to plough through the whole business plan. Your executive summary should:

- Begin with an overview of the type of business, or business opportunity. Briefly describe the products or services, confirming that the business can manufacture or outsource and deliver the products to the potential customers. In the case of a retail store, confirm that you can buy the goods and sell them to the potential customers.
- Confirm the products are unique and that there is a market (general or niche) for the products - this may be supported by the market research and initial sales. Give details of potential sales, market growth, competition and protection (registration, trademarks). Outline how your products will be promoted and advertised to create awareness and establish the brand image.
- Provide brief financial statements; cost breakdown, income breakdown, breakeven point analysis, payback period and a forecast profit and loss statement. Develop a cashflow forecast to outline the borrowing requirement, when and how much money is needed, and when the investors can expect to be paid back, together with a forecast return on their investment (ROI). Outline the risk assessment of your venture, the main risks and likely responses.

2. Product/Service Plan

The product or service plan outlines your products in detail, the type of industry and the market in broad terms – this would be the fashion industry in general and could be womenswear, menswear, high end fashion, accessories, etc. in particular. It outlines:

- The main operations of your business in terms of its current and proposed business activities and objectives of the business in the short term (1-2 years), and long term (2+ years). Describes the products in terms of competitive advantage (unique features), any legal protection obtained (copyright, patents and trademarks), and planned expansion with future products (another label or product area, such as, menswear). This could also be shown by presenting samples, presentation boards and PowerPoint presentations.
- Where the business sits in the supply chain and how the products are received, processed (value added) and passed on to the next link in the chain.
- What support services are required, including suppliers, contractors (CMT), outsourcing, advertising, promotions and customer service strategies.
- Details of who owns the premises, the present valuation and age of the building(s) and, if the premises are leased, the details of the lease (period, rental, option to renew). The details of the floor area and scope for expansion and the suitability of the premises for the proposed type of business, particularly in the case of retail businesses where the customers visit the premises. The following headings can be used as guidelines; visibility, size, image, accessibility to target markets, vehicles (parking) and pedestrian traffic flow, together with future growth and development in the area which may influence the business.
- The name of the local authority and other governing bodies, and the official approvals that are required for the operation of the business.

James Caan, *'There's no question Dragons' Den has had a substantial impact on the rise in start ups. My own website gets 200,000 hits a month [Google 'James Caan']. The level of interest today by people that want to be entrepreneurs is incredible, and I really think that's because of shows like ours and The Apprentice. It's the first time in Britain it's actually cool to be an entrepreneur.'*

Fashion entrepreneurs could offer a service in textile design.

Fashion and Textile Designer: Lidwine Grosbois

3. Organization Plan

The organization plan establishes the credibility of the people involved in the business (yourself [entrepreneur], fashion designer, design team, sales and marketing, accounts department, suppliers and contractors, outsourcing companies) and their ability to achieve the new venture's goals and objectives.

People are an organization's most valuable asset so the focus here is on the people in the business and not the products, the rationale being that if you have the right people, and the right team you will be in a better position in the future to spot opportunities and make them happen. Your organization plan should:

• Introduce the business with a brief history of who, why and how the company was originally formed. Provide details of its legal identity and registration – this would typically be a sole trader (UK) or a sole proprietorship (US), a partnership, a limited company (UK) or a limited liability corporation (US), or a franchise.

• Identify all the key people in the business, outlining their roles, qualifications, appropriate work experience and knowledge of the industry, together with any other special attributes they bring to enhance the competitive advantage of the business (see Figure 6.2). CVs (résumés) should be supplied where appropriate.

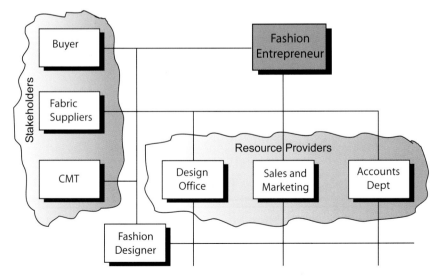

Figure 6.2: Organization Matrix - shows how the fashion entrepreneur interfaces with the fashion designer, design office, sales and marketing, accounts dept, CMT, fabric suppliers, and the buyers (customers/clients).

4. Sales and Marketing Plan

The sales and marketing plan outlines how you intend to market and sell your products or services. Sales and marketing can be subdivided into three sections:

1. **Market Research** - confirms there is a market for the products/services and assesses the customer needs and competition (strengths and weaknesses). This should be supported where possible by tangible market research which covers the five Ps; People, Product, Price, Place, Promotion. This is where the target customer's profile should be discussed, so that you can clearly visualise the customers putting their hands in their pockets and buying your products – the 5 Ws + H; what, who, when, where, why, and for how much.

2. **Marketing and Branding** - promotes your brand and products to create an interest.

3. **Sales and Negotiation** - sells your products to the customers and closes the deal.

The sales and marketing plan should:

- Estimate the size of the market and its future growth potential - local, national and, increasingly, international through the Internet.
- Assess the competition and suggest why someone would buy your products in preference to the competitors'.
- Estimate your share of the market; note here if the products are for a niche market or general market. Based on the above information, estimate the future sales figures over the next three years. Identify the competitors, their size, market share and possible response to the products and price strategy.
- Outline the price strategy, relating to the identified competition. This is the place to comment on penetration price, price skimming and discounts (if appropriate).
- Comment on how the promotion and advertising of the products will reach the target market. This could be broad based advertising (newspapers, radio and television), through the internet (websites, viral marketing) to a wide market, or direct promotions to a niche market.
- Indicate how you plan to develop the brand image and what image you want to portray. This includes; company name, product name, labels, logos.
- Indicate how you plan to sell your products or services - where and to whom, generate the sales, and close the deal.
- If your company intends to sell directly to the general public, this is where you discuss your retail plan. Retail is the final link in the supply chain, the link to the customer and end user. You need to discuss the retail store, the sales people, the changing rooms, the store layout and visual merchandising.
- Comment on how you will deal with customer service and respond to customer enquiries and problems. Friendly customer service is essential to ensure customers are dealt with quickly and efficiently. It is also the best way to ensure repeat business, which in turn should reduce future marketing costs. It is easier to keep a customer satisfied than to go out looking for new customers.

Below: *An example of a fashion entrepreneur's retail store layout.*

Fashion Entrepreneur and Designer: Kerry Hobbs

5. Production and Distribution Plan

Production: The production section describes how the products are made, detailing the critical elements of the manufacturing process. It confirms what special equipment and expertise are required, together with availability; specialist staff - a tailor, milliner, lingerie expert; specialist equipment for digital printing, embroidery, laser cutting. It also highlights to what extent the business has production and price advantage over the competitors. For example, if you are producing 1000 pairs of jeans using a factory with automated production lines, this should give an economy of scale which lowers the unit cost of the products.

It confirms if you plan to manufacture the products locally or outsource work as a means of gaining competitive price advantage, and discusses what is involved in making the products or services. This includes outlining:

- How the products or services are designed.
- What raw materials are used, who the main suppliers are, and what credit terms are enjoyed (60 to 90 days before payment is due).
- What manufacturing equipment and plant are required.
- How the production planning will be managed.
- How quality will be assured, inspected and controlled.
- The risk assessment of the manufacturing process.
- The experience the management team brings to the manufacturing process.

Distribution: This is the section to discuss the warehousing, inventory control and the distribution strategy. This includes outlining:

- The proposed holding stock, inventory control system, and delivery lead time (JIT), together with any special storage facilities.
- How the products or services will be distributed and delivered, and what vehicles and handling equipment are required; hub and spoke distribution, hub to hub distribution.
- The present and future production capacities; relating this to the sales figures and growth projections.

Product samples: Now is the time to create the samples of the products, for example, make the first samples for the range and prototypes to show to the potential investors and stakeholders.

The production and distribution plan is where you discuss if you intend to outsource your production and distribution.

Above: *Manufacturer's design room, and the administration area where the fabric, trims and production process is planned and controlled.*

More than half of all new businesses fail within the first three years - lack of business management planning has been identified as a major cause of this failure. A good business plan is, therefore, essential to help pinpoint unrealistic marketing, potential competition, and unforeseen problems.

6. Financial Plan

The financial plan is primarily concerned with the money issues of running a small business. For private investors thinking of investing in your new venture, the financial statement is one of the key sections, together with growth potential. You need to clearly demonstrate that you have a sound financial plan which you can manage and control. The accounts and financial statements should estimate and collate all the costs involved in setting up and running the new venture. For the purposes of this book these may be presented as:

- Setup costs (seed money and sunk costs).
- Production costs (variable costs).
- Overhead costs (fixed costs).

Financial Forecast: The investors will want to see your financial forecast for the next few years; these are best presented as the following:
- Profit and loss statement.
- Cash flow statement.
- Breakeven analysis.
- Payback period.

The **forecast profit and loss statement** is used to show how the new venture will make a trading profit.

The **cashflow forecast** gives a monthly snap shot of the bank balance and the need for short term finance. The cashflow forecast should also include proposed funding and repayments over an extended period of two or three years, and property loans over ten years.

It should use the **breakeven point** analysis to assess the financial risk by quantifying the number of sales required to cover the set up costs, and use the **payback period** to quantify the time to reach the breakeven point (see the *Small Business Accounts* chapter for calculations).

Managing the Accounts: Outlines how you intend to manage the accounts on a daily basis and any other statements to quantify the company's financial position. Two popular statements are:

- Cash book (lists all the incomes and expenses).
- Balance sheet (lists all the assets and liabilities).

Sources of Finance: Outlines any existing funding including the terms and conditions (see the *Sources of Finance* chapter).

Dance wear - niche market
Fashion Illustrator: Montana Forbes

7. Risk Management Plan

The risk management plan should identify all the potential risks and problems that could prevent your new venture reaching its objectives, the production schedules and sales targets, and how you propose to respond to the risks. This could be to eliminate, mitigate, deflect or accept the risks. If you are accepting the risks, this is the place to outline the contingencies. For example, if the fabric for your production is not delivered on time you may have to consider using a substitute fabric or, if your customer/retailer rejects an order because of a late delivery you may have to sell those garments at a mark-down to someone who buys surplus stock and ends of lines.

Other potential risks are; the competition taking your competitive advantage, the market changing and wanting a different type of product or fashion, left over stock that needs to be sold off cheaply, having to put products on sale or mark-downs, the exchange rate going against you in regard to your international sales of merchandise.

Disaster Recovery: This is the section to outline what measures will be put in place to respond to the ultimate risks (fire, floods, lost data). In particular, how you will ensure the business will be able to continue operating in the event of a such a disaster, and how your data and information will be backed-up and recovered. Statistically, most small businesses that have a fire take so long to recover that their clients move on.

Developing a realistic business plan could help to prevent you pursuing a fashion venture that is doomed to fail. If a new venture is marginal, at best, the business plan should show where and why the venture is questionable and the risks that require further investigation.

Your business plan is the flip side of innovation and opportunity. Without innovation and creative ideas there is no small business venture to consider but, conversely, without a sensible business plan there may be no more ventures because you could have sunk all available funds into a white elephant. There are endless business opportunities in the fashion and creative industries, and many small business fashion entrepreneurs who have developed successful businesses - so let yours be one of them with an effective business plan to set you on the runway to success!

Top: *Risk management: Have a back-up plan in case of loss!*
Illustrator: Maria Cardelli

Above: 'High Tide Heels' - *is this people committing crimes of fashion, or risk management in anticipation of, the all too familiar, flooding?!*
Courtesy of designer, photographer and retailer - unknown!

Exercises:

Develop a business plan for:
1. Starting up a new fashion venture from home, specialising in a niche market.
2. Starting up a new retail business in the young, up and coming area of London's Brick Lane, New York's Greenwich Village or a trendy part of your local area.
3. An Internet fashion business offering clothing and accessories.
4. A fashion service or agency working closely with the fashion industry.
5. Make a one minute sales pitch in front of the Dragons' Den or to a panel of prospective investors inviting them to invest in your business for a 20% equity stake.

BLACK COTTON DRILL JACKET BY SATYA JAMES

Fashion Designer: Satya James

Illustrator: Sarah Beetson

7

Starting Your Own Business

Emerging fashion entrepreneurs are inspired and motivated by the idea of starting their own fashion businesses because this should give them the ideal platform, freedom and independence to develop their own creative ideas and offer the latest fashion products or services.

Statistically, fashion designers are five times more likely to start their own business compared to those in other professions (US Bureau of Statistics). This is because they have the ability to design, make and sell their products (fashion clothing and accessories), and offer a product or service within their specialist field. Therefore, as a fashion design entrepreneur, 'starting your own business' is a realistic career path. Starting a business can be achieved by one of the following ways:

• Start a small business from scratch.
• Buy an existing business.
• Buy into a franchise business.

black lace-up corset *jacket* with red ribbon
SATYA *JAMES*
silver pistol charm earring
WILLIAM L. GRIFFITH

Starting a New Business: Starting a fashion business from scratch gives entrepreneurs the freedom to explore their own innovative ideas and test the business opportunities they have spotted. Being the boss means they have to make all the decisions, they can keep all the profit, but they must also except all the associated risks (see advantage and disadvantages below).

Buying a Business: Why would someone go to all the trouble of starting up a new fashion business when an established fashion business can be bought off the shelf? Buying a ready-made business means the entrepreneur can hit the ground running. An established business should have an established team, a marketable product, an established supply chain and a loyal client base. It has the advantage that its previous and current performance can be confirmed – there is more certainty about the success of the product and the market than when starting from scratch.

Buying a Franchise: Buying a franchise business has become a popular way of starting a business. This is encouragingly supported by the statistics that show a franchise business has a higher success rate than an independent start up business.

Buying a franchise business means the franchisee (the entrepreneur) buys the rights to use the franchise's brand name and products which are already developed and established in the market place. The franchisor (them) usually supports the new business with business plans, training, management systems and a mentor.

Of the three ways to start a business, this chapter will focus on starting a small business from scratch. However, the other two options should not be completely dismissed because they may be more appropriate for certain types of products, certain locations and certain types of entrepreneurs.

Fashion and textile design entrepreneur, Camilla Ramirez winner of the Clothes Show Live 'Design a Print' competition had her collection taken up by Marks and Spencer. They produced a Limited Edition of her designs which flew out of their flagship stores. She is currently building up her business and retail skills managing 'The Laden Showroom' which houses up and coming fashion labels.

Camilla advises, 'It's not just about the pretty dresses, it's the business side and what sells.'

Showcasing fashion collections during the academic year, during Graduate Fashion Week, through fashion and textile trade fairs and fashion events, present excellent opportunities for emerging entrepreneurs and graduates to network and gain competitive advantage.

There is also the potential of making the right contacts to trigger 'starting a business' as there are always plenty of potential private customers, including buyers, at these events on the lookout for the 'next new designer in the making'.

Pros and Cons of Starting Your Own Business

Before rushing out to start a new business, you should appreciate that the small business environment is highly competitive and ruthless. It is, therefore, important to consider the pros and cons (the opportunities and risks) before embarking on such a venture so that an informed decision can be made as to what type of business to start.

Some of the **advantages** of setting up your own small business are:

Own Boss	You can be your own boss, work independently and be in control of your life.
Passion	You can develop your passion for fashion, interests and hobbies into a small business.
Achievement	You will feel a great sense of achievement as your business products will also be your personal products.
Recognition	You will receive personal recognition for the design and quality of your products.
Responsibility	Owning your own business means you are responsible for its success. This responsibility heightens your awareness, your sense of achievement and recognition.
Freedom	Running a small business will give you the freedom to pursue marketable opportunities as you see fit – you do not need to ask anyone (a boss) for permission.
Maximise Return	You will be able to maximise the return on your investment which may be expressed as making the best use of your time or potential to earn a lot of money.
Financial Leverage	You have a greater opportunity to maximise your income through leverage. You do this by earning a portion of your employees' labour rate and a profit share from every garment sold.
Business Growth	You can grow your business by expanding vertically up and down the supply chain, horizontally by offering more products, and 'Z' by finding more customers.
Income Security	You can increase your income security by offering a range of products to a wide client base (this reduces the risk of having all your eggs in one basket).
Gain Experience	It is a great way to gain first hand experience. In this sink or swim situation you make your own mistakes and learn quickly (this is a good example of problem based learning).
Employment Block	By supplying a product you do not have to confront the age discrimination employment block (not enough experience for the job - this may be the trigger to start your own business).

Starting your own business is not as risky as the statistics may first appear. Although, statistically 50% of small businesses cease trading within three years, many cease trading for legitimate reasons which might be as simple as a company name change, moving to a different location, selling the business, or merging with another company.

The exciting thoughts of starting your own company could soon turn into a financial nightmare if you blindly rush into a new venture without considering the following **disadvantages**:

Lose Investment	Your new venture and business could fail and you could lose all your investment, including any investment from your family and friends who you have persuaded to invest in your 'hare-brained' scheme.
Uncertain Income	An irregular supply of work and sales will lead to an irregular and uncertain income - in this feast or famine situation it is difficult to budget ahead.
Tight Budget	You will be working to a tight budget as you try to cut costs and do everything on a shoestring. Meanwhile your corporate contemporaries are working in style with the latest technology, sample machinists, house models and a travel budget to see the top fashion shows around the world.
Long Hours	Working long hours (24/7) driven by passion and enthusiasm for your product, will leave little time for your family and friends, and no time to live a life pursuing your hobbies and interests.
Stress	Working long hours with little time for relaxation and holidays will increase your stress levels and could have a detrimental impact on your health and, further, stress on your family.
Problem Solving	You will be continually under pressure solving problems and juggling resources to meet deadlines and customers' expectations. A poor decision means your personal assets are at risk along with your reputation.
Perform Every Job	As you start your own business, you will have to perform every job - from being the boss to cleaning up. This will leave you little time to do what you really love – designing a fashion collection.

Top: *Sarah Beetson, fashion illustrator at work. Bursting with ideas and passion, her dedication and enthusiasm gets her through the long hours to get the job finished.*

Above: *Success, the job is finished!*

Illustrator: Sarah Beetson

Starting your own business is a major decision and commitment of your time and resources. Although the statistics for small business survival are a concern, the reason for business failure is usually due to poor small business management and project management skills. With this in mind, you need to strike a balance between fashion time and business time, or take on a partner who has complementary skills so, between you both, you can address all aspects of the business.

Finance: *One major problem for new fashion entrepreneurs is lack of funds. Buying a business or buying a franchise incurs relatively high upfront costs which entrepreneurs are unlikely to have. Both types of business may cramp the style of the true entrepreneur, particularly a franchise business which has strict procurement policies. Ultimately, most fashion entrepreneurs prefer to do their own thing and learn by their own mistakes.*

Steps to Starting a New Business

When setting up your own business it is essential to have an overview of the starting a new business process. Starting a new business involves a number of one off tasks which are best approached as a repetitive process. Embedded in starting a new business is the design and production process (see the *Design and Production Cycle* chapter which has its own iterative spiral). These one-off tasks are presented here as:

Step 1: Business Plan

Step 2: Company Registration

Step 3: Budgets

Step 4: Setting Up Your Premises

Step 5: Buying Equipment

Step 6: Design and Production Cycle

Step 7: Trigger

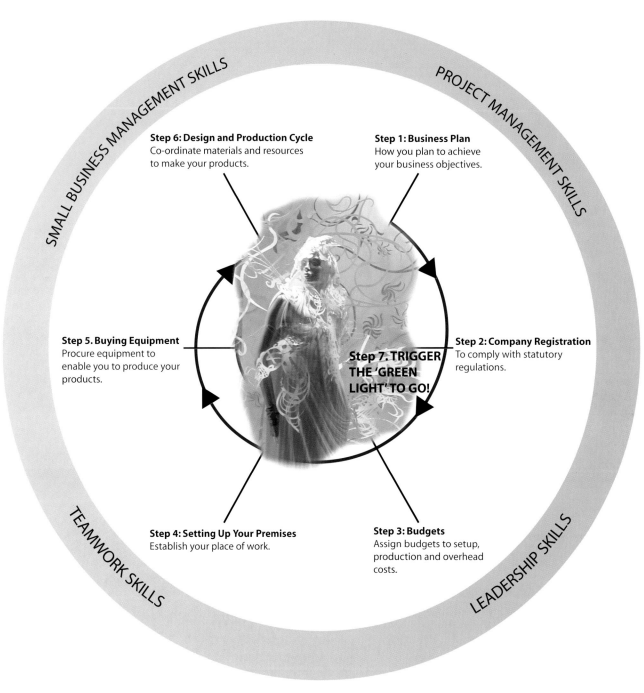

SMALL BUSINESS MANAGEMENT SKILLS

PROJECT MANAGEMENT SKILLS

TEAMWORK SKILLS

LEADERSHIP SKILLS

Step 6: Design and Production Cycle
Co-ordinate materials and resources to make your products.

Step 1: Business Plan
How you plan to achieve your business objectives.

Step 5. Buying Equipment
Procure equipment to enable you to produce your products.

Step 7. TRIGGER THE 'GREEN LIGHT' TO GO!

Step 2: Company Registration
To comply with statutory regulations.

Step 4: Setting Up Your Premises
Establish your place of work.

Step 3: Budgets
Assign budgets to setup, production and overhead costs.

Figure 7.1 Starting a Business Spiral – shows how the key topics are inter-related, together with an outer circle of small business management skills, project management skills, leadership skills and teamwork skills. The iterative spiral helps to explain how opportunities evolve into products and companies - until you achieve the Eureka moment!

Step 1: Business Plan

Producing a business plan is the natural starting point for starting your own business, because it confirms the proposed business is feasible and should make the best use of your resources. In fact you may produce a number of business plans for different businesses and opportunities before deciding which venture to start. True fashion entrepreneurs are intuitively developing thumb nail business plans in their heads as they continually look for opportunities to gain competitive advantage (see the *Business Plans* chapter).

Step 2: Company Registration

All companies need to register and obtain licences to comply with local rules and regulations. This may include registration for personal tax, company tax and VAT, together with a licence to practice, register trademarks, apply for patents and apply for professional indemnity insurance.

When you set up a new business you need to establish a legal identity for the new enterprise to comply with statutory rules and regulations. There are three main legal identities to consider:
- Sole trader
- Partnership
- Limited company.

Businesses come and go but, the astute entrepreneur who starts and develops a successful business and keeps an eye on new products and services will keep on going.

1950s advertising posters, London.

Sole Trader (UK), Sole Proprietorship (US)

A sole trader/proprietorship is a business owned and operated by an individual. It is one of the most common types of small businesses as it has the minimum amount of bureaucracy, the least amount of paperwork and the least amount of interference. Consider the following **advantages** and **disadvantages** of registering as a sole trader:

Advantages	Disadvantages
The biggest advantage of this type of business is that it is simple to set up, is the quickest business structure to get started and is simple to run as it has the least amount of formalities. You can simply start to conduct business - although it may be necessary in some locations (countries, cities, states) to file for a business licence.	You will personally have to accept unlimited liability for all business debts and legal claims against the company.
As you are in complete control of the business and do not have to report to anyone, you make your own business decisions and can respond quickly to market forces.	Your personal possessions such as your car, house and furniture can be seized to pay business debts.
You keep all the business profits and use them as you deem fit without having to justify your spending.	
Apart from tax returns, you are not required to divulge any information about your business.	
The sole trader structure has the least amount of red tape and, therefore, the least amount of compliance costs.	

At a later date, as your business grows, you can always register as a partnership or limited company (limited liability corporation, LLC [US]).

Partnership

A partnership is a legal agreement between two or more people working together. The earnings are distributed according to the partnership agreement and then treated as personal income for tax purposes (See Burke, Rory, *Small Business Entrepreneur*). Consider the following **advantages** and **disadvantages** of registering as a partnership:

Advantages	Disadvantages
The more partners, the wider the range of complementary skills. For example, a fashion designer with creative skills and pattern making skills could team up with someone who has sales and small business management skills.	All the partners share the liability of the partnership. This means you are all equally responsible for the other partners' debts.
Interaction and synergy between the partners should generate more creative ideas compared to the members working individually.	Unless there is an agreement to the contrary, the profits will be equally shared between the partners irrespective of who does the work - this can cause conflict.
The more partners there are, the wider the network of useful contacts, and more opportunities to generate more business.	Compared to setting up as a sole trader there is more paperwork required to set up a partnership agreement, making it more time consuming and more expensive.
To extend the survival period, the more partners working in lieu of income reduces the up front impact on the cashflow.	With two or more people of equal status involved in the partnership, who makes the decisions? And who is the boss?

It is recommended that a well structured partnership agreement be drawn up to legalise the partnership. This will help to avoid and clear up any disputes which may arise concerning profit, liabilities and responsibility.

Limited Company (UK), Limited Liability Corporation (LLC [US])

Unlike a sole trader and a partnership, a limited company/LLC is a legal identity in its own right. Its shareholders and directors may change, but the company continues to exist as a separate identity. As the name suggests, it limits the liabilities of the shareholders should the company fail or be sued. In the worst case the shareholders' liability would be limited to their share capital.

Consider the following **advantages** and **disadvantages** of registering as a limited company:

Advantages	Disadvantages
Limited liability means your loses are limited to the money you invested in the company, but not your personal assets (house, car).	The limited liability protection may be overridden by investors requiring personal guarantees from directors for a particular project/contract (your house could still be on the line).
Increased credibility with lending agencies, customers and suppliers (stakeholders). Banks are often more willing to lend money (provided there is sufficient security) since it is a business structure they are comfortable with.	There are increased regulatory burdens and company audits.
The company name is protected as the registration process registers the name as well as the company.	You have to share the profits with the other shareholders.

Unless there is a special reason, small businesses do not usually start trading as a limited company because of the additional costs and regulatory requirements. It is much easier to start as a sole trader/sole proprietorship or a partnership.

Intellectual Property (IP)

Within hours of the models strutting down the runway at the top designers' seasonal fashion shows, many of the designs are being copied all around the world. Although, it is very difficult for companies to protect their products there are a number of steps that can be taken to limit the impact.

The purpose of IP is to give companies the ability to protect their investment, creativity and designs (products and brands) to ensure they have the right incentives to continue to innovate. IP can be protected by establishing name protection, branding, trademarks, patents and copyright.

Company Names: From a statutory point of view, it does not matter what name is registered – that is between the company and the government – although registration will give name protection. But a trading name and label are important because they form the cornerstone of the company brand (see the *Marketing and Branding* chapter).

Branding: Branding signifies ownership and identification which enables people to make a decision based on the reputation of the brand and company. Branding helps the customer distinguish between a high quality product, its associated value, and an imitation (even though both products might look similar, be a similar price, or more commonly a cheap imitation). See the *Marketing and Branding* chapter.

Working in the creative industry you need to be aware of your intellectual property rights. IP can allow you to own things you create in a similar way to owning physical property. IP distinguishes the goods and services of one trader from those of another. You can control the use of your IP and use it to gain reward. The four main types of IP are:

Copyright ©	Copyright © protects material, such as, text books, literature, art, music, sound recordings, films and broadcasts.
Patents	Patents protect the technical and functional aspects of products and processes.
Trademark ™ or ®	Trademarks protect and identify a company's image; Louis Vuitton, Prada, Gucci, Yves St Laurent etc. A registered trademark might be a word, phrase, symbol, design, even a colour.
Passing Off	Passing off is the illegal use of a trademark by another company or person.

Trademarks: To be registered, your trademark must be:
- Distinctive for the goods and services applied for.
- Not similar or identical to any earlier marks for the same or similar goods and services.
- Not deceptive, or contrary to law or morality.

Your trademark does not have to be registered but an unregistered mark will have to rely on the common law of passing off.

Passing Off: If you have not registered your trademark you may still be able to take action against someone who uses your trademark without your permission, by using the common law of passing off. To be successful in a passing off action, you must prove that:
- The mark is yours and you have built up a reputation in the mark.
- You have been harmed in some way by the other person's use of the mark.

It can be very difficult and expensive to prove a passing off action. But if you register your trademark, it is easier to take legal action against infringement of your trademark.

Complementary Skills: There are many examples of designers who have worked together and whose skills have complemented each other such as; Domenico Dolce and Stefano Gabbana for Dolce and Gabbana; and Heidi Middleton and Sarah-Jane Clarke for Sass and Bide.

Family Business: Many family businesses reach fashion success such as; Donatella Versace for Versace, who took over from her famous brother, the late Gianni Versace; and Miuccia Prada, for Prada, who entered the family business in 1978 and was to soon revolutionize the appearance of its products.

Step 3: Budgets

When starting a new business there are typically three types of costs to quantify.

1. Setup Costs (also known as seed money and sunk costs) are the activities and costs required to set up a new business (see table below). Set up costs are called seed money as they stimulate the growth of the business. But they are also called sunk costs because, once spent, they cannot be recovered.

2. Production Costs relate to the design, manufacture and distribution of your fashion products. These are variable costs as they relate directly to the number of garments produced.

3. Overheads Costs relate to the activities and costs required to run your business on a day-to-day basis. For example, rent, staff salaries and services. These are typically fixed costs because the company will incur them irrespective of the number of garments produced.

It is sometimes difficult to separate setup costs from production costs and overhead costs as there is a certain amount of overlap and interpretation between the three. But it is important to understand the difference as you need to separate these costs to calculate your breakeven analysis and payback period.

The setup, production costs and overhead costs can be identified as:

Fashion entrepreneur, Nikki Burns has used her design and entrepreneurial talents to create her very successful company, 'PinkNik'. She offers a design, printing and embroidery service where she customizes clothing and gifts. Nikki does this through logos and designs that are created by PinkNik or by the client. These designs are printed or stitched on to anything from clothing to guitar straps to coffee mugs. She runs her company from her design studio where she meets her customers in person, on the telephone or online.

Setup Costs (Seed Money)	Production Costs (Variable Costs)	Overheads Costs (Fixed Costs)
Market research	Market research	Staff salaries
Registering a business	Product development - designing and making the products	Utilities - power, water, telephone
The logo design, company names, marks	Maintaining a sewing machine	
Buying equipment, a sewing machine etc.	Buying fabric for your product	
Buying stock fabric	Manufacturing	
A deposit to rent a premises	Warehousing and distribution	Monthly rent
Buying office equipment, shop fittings and company stationery		Servicing office equipment and replacing company stationery
Marketing and advertising		

Typically, entrepreneurs add another dimension; if they cannot afford to buy something, they will beg, borrow or befriend their network of useful contacts!

Sources of Finance: Ready cash and seed money are the life blood of starting your own business. With your budgets established, now is the time to approach your sources of finance for funding and seed money.

Step 4: Setting Up Your Premises

Your business premises are where you conduct your work and, depending on your product or service and your type of business, this will influence the type of facilities required and the location (see the *Sales and Negotiation* chapter).

- Fashion Designer - the premises required could be a studio, an office, a spare room at home, a retail outlet, a retail store.
- Fashion Retailer - the premises required could be a retail store or retail space.
- Fashion Manufacturer - the premises required could be a factory, industrial premises, and could include; production area, storage space, warehouse space for material handling and orders.

To decide what premises you require you also need to consider the following:

- Do your customers come to you or do you go to them? If customers come to your premises you will probably need to be in a particular location; for retail customers this is the high street, shopping malls or a trendy part of town to get the passing traffic. If your customers go to your website to buy your products your location is not important.
- Do you need to be in a fashion cluster where you can network and easily find plenty of business opportunities? The fashion cluster is where you find supporting trades and services/skills all working within the fashion industry (see *Networking* chapter).

Working From Home: Working from home is becoming increasingly popular and increasingly feasible with new technology (broadband) and new ways of doing business (outsourcing). Garages, spare bedrooms, and even the garden shed are being converted into work places and offices. On the **positive** side, working from your home:

- Reduces your overheads - there is no office rent and no additional telephone line charges.
- Allows you time to test the market and slowly grow your business before taking the leap into expensive business premises.
- There is no 'dead-time' travelling to the office. This could be more than a couple of hours a day of productive time gained.
- Reduces the travelling costs – car (fuel), buses, trains or ferries.
- Should allow you to be more flexible with your time to suit your lifestyle and increase job satisfaction.

On the **negative** side, working from home may be cocooning you from the real world. You may need outside interaction, to bounce ideas off others to achieve a cross flow of vibrant, motivating and stimulating ideas keeping you up to date with what is happening in the creative world.

Private Customers: If private customers come to your home, you will need the right kind of home to suit your target market, a home that your customer would want to visit, one that is easy to get to, and with easy access to secure parking. As you build up a number of private clients this can work well, and from small beginnings you can gradually build up your client base. Initially working from home could be a cost effective option, and as your business grows you might consider renting larger premises and moving out.

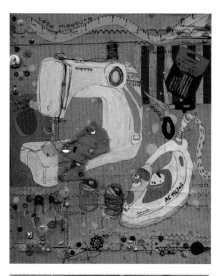

Setting up a business at home is a feasible option for many emerging fashion entrepreneurs.

To reduce your overheads you might start your business in a spare room with just the basics, a sewing machine and scissors! You might develop a list of private clients who eventually come to you for their complete wardrobe!

Illustrator: Sarah Beetson

Step 5: Buying Equipment

Fashion entrepreneurs are in the fortunate position that they can start small (low barrier to entry) and build up a business slowly as their sales increase.

By starting small, a few key pieces of equipment might be all that you require. You can always hire expensive equipment as needed. Key pieces of equipment could be:

Sewing machine and overlocker	Iron and ironing board
Buttonhole machine	Material and paper scissors etc.
Cutting table	Computer
Mannequin (Dress makers form/dummy)	CAD software - Photoshop, Illustrator
Full length mirror	Basic office equipment

Beg Borrow and Befriend: A classic entrepreneur trait is to beg, borrow or befriend when you need something you cannot afford, particularly equipment for your first collection. Consider:

- Cutting your patterns at university/college or work where there is a large cutting table.
- Borrowing or hiring special machinery; an industrial sewing machine, buttonhole machine, embroidery machine .
- Outsourcing reduces your capital up front expenditure on machinery and equipment. For example, if you occasionally need material specially laser cut, embroidered or printed logos, even buttonholes, this could be outsourced.

Above: *Fashion and textile designer, Samantha Payne sourced her design inspiration from Italian architecture to create her fabrics and garments. She used a special laser cutting machine to cut the fabric for these designs and foil printing to enhance the look.*

Fashion and Textile Designer: Samantha Payne

Step 6: Design and Production Cycle

Registering your business and setting up your premises gives you the platform to design, make and sell your product or service. Whether you are producing your collections twice a year or involved in fast fashion, you will have a design, manufacture, distribution, sales and marketing cycle. This is discussed in detail in the *Design and Production Cycle* chapter.

The first two or three times you go through the design and production cycle might be considered as part of the start up phase as everything will be new. You will be looking for new suppliers and contractors, new manufactures, new distributors, new retails, and new clients/customers. But with successive cycles you will start to use the same companies, therefore, the cycle will become less of a one-off project and more a production process.

Step 7: Trigger

It is not unusual for entrepreneurs to hover on the 'starting blocks' waiting for a trigger to give the green light to go. Once all your plans and registration are in place and the business plan(s) for starting your own business have been produced, there are usually one or two events that need to happen before you can start the new venture – these events are referred to as triggers. The trigger could be any of the following:

- **Seed Money:** The availability of seed money to start the venture; this could be support from family and friends, or the approval of a loan (see *Sources of Finance* chapter).
- **Potential Partner:** You find a potential partner with complementary skills. You may be good at design, but the other person has excellent small business management skills. Even the most talented fashion designer is unlikely to be an expert in all fields of fashion design and small business or have time to do everything, especially as the business grows.

Sportswear design board: *Once you have everything in place to start your business and are ready, at the starting block, you may just need the trigger to go for it!*

Fashion Designer: Marlies Ball

• **Sizeable Order:** The award of a sizeable order might make it worthwhile giving up your day job. Many fashion entrepreneurs work for a fashion company during the day then, in their spare time, pursue their own small business ambitions. This enables them to establish their business skills, product range (samples) and develop a network of useful contacts over a period of time while they are still receiving a secure income.

• **No Job:** You are unable to find a job. One more job application rejection may just be the trigger you need to take control and determine your own future.

Exercises:

1. Discuss the pros and cons of starting your own business from your perspective.
2. Discuss the pros and cons of the company registration method you plan to use.
3. Discuss how you plan to protect your intellectual property (IP).
4. Discuss what premises you need for your business.
5. Discuss the feasibility of working from home.

Melanie Casper, 'Munko', successful fashion design entrepreneur advises, 'You must be really serious about your business and what you want to do. You need to make a plan – you cannot be everything to everybody. You must be really passionate and disciplined - there are no 9 to 5 days! You should start small, maybe start at home or rent a small place – you do not want to spend a lot of money on premises until you have really made it. Do not spend money on fancy advertising – direct calling and word of mouth is the best. You should not get carried away when you receive a big order or when the thousands start coming in as you will need this money to finance your next collection and production run.'

8

Market Research

Behind every successful fashion story is an innovative product, and behind every successful product is **market research**. Fashion entrepreneurs can be prone to myopic vision focusing on their product's design and features in complete isolation to their target market. This does not mean that they cannot be innovative and follow their passion at the same time, but market research will prevent them from pursuing an idea and rushing off making products for which there are insufficient customers, and prevent them from wasting their precious funds and resources. The key is to have the customers in mind when developing new products.

The previous chapters have discussed a number of ways to identify opportunities and generate creative ideas. This chapter, and the next two chapters, will discuss the 'sales and marketing flow chart' (Figure 8.1).

- Where **market research** investigates what products the target market/ target customer wants and how to make the crucial link between the product and the market,
- **Marketing and branding** promotes an awareness and creates an interest in the products, and
- **Sales and negotiation** directly engages potential customers and closes the deal.

Figure 8.1 Sales and Marketing Flow Chart - shows Opportunity and Market Research in a closed loop where new ideas and customer feedback converge on an optimum design or product. This is then followed by Marketing and Branding, and Sales and Negotiation.

> **Definition: Market Research** may be defined as, *the study and questioning of groups of people to help determine the target market, determine what products they want, and determine the competition, to ensure a product has competitive advantage and the best chance of success.*

Your market research will provide you with objective data that will enable you to make better business decisions about the product development and marketing of your new venture. It will help you confirm that your venture is worth pursuing by establishing that there is a market for your idea, that people will buy your products, and that there is potential for growth.

Based on your market research you should be able to tailor your products to appeal to the greatest demand - you might even come up with another opportunity to develop a product you subsequently found missing in the market.

Figure 8.2 Market Research Strategy Flow Chart - shows the 10 step market research process.

Market Research Strategy

The market research strategy outlines a simple 10 step process to follow (see Figure 8.2):

Step 1: Market Research Brief
Step 2: Identify Sources of Information
Step 3: Market Research Information
Step 4: Determine Your Target Market
Step 5: Become a Customer for a Day
Step 6: How to Conduct Market Research
Step 7: Trend Research
Step 8: Know the Competition
Step 9: Pricing Strategy
Step 10: Speed to Market

Step 1: Market Research Brief

The market research brief initiates the market research process by outlining the scope of what you want to achieve. When starting a business this may be to confirm there is a market demand for your company and your products. As your company grows your brief will become your instruction document with responsibility, scope, budget and report back dates to integrate with your production schedule.

Step 2: Identify Sources of Information

The sources of information for your market research can be subdivided into; customers, the fashion industry, and sales data (see Figure 8.3). These can be identified as:

- **Customers:** Existing and potential customers, individuals and focus groups.
- **Fashion Industry:** This can be subdivided into; retail buyers and sales staff, trend forecasts and trade fairs (fashion shows, fashion trade fairs, textile trade fairs), the media (trade journals, periodicals and fashion magazines, fashion television), and published reports (information in papers and on the internet, government statistics).
- **Sales Data:** The company's sales data supplies historic information with actual sales figures which helps to identify the sales trends (new businesses may not have this information as yet, or have very little).

Market Research / Sources of Information						
	5 Ps + C					
		People	Product	Place	Price	Promotion	Competition
Customer	Existing/Potential	?	?	?	?	?	?
	Focus Groups	?	?	?	?	?	?
	Become a Customer	?	?	?	?	?	?
Fashion Industry	Buyers (Retail)	?	?	?	?	?	?
	Sales (Retail)	?	?	?	?	?	?
	Trade Shows	?	?	?	?	?	?
	Trend Forecasts	?	?	?	?	?	?
	Media	?	?	?	?	?	?
	Published Reports	?	?	?	?	?	?
Sales Data	Sales Data	?	?	?	?	?	?

Figure 8.3 Market Research Matrix - shows the sources of information and the scope of information required.

As part of your market research you need to establish what are your potential customers' needs and wants.

Illustrator: Maria Cardelli

Step 3: Market Research Information

Five Marketing Ps + C, and Five Ws + H: It is easy for the scope of market research to become open ended and too broad. To help focus your market research consider using the 5 Ps plus Competition, and the 5 Ws plus How. The 5Ps are often referred to as the *Marketing Mix*. There is a certain amount of overlap between the 5 Ps + C, and 5 Ws + H, to clarify see below:

5 Ps + C	5 Ws + H	
People	Who	Although you will have an instinctive idea of **who** your potential customers are, you need to identify your target market in more detail so that you can establish your potential customers' needs and wants.
Product	What	You need to ensure that you have the right products or services directed at the right target /niche market.
Place	Where	You need to identify **where** your customers will purchase your products and your distribution channels - retailers, designer markets, online.
Price	How Much	You need to determine your pricing strategy; the price your customers are willing to pay for your products or services (they must see value in your products). The price must be right for your target market - you will need to compare it with your competition.
Promotion	How and When	You need to determine the best way to inform your customers about your products and the right type of promotion (marketing and advertising). **How** refers to the method of promoting information to your customers. **When** you promote is determined by the fashion calendar; seasons, specific holidays, sale times, and customers' buying behaviour.
Competition		You need to consider how your competition will react to your products and pricing strategy.
	Why	Refers to the company's marketing goals and objectives

Fashion entrepreneurs and especially fashion designers, by their very nature, are 'streetwise' and intuitive. They rely on a certain amount of 'gut' feel, believing they have the designs and products the market wants. Through their market research they are able to target their products to their niche market giving them the 'competitive edge' over their competitors.

Illustrator: Maria Cardelli

See the Fashion and Textiles Calendar *in the* Fashion Entrepreneurs' Runway to Success *chapter.*

Figure 8.4 Market Research Information Matrix - shows how the 5Ps +C, and the 5Ws + H can help structure your market research checklist.

Types of Data: Market research can be subdivided into primary and secondary data. **Primary** data is data you have obtained through questionnaires, interviews and focus groups. **Secondary** data is obtained through published information, government statistics, etc.

Data can be further subdivided into quantitative and qualitative data. **Quantitative** data is based on numerical information (sales figures, people's sizes), while **qualitative** data based on a customer's attitudes, views and feelings.

The more established companies typically subscribe to commercial providers that conduct research specifically targeted to their clients' needs.

As an emerging entrepreneur, there is plenty of 'free' market information available from various sources; via the internet, from libraries, as published reports from government statistics, national newspapers and local banks, through local community business start up agencies, and incubators.

Reports can be found on population (age, gender, marital status), income, wholesale and retail trade (online sales, shopping centres). For example, search on the internet for your local government's statistics (www.statistics.gov.uk, www.census.gov).

Market research will help you identify your customer/target market.
Top: *Are your potential customers male or female?*
Illustrator: Ella Tjader

Above: *What car do they drive?*
Illustrator: Maria Cardelli

Step 4: Determine Your Target Market

The key to determining your target market is initially to ask yourself, *'Who are my potential customers? Why will they buy my products?'* Can you identify your customer? Can you visualise a customer selecting your garment in store, trying it on and taking it to the sales person and paying for it?

This section will help you determine your target market by asking a series of questions and help you prepare your own targeted questionnaires.

Market Segmentation: The fashion and clothing industry can be segmented in three distinct ways; womenswear, menswear and childrenswear. There are many other ways to break it down but the most common are:

- **Geographic** segmentation based on location; where the consumer lives.
- **Demographic** segmentation based on measurable statistics; socioeconomic groupings, age, income levels, ethnicity.
- **Psychographic** segmentation based on lifestyle preferences; fashion attitudes (fashion followers, trend setters).

Self Questionnaire: By considering the above and by asking yourself the following questions, you should be able to establish your customer profile and the merchandise customers might want (consumer behaviour), and then prepare your own customer focussed questionnaires, updating them as required:

Target Market (customers)

1. Are your potential customers male or female? Or will your product sell to both?

2. How old are your customers (age group)? (Demographic)

3. What is their occupation/profession?

4. What is their income range? Do they have disposable income, or are they on a tight budget? What is their socio-economic group?

5. Are they single, married, with children or dependants?

6. Where do they live? (Geographic)

7. What are their hobbies and where do they go on vacation?

8. Do they go to clubs, restaurants, movies, concerts?

9. Do they drive a car? What car do they drive?

10. What life stage are they at? Are there certain clothes they would not wear?).

Consumer Behaviour - Why We Buy: If you understand why we buy this will help you clarify why customers might buy your products.

Statistically we buy products because we **need** or **want** them. In today's consumer market the **want** is usually bigger than the **need** but it is important to appreciate the difference between the two. We might **need** a uniform, protective clothing or more practical clothes for work , but out of work we may **want** to create a highly fashionable image. We might **need** practical clothes for tramping, sailing or going to the gym, but we may **want** to create a more fashionable image in these situations and, therefore, we only buy the latest branded sportswear - Nike, Puma, Adidas, perhaps a designer label, Stella McCartney, Gucci or Chanel.

We all need clothing but, above all, we dress the way we do because we want to look perhaps; younger or older, more successful, the height of fashion, to fit in or stand out amongst the crowd, to look sexy or classic, to make our friends admire us, even envious of us. It is this desire to be admired by others, to make us feel special, and even boost our self-confidence and self-esteem that 'fashion' caters for, and why the fashion trends affect our needs and wants.

The following questionnaire will help you to establish your customers' consumer behaviour in regard to their fashion purchases:

Consumer Behaviour (Fashion Attitude)

1. When do they shop, and how often do they shop?

2. What do they buy? What products, magazines, music do they buy?

3. How much do they spend a year on fashion clothing and accessories?

4. Why do they buy certain products? Are they young and want the latest, cheap fashion, or are they older and looking for quality clothes that do not date quickly? Do they buy because of the functionality of the product or is it because they are brand driven?

5. Are they brand loyal? Is image important to them? Do they buy for the image of exclusiveness - Lanvin, Dior, Chanel.

6. Where do they shop - in shopping malls, in the high streets, in the trendy backstreet areas or designer markets, online, through catalogues?

   a. Designer Labels: Do they only buy high end designer labels – Alexander McQueen, Stella McCartney, Marc Jacobs, Prada, Dolce and Gabbana, Chloé, Marni?

   b. Luxury Brands: Are they into luxury designer brands – Louis Vuitton, Gucci, Balenciaga?

   c. High Trend Driven Brands: Are they into more trendy brands - Diesel, Guess? Classic Brands: Burberry, Ralph Lauren?

   d. Department Stores: Do they shop at department stores - Harvey Nichols, Selfridges (UK); Barneys, Saks Fifth Avenue (US)?

   e. Independent fashion stores/boutiques: Do they prefer buying from Indie designers, where they find more unique products?

   f. High Street: Do they buy from the high street shops - Top Shop, Zara, H & M, Abercrombie & Fitch?

   g. Ethical Fashion: Is ethical and sustainable fashion important to them? Do they buy Eco labels?

Step 5: Become a Customer for a Day

To be a successful fashion entrepreneur you need to know what your customers want and how they buy. Are customers buying on features, the latest fashion, the price; or are they buying on quality and service? These are often at opposite ends of the product continuum - low end, Chinese imports to the highest end, haute couture.

Becoming a customer for the day, shopping for similar products and services to those you anticipate selling to, will help you gain the all important customers' perspective and provide another source of information towards your market research. This role reversal puts you in 'their' shoes, which should help you to improve your business decisions, your product design, and the way you market and promote your products. You could do store visits and note how you are approached and helped by the sales staff; is the selection of merchandise exciting, do you walk in and feel excited by the visual merchandising and ambience, do you feel you want to buy everything in the store, and are the prices right?

You may spot a weakness in your competitors' products - this could become one of your unique selling points (USP). Conversely, you might find a weakness in your own product which you need to fix!

Becoming a customer for the day will help you gain the all important customers' perspective.

Illustrator: Maria Cardelli

Step 6: How to Conduct Market Research

With your clipboard in hand, this section will discuss how to conduct your market research. Initially, your best sources of market research will be through your personal network of fashion and business contacts and stakeholders (see the *Networking* chapter). In addition, you could visit the fashion retailers and talk to the buyers, the store managers and the sales people. Armed with your questionnaire (as discussed in the previous section), and your product samples (if available), you could:

- **Customers:** Approach existing and potential customers for feedback and talk through their needs and wants.
- **Focus Groups:** Set up a focus group, or small discussion group, to brainstorm situations and topics relevant to your research. You could use your list of stakeholders as a starting point to get a focus group together.

  The feedback you receive from this form of market research will help you plan and improve your products' features and design. However, the results you receive will need to be carefully analysed as, within such groups, opinions can be biased; some people may not voice their true opinions for fear of sounding ridiculous and can be swayed by the strongest group members.
- **Retail Buyers:** Retail buyers and sales staff should have the best feel for the market because they are dealing with customers everyday.

Above: *Through your market research you might find an opportunity to offer another product or service - perhaps a fashion design service offering design and make for private clients.*

Below: *Focus Groups - you could set up a focus group, or small discussion group, to brainstorm situations and topics relevant to your research and your products.*

Illustrator: Maria Cardelli

Definition: Focus groups in the fashion context may be defined as, *a form of qualitative research where people (fashion consumers, users, buyers) are brought together to openly discuss their thoughts on a particular product, service, concept, the price, the packaging, advertising etc.*

Step 7: Trend Research

Awareness: As a fashion entrepreneur you need to be aware of trend directions as they will influence the design of your products, and the products your customers will be looking to buy. By tracking fashion and lifestyle trends (past, present and future) you will begin to appreciate how they impact on the global market, how they impact on the mainstream, and how they are a key factor of emerging consumer groups, influencing their needs and wants. In terms of market changes, this will help you establish the design of your product and the changes you may need to make to develop a better, more saleable product. You need to be aware of:

Hand crafted shoe (made in eco-friendly materials).

Silhouettes and styling	The latest silhouettes and styling - seen at the major designer shows; John Galliano, Lanvin, Versace, Balenciaga etc.
Textiles	The latest textiles and developments in fabric technology - first seen at the textile trade fairs.
Colours	The upcoming seasons' colours, trend shades, colour combinations, colour palettes (trade fairs, forecasting publications).
Current Trends	The latest trends in store, the visual merchandising, analyse the looks and note what celebrities are wearing.
The Youth Market	Young style leaders, renown for soaking up new trends and starting them, from street culture to subversive street edge, from consumer mindset to pop culture.
Art to Lifestyle	Art, architecture, photography, film, music, graphics, lifestyle, all have an influence on the fashion trends, from Salvador Dalí, Gustav Klimt, Mario Testino, Madonna, to Gwen Stefani.
Historical and Cultural References	Historical and cultural fashion is always being redesigned to become the latest big trend - fashion from the 60s to the 90s and even previous eras - Chanel suits, Indian saris, Japanese kimonos.
Technical Developments	iPhone, MP3 players, Second Life, the internet - all influence or impact on the fashion trends.

Market research indicates that there is a correlation between a unique selling point (USP) and market performance. New products and new designs help capture market share which leads to increased profitability for a business.

Even for established businesses it is important to offer new innovative features and new products to keep customers interested. Consider the growing global interest in eco/sustainable clothing, and in high tech fabrics - fabrics that, at a touch, will connect you to the internet!

Illustrator: Maria Cardelli

Trend Forecasting: Trends do not just begin with some wild idea for no reason, but through professional teams of people whose job it is to analyse and research the market and who work strategically in various parts of the globe, and collate the information into qualitative research trend reports. These teams include designers, stylists, trend scouts, cool hunters, analysts, forecasters, planners, strategists, cultural academics, illustrators and writers. By the time a trend is reported you could almost say *"the future has already happened"* but it is through identifying the hottest new trends that products are developed and are commercialised in the market place.

Trend Sources: You can source trend information to help you develop your products through:
- Forecasting publications/online: WGSN, Promostyl, Peclers Paris, Nelly Rodi.
- Trade shows: fashion, textiles, design; events held all over the world (Prêt à Porter, Magic Show, Premier Vision, Igedo).
- Trade journals, magazines and the Internet.
- See *Internet Resources* at the end of this book for more information.

Attention to 'Style and Design' has become a key factor of virtually every product, from fashion, beauty, interiors, music, film, to technology, lifestyle and the media. It influences what people buy, from the mega rich consumer to those on a 'shoestring' budget. Through the media (the internet, television, magazines, newspapers) we are constantly kept up to date with the current products, commercial trends and fads.

Too Trend Driven: You need to be careful of your products being too trend driven, as you can be in danger of losing your identity and niche market. But by finding the right balance between trends, innovation and creativity, and interpreting the trends in relation to your target customer, you can use this knowledge to help you produce a successful product.

Faster Communication: This means that as soon as the latest fashion trends are seen on the runways in London, Paris, Milan, and New York, the hottest looks are frequently being copied by companies that will make similar, but usually inferior quality merchandise (less attention to quality, materials, detail, fit); and sometimes getting it into the stores before the genuine articles. When a trend really takes off commercially it can very quickly saturate the market worldwide, evidence of which can be seen in the thousands of cheap 'rip-offs' of designer bags, designer watches, designer sunglasses – Louis Vuitton, Gucci, Chanel, Prada etc.

Fashion Trends Lifecycle: The fashion trends lifecycle, Figure 8.5, shows the sales of the three key fashion categories and how they are adopted by the consumer.

• **Fashion Fads** are adopted by the younger consumer or sub-culture, hit their peak and saturation point almost instantly, but just as quickly, drop and go out of fashion never to be reintroduced, as another fashion fad takes its place. This gives a short window of opportunity for the fashion entrepreneur but is a high risk area.

• **Fashion,** adopted by a larger number of consumers of varying ages, takes a little longer to reach its peak and saturation point, maybe a season or two, and also declines more slowly than 'fad fashion'. A few years later these trends may become fashionable again (the mini).

• **Classic Fashion**, such as, the Burberry trench coat and Gucci handbags, and **basic fashion** products, such as, tee shirts and blue jeans, have the longest lifecycle compared to a fashion product or 'fad'. The styles continue selling for several seasons, or years in some cases, with very little design change, but when they do decline they can often re-appear several years later.

Knowing where your products fit in the fashion trends lifecycle will influence the way you design, produce and merchandise your range, and how you develop your product mix. For example, if you balance your range to include some basic or classic styles along with trend driven designs, you should be able to fully maximize your sales potential and customer base.

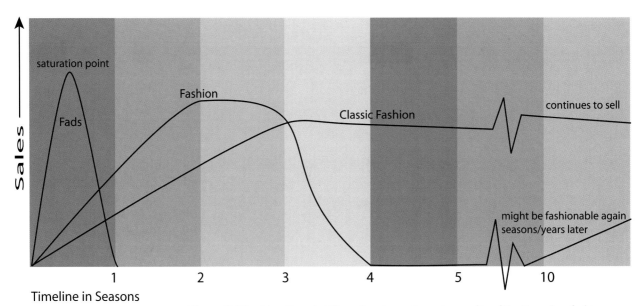

Figure 8.5 Fashion Trends Lifecycle - shows the sales profile of the three key fashion categories and how they are adopted by the consumer.

Step 8: Know the Competition

Competition plays a big part in the business strategy as there are many companies with similar products chasing the same customers. Knowing your competition's products will help you make better decisions about your products and help you build a successful business (see the *Competitive Advantage* chapter).

Size of the Market: Estimating the size of the market for a product can be extremely difficult especially if you do not have any previous sales figures to base it on. Basic economics influences the size of the market - this is called the supply and demand curve. Typically, as the price of a product reduces, the demand for the product increases . With larger production runs, unit manufacturing costs will reduce and give you better buying power which will influence the cost of your products.

The next step is to estimate what percentage of the market you hope to capture with respect to the competition. Knowing the size of the market and establishing your competition will help you determine your potential share of the market. This involves establishing:

1. What is the potential size of the market? How much of the product would the potential customer buy and how often?
2. How many other companies are offering the same or similar products?
3. What is the percentage of the market you could capture?
4. Is the market trend growing, steady or declining?

Step 9: Pricing Strategy

When deciding on a price for your product you need to establish:
1. How much it costs to make the product?
2. How much the customer is willing to pay? What price can the market stand?
3. How much is the competition's product and how will they react to your price?

The price you decide to charge the customers for your merchandise is a market strategy decision. While you need to determine a base price to cover the expenses, the final selling price is determined as the result of where to place the product with respect to the competitors' products and the customers' willingness-to-pay (supply and demand).

Compare the prices of well known high end designer brands to those emerging designers selling their collections in independent stores. Some customers are willing to pay more for the high end brand (brand loyalty) compared to labels which design wise may be equal but, have not yet established their brands (see the *Market and Branding* chapter).

Right Price: Fashion entrepreneurs supplying a niche market find that consumers are prepared to pay for quality services, quality products, good design, and exclusivity. In contrast, there are consumers who want the latest trends regardless of quality and exclusivity – this is where the cheaper, mass produced clothing made in countries, such as, China have taken the market share. Regardless of which end of the scale, the price of the product must be the right price and be competitive.

Value: The product should be worth the asking price; good value for money. Whatever the product, low end mass market, mid-range brands, high end designer brands, the consumer still demands perceived value for money. Value may be seen as not only a lower price but the price a customer pays for exclusivity and image.

Levi's jeans, *which at one time had the majority share of the jeans market, has seen heavy competition over the last few years from high end designer labels, such as Diesel, Guess, Armani, Gucci , and numerous 'cool' , 'trendy' labels. These companies, through research and impressive marketing, have developed a better understanding of their customers' desires and successfully tapped into the share of the jeans market with their branded fashion jeans. This has forced Levi's to reassess their market. At the same time this competition has grown the size of the jeans and denim market.*

Your products should be the right price for your target market.

Illustrator: Maria Cardelli

Learn from a highly influential and successful entrepreneur: Sir Paul Smith, one of the UK's most successful fashion labels, began his career in menswear design. Observer interview, 'The success of his business is due to his understanding of the roles of both designer and retailer; the success of his designs is attributed to his combination of the classic and the quirky, which he has described as, 'Savile Row meets Mr Bean', and which allows men to purchase relatively traditional (and hence commercially popular) designs but which offer a 'twist' of individuality. He states, 'I'm certainly not above working in my own shops. People do a bit of a double-take. I guess they wouldn't expect Donatella to pop up from behind the Versace counter!'

Profit: A product should not only be competitive on price, but also make a profit. There are basically three ways to increase profits; cut the costs, increase the sales, or increase the price. If your market is highly competitive it may not be possible to make a profit - in which case you will need to look to other options which could include; offer a different product, improve your product, or even enter at a different level on the supply chain (instead of just offering a fashion design service, actually make the garments as well).

Diffusion Labels (secondary lines): To capture more of the market share, many fashion brands offer the customer a less expensive label - brands such as Giorgio Armani, whose more affordable collection is Armani Exchange (AIX), and their Armani Jeans denim collection. The danger here is that the main brand could be diluted.

Price Skimming: Certain sectors of the fashion industry are able to achieve price skimming where the **first to market** is able to achieve a high price for a new product or the latest fashion (novelty and availability). A high pricing structure might last for a short time period, taking advantage of early demand for a new product and the lack of competition. This is a clear willingness-to-pay situation where affluent customers and those that will pay anything to have the latest fashion are prepared to pay a higher price to have the product now rather than later. With competition, the price will reduce as other companies try to achieve competitive advantage by lowering their prices. Towards the end of the retail fashion cycle or season left over stock will be put on sale in store, sold through factory shops (outlets), or sold off to jobbers. Price skimming is evident with fashion items such as; the latest Gucci 'must have' handbags, the latest iPods and iPhones.

Penetration Price: The opposite to price skimming is a penetration price, which is a low price to encourage people to buy a product and try it, with the rationale that, if they like the product they will come back for more (repeat customers). In the short term this is an effective marketing strategy for the entrepreneur to build up sales quickly and help establish the brand.

Low Price: Unless your product can achieve a substantial cost advantage over the competitor's product, you should not try to compete on cost alone. For example, it is difficult for many fashion designers to compete against imported clothing from China, but easier to compete on quality (fabric, make) and uniqueness of design.

Low prices often bring their own problems as they can only be achieved by cutting the profit margin. Lower profits can lead to a struggle to survive. If you compete aggressively on price, remember your competitors are likely to respond aggressively. They might even be able to under-cut your price by running at a loss to drive you out of the market, particularly if they have other profitable products to support the loss makers.

Profit Margins: In regard to the profit you wish to make, you can use 'differential profit margins' as a balancing strategy - the same margin doesn't have to be applied to everything (every garment). This approach would need to be reviewed for the next season though, as some adjustments might have to be made according to what sold well at what margin etc.

Step 10: Speed to Market

Your market research needs to determine: When will the customers buy your product? Is there a particular time of the day, week, month, year or season? When do you need to promote your product?

If a product is too ahead of its time, too unique or too trend driven it may not sell – but conversely you must not be too late, or too far behind your competitors. You need to take into account the seasons, the buying cycles, and customer behaviours. You need to consider the design and production cycle, from the design and make of the first sample through to the production process, sales and distribution. This will determine when your new products need to be promoted and when they need to be in store.

Retail buyers traditionally place their orders 6 months ahead of the date the merchandise is needed in store but, as consumers demand more 'instant fashion', this creates much shorter lead times. This cycle will depend on who you are selling to, your product and where you are on the supply chain. Fashion buyers may place their retail orders during 'Fashion Week', twice a year, four times, perhaps every other month. In retail, high sales periods typically occur at the end of the month when people are paid, and prior to and during special holidays, festivities and events; for example, Christmas, Easter, New Year, the start of summer or the first winter chill.

Analysis: Your market research will establish if there is a demand for your product and clarify the market potential with respect to the latest fashion trends and your competition. The feedback from your market research will help you converge on an optimum product, new venture or service and will form the basis of your marketing mix – a key component in your business plan and marketing (see the *Marketing and Branding* chapter). By implementing the results from your research you will be able to design and improve your products in relation to the market and to your consumers' needs, and position yourself on the runway to success. The design process is discussed in the *Design and Production Cycle* chapter.

Speed to Market - your products should not be too ahead of their time, too unique or too trend driven, conversely you must not be too late, or too far behind your competitors.

Illustrator: Maria Cardelli

Exercises:

1. Discuss how you link your product's features to the market's needs and wants.
2. Discuss how you would organise a focus group and prepare your questionnaire for feedback.
2. Outline how you would conduct your market research and your sources of information.
3. Develop a market comparison between your product and your competitor's product.

DEVORE BUG TOP BY ADRIAN, TO ORDER

LACE PANTS BY ALEXANDER MCQUEEN

Illustrator: Sarah Beetson

9

Marketing and Branding

Designing and developing a creative range of products is only half the story - the other half is marketing and branding. Marketing gets your product 'out there' by promoting and advertising your products, capturing new customers and, just as importantly, maintaining existing customers. Branding communicates an identifiable signature and image which links your product to your company, creating your 'brand identity'.

Creating the 'right' image is a key factor when producing a marketable product. This particularly applies to the fashion and creative industries as consumers have become much more 'brand conscious' (a brand's perceived status and reputation).

The previous chapter, *Market Research*, discussed ways to identify your customers and determine what they want to buy, when and where; this chapter will discuss how to develop and implement a marketing strategy to advise your potential and existing customers of your products and create an interest (see Figure 9.1).

Marketing and Branding/Market Research Cycle: Marketing and branding forms an interesting cycle with market research where the company conveys marketing and branding information to the customer via; promotion, advertising, social networks, etc., and market research conveys customer feedback via; interviews, focus groups, questionnaires and direct feedback to the company.

Figure 9.1 Sales and Marketing Flow Chart - shows Marketing and Branding's relative position in the flow chart between Market Research and Sales and Negotiation.

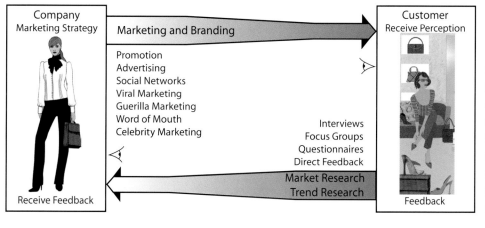

Figure 9.2 Marketing and Branding/Market Research Cycle - shows how Marketing and Branding conveys information from the company to the customer, while Market Research conveys feedback from the customer to the company.

A brand's message may be an expectation of quality (tangible), or an association of its fashionability (intangible).

Marketing Strategy

It is important to have a coherent marketing strategy which co-ordinates the marketing process because, a great product that no one knows about will not sell - your potential customers will live in ignorance and you will soon go out of business - it is crucial to get your message across. Marketing is not a 'one off campaign' but should be a continuous process throughout the year. Your marketing strategy should outline how you plan to achieve your marketing objectives by using the following key steps:

Step 1: Marketing Brief - initiates and outlines your marketing process.
Step 2: Market Research - determines your target market.
Step 3: Branding - develops an image of your company and its products.
Step 4: Marketing Kit - develops promotional tools and presentations.
Step 5: Public Relations - publicizes your business and products to the media.
Step 6: Advertising - advertises your products.
Step 7: Implementation - actions your marketing plan.

Step 1: Marketing Brief

The marketing brief initiates the marketing process by outlining the scope of what you want to achieve. When starting a business this confirms the type of marketing you need and how you are going to inform your target market about your products and new venture. Initially this will be through direct contact via telephone and follow up emails.

As your company grows your marketing brief will become your instruction document with details of who is responsible for the marketing (you or a team member), the scope of work, your marketing budget and the timing of your marketing (this will integrate with your production schedule, together with any key dates, such as, the fashion seasons, the fashion calendar, and the production schedule).

Step 2: Market Research

As part of your marketing strategy, market research discusses ways to identify your target market (customers) and determine what they want to buy, when and where. It confirms your venture and products are worth pursuing and helps you to develop a better product (see the *Market Research* chapter).

Learn the rules of fashion entrepreneurship and catch the express train to success! A company's brand logo is unique and identifies the company and its products.

Marketing & PR Assistant: Joanne Hill, Graff Diamonds Limited

Graphic Designer: Robert Stapleton

Step 3: Branding

The concept of branding can be dated back to 2000 BC when cattle were branded as a sign of ownership; by 1300 BC potters were using *potters' marks* to identify their work. Today these marks are associated with a company's unique image and their unique products. For example, Gucci's unmistakable 'G' monogram and Louis Vuitton's 'LV' are globally recognized signatures expressing luxury and glamour and have become identifiable status symbols in the fashion world.

> **Definition: Branding** may be defined as, *the process a company uses to identify and communicate its product or services and provide customers with assurances of a level of quality and consistency of standard.*

Branding is predominantly the reason consumers choose to buy one company's product or service in preference to another. It plays an important part in a company's marketing mix. Effective branding is achieved through an integrated development of the following: company name, product names, domain names, trademarks and logos (graphic representations, colours, terms, catch phases and even sounds), together with the way a company does business (customer service). A company's branding:

- Indicates ownership.
- Identifies a company and its uniqueness.
- Conveys a message from the company to the customer.
- Creates an association which is translated by the customer.
- Creates an expectation of a certain level of quality and standard.
- Helps develop brand loyalty.
- Offers protection.
- Benefits from celebrity endorsement.

Ownership: Branding indicates ownership which gives the brand name and product legal protection. This is achieved through registering trademarks, copyright and patents (see the *Starting Your Own Business* chapter).

Identification: Distinctive branding (logos, swing tickets, packaging) helps to make a brand stand out amongst all the other brands, for instance; the signage of stores in the high street, the labelling and swing tickets on clothing on a clothing rack, the cover design of magazines on a book shelf.

Message: Branding conveys a message about the company and its products to the customer (see Figure 9.2). The message may be an expectation of quality (tangible), or an association of its fashionability (intangible).

Translation: The customers' socio-economic group (backgrounds, culture, education) and their market sector (fashion followers, trend setters) influences how they translate a branding message into an association which makes them either interested in the company's products or not. This may be an association of quality, fashionability, lifestyle, uniqueness, exclusivity etc. Positive association is the key to effective branding.

Quality: Branding gives an assurance to the customer of a certain level of quality and consistency. For example, Chanel, Dior and Nike symbols, and names such as Prada, Marc Jacobs and Alexander McQueen, through their branding, all aim to convey a guarantee of quality and the latest fashion styling.

Brand Loyalty: It is a human trait that people prefer familiarity so, if customers are happy with a brand and its products, they will remain loyal to the brand and continue to purchase the brand's merchandise - 'brand loyalty' means the company will get repeat business.

Distinctive branding and signage makes a store stand out from all the other stores in the street. Independent designer stores in Paris.

'...fashion has become more and more entwined with celebrities, and the fashion stylists have also become more and more entwined with those stars.' Vogue (Australia) Editor, Kirstie Clements.

'Brand development' has become a fashion company's method of gaining competitive advantage. The luxury super brands such as Prada, Gucci, Dior are global companies that appeal to those customers who want to be seen wearing a quality, high end fashion label, and be part of the trend setters and 'it' crowd.

Top: *Marithé & François Girbaud, Paris: You do not always need bold signage - images often replace words. Here the image in the window says it all!*

Middle and Above: *Store with no name! When your brand is so successful you do not even need signage to display your name or logo, surely you will have made it!? Prada store, Rodeo Drive - even the visual merchandising in the floor of the entrance does not identify the brand name!*

Protects the Market: A well established brand tries to not only protect the product's market share but also protect the customer from unknowingly buying inferior products. For example, the Levi's brand is traditionally known for making quality jeans from quality denim; jeans that will not fall apart or lose their shape the minute they are washed.

Celebrity Endorsement: Celebrity endorsement has become a powerful way to enhance a brand's image. By having a celebrity supporting or wearing the product, the celebrity essentially confers their own branding on to the product enhancing the product's appeal. Celebrity endorsement may be through; advertisements (you just have to turn the pages of a fashion magazine to see who is the next big celebrity endorsing the latest products), and by the celebrity wearing a brand's latest designer label to a 'chic' social event (the Oscars).

And celebrities like model Kate Moss, have taken celebrity endorsement a step further, by signing a contract with the UK retailer, Top Shop, for a *Kate Moss* collection. By having her name and image associated with Top Shop, the retailer does little advertising, relying on 'star power' to sell its products.

Company Name and Label

People associate very closely with company names and product names; certain words, names, numbers and catch phrases stick in their minds. Therefore, your company name or label should support your brand image, sound interesting to your customers and catch their attention.

Domain Name: A domain name is your address on the Internet. Every website must have a domain name or IP address (Internet Protocol). Registering your domain name gives you ownership and protection. Your website is an essential communication and marketing platform, therefore, before investing in developing your company name, product names or labels, it makes good business sense to first check the domain names are available or can be purchased either as a; .com, .net, .org, .co.uk, etc.

Your Own Name: One of the easiest names to choose for your business is your own name. Your own name reinforces and associates the person, the product, the brand and the company name – for the customer it makes it simple as there is only one name to remember! Although using your own name may seem unimaginative, consider how many of the most successful fashion designers use their own name for their branding; Vivienne Westwood, John Galliano, Matthew Williamson, Marc Jacobs.

Name and Product: Considerable benefit can be gained from the customer being able to associate your company name or trading name with your product, where your name immediately conveys a sense of what the brand is about. Industry examples include; London College of Fashion (LCF), Royal College of Art (RCA), Fashion Institute of Technology (FIT), The Fashion Bookstore (LA), Worth Global Style Network (WGSN), and website addresses *www.tagillustrate.com, www.apparelsearch.com, www.fashionbooks.info.*

Numerical and Alphabetical: Company names that include a number are also easily remembered; 4711 (classic perfume), Line 7 (sportswear), Hang Ten (surfwear clothing). To come up first on a list, some companies pick numbers or the letter 'A' - numbers 1,2, 3 etc. precede 'A'.

Logos

Logos are an important part of the 'brand image' because they are quicker to recognise than text. Identifiable logos can be based on symbols, images, design details, colours and even catch phrases.

Fonts: Although most fashion brands today use a particular font and colour to identify their company name, there are many other ways to create a brand logo.

Graphic Symbols, Images and Colours: In its simplest form, long before learning to read and write, we learn to associate images and colours; for example, a cow indicates milk to drink and white is its associated colour, an apple indicates food and green or red is typically its associated colour. Today's highly identifiable brand logos include: Apple Mac and their white apple symbol; Coca-Cola which can be recognised simply by the shape of the bottle and its signature red; U2's *Make Poverty History* campaign which uses the name RED and the colour as its logo on clothing labels; Breast Cancer Awareness which uses a pink bow.

Catch Phrases: Catch phrases are frequently used in advertising - L'Oreal Paris, *"Because you're worth it"*, Diesel's slogan, *"For successful living"*, Coca-Cola, *"It's the real thing"*.

Logo Positioning: As a design feature, the positioning of a logo or label can be an important part of the branding - placing a logo on the outside of the garment on a pocket, collar, hem; Lacoste's alligator logo is stitched on the breast pocket of their tops, and Levi's jeans use a large leather label on the outside back waistband and a red side winder label on the back pocket of their jeans.

Above: *The name of this website clearly identifies what the site is about.*

Left: *Sprite's imagery identifies and appeals to its target market with a carefully considered logo, images and colours.*
Illustrator: Abdul Yusufu

Below*: As part of the company's branding, Levi's places great importance on the type of label it uses and where it is placed on its products.*

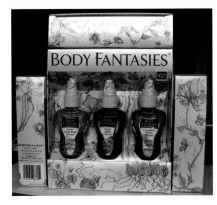

Avne Patel's distinctive imagery and logo design on her clothing labels and packaging identify her unique brand name and company signature .

The packaging of products plays an important part in the branding and marketing of products. (This is an opportunity for a fashion illustrator).

Illustrator: Ella Tjader

Step 4: Marketing Kit

The marketing kit develops the promotional tools you need to promote and advertise your business and your products. Promoting your product can take a lot of time, resources and finance, therefore, you need to consider the best and most effective marketing and branding methods.

As a start up business you should consider starting small, local, within a niche market and contacting customers directly. As your sales increase and your business grows, you could increase your marketing and branding budget - even consider national and broad-based advertising through the media. But where applicable, your branding logo, contact details and website details should appear on your marketing material and products. Your marketing kit could include; business cards, garment labels, brochures, press kits and websites.

Business Cards: Exchanging business cards is almost a ritual when meeting new clients, customers and suppliers at fashion presentations, meetings, trade fairs and exhibitions. Your business card is often the first opportunity you have to convey an image of yourself and your company. It should contain all relevant contact details; name, company, position, telephone number, email and website address, together with your logo (perhaps an image of your product). As a marketing tool, people will remember you and be reminded to checkout your products on your website.

Garment Labels, Swing Tickets, Company Stationary and Packaging: Your brand identity should follow through to your garment labels (sew-in labels, swing tickets) and your company stationary (letterheads, perhaps order forms and invoices) and, as your company grows, it could be on clothing hangers, note pads and packaging (paper bags, carrier bags, tissue paper, gift wrap).

Brochures, Product Postcards, Promotional Mailers: These are excellent ways to present information about your business and products to potential and existing customers. They should include; your business details and logo, product details and visuals (stylish artwork/photographs) of your latest products. They can be fairly inexpensive to produce compared to press or sales kits, and can be mailed, sent digitally and handed out at trade fairs etc. to interested buyers and customers.

Press Kits, Sales Kits, Look Books and Line Sheets: These are your portfolio approach to introduce your company and your products to buyers and the press. Presentation could be in the format of a two-pocket folder containing: an introduction to your company and your brand, business card, a 'look book' (photographs or fashion illustrations of your collection) and/or line sheets (detailed drawings of your products), a description of your products (fabrics, colour range, sizes, availability and price), and copies of your latest relevant press coverage. These kits can be expensive to produce so you should give them only to serious customers/buyers, or the press who are going to review your collection. It is becoming increasingly more common for these kits to be presented in digital format on a disc or sent as a PDF email attachment.

Website: The Internet has become a key marketing platform for all businesses so it is essential that you have a website to display your business details and your products or services. Your website should follow your brand image, be simple in layout, easy to navigate, with clear visuals and just the right amount of text to be informative (people do not want to wait for large images and videos to download). You should not upload the whole of your latest collection before it has reached the retail stores for risk of it being copied - a few images to create an interest in your products would be sufficient.

You need to ensure that your website can be found easily so, as well as putting your website details on your marketing material, you also need to be found by search engines. As your business grows you might consider having a site developed by a professional web designer who can manage your site and perhaps you could even consider selling online (see the *Sales and Negotiation* chapter).

Step 5: Public Relations (PR)

PR effectively communicates information about your company and products through the media. Press coverage helps generate an interest in your products and establish your brand. The advantages PR has over paid advertising is that it is usually free of charge and, as the information is presented as editorial or a news item, it has greater credibility in the consumers' eyes.

PR is communicated through editorials and reviews and through all aspects of the media; newspapers, magazines, trade journals, radio and television. The media prefers the information to be 'today's news, not yesterday's news, so newsworthy fashion topics could be; a new product launch or fashion show, the opening of a new fashion business, an entrepreneurial fashion business receiving a large order from overseas, a milestone fashion event or anniversary, a celebrity opening.

Press Release: By writing your own informative press release you will make the media's job easier. You need to include:
- An attention grabbing headline to indicate what the news is about.
- Short informative/descriptive details of the event/products and, where relevant, release dates, advantages and prices .
- Great photos to catch the editor's attention and the reader's eye - consider images that include appropriate backgrounds, people and suitable poses, the products displayed to their best advantage, the props and the lighting.
- Press samples - in addition to your range samples you might need to make 'press samples' especially if the media require your products for several days.

Step 6: Advertising

The closer you are to your customers, the less you need to advertise - this is the classic niche market position where it is possible to identify and contact customers directly. But, the further you are removed from your customers, the more you will need classic, broad-based advertising to inform customers of your new products and where to purchase them. Your method of advertising will depend on whether you are trying to reach a niche market or a broader base/ national market. Advertising in the local press, local radio, and on notice boards is a lot less expensive than advertising in the national fashion magazines and television, and will probably be all you need initially.

Guerilla Marketing and Viral Marketing (Advertising): These are the latest innovative methods of marketing and are particularly suited to small fashion business entrepreneurs with small budgets. Products are promoted by using creative methods; through the Internet, mobile phones, referrals, word of mouth and also direct marketing. Viral - think computer virus. A message is passed from person to person using social networks (Facebook, YouTube, MySpace), and through viral promotions such as, video clips, interactive Flash games, e-books, and text messaging. Guerilla and Viral marketing have become a significant share of a highly sought after demographic of social Internet users and a successful way of marketing for many companies.

Above: *Fashion Stylists package and promote a brand's product.*

Stylist and Illustrator: Lucy Laucht

Guerilla Marketing *definition, source* www.*businessdictionary.com,* *Tactics available to every small firm to compete with bigger firms by carving out narrow but profitable niches. These tactics include (1) extreme specialization, (2) aiming every effort at favourably impressing the customers, (3) providing service that goes beyond the customers' expectations, (4) fast response time, (5) quick turnaround of jobs, and (6) working hours that match the customer's requirements. The term 'Guerilla Marketing' is a registered trademark of author Jay Levinson who popularized it through his several 'Guerilla' books.*

Above: Fashion Entrepreneur, Hannah Marshall, *a talented fashion designer has used her business and entrepreneurial skills to establish her business. She has all her marketing and promotional tools in place along with a professional, informative, navigable website.*

Left: Hannah Marshall - *design from her winter collection.*
Photographer: Victor de Mello

Step 7: Implementation (Action Your Marketing Plan)

The implementation of your marketing plan starts the process of informing your potential customers about your products. This can be actioned through a number of methods; direct contact (the best method when starting your own small business), PR, advertising, promotions, mailing lists.

Marketing Timeline: The marketing timeline (Figure 9.3) links the marketing process with other activities in the design and production process. You need to inform customers when your products (latest collection) will be available. In many cases this will be targeted to the fashion calendar, fashion seasons, special holidays and festivities (Christmas season, graduation parties, back-to-school, etc.). Depending on the type of business you are running, you may need to contact them once or twice a year or more frequently. It would probably be a waste of resources if you promote your products before they are available because, if your customers cannot purchase them immediately, they will either forget about them or buy a competitor's product. Conversely, if you promote too late the garments will be in the shops but no-one will know about them or worse, you will miss the season completely and your products have to go on sale at a reduced price - timing is therefore crucial.

Scope of Work	Aug	Sep	Oct	Nov	Dec	Jan	Feb	Mar	Apr	May	Jun	July	Aug	Sep
Market and trend research, designs	A/W						S/S							
Marketing Kit, website					▬						▬			
Sales and marketing							▬						▬	
Pre-Production, Production									▬					
Shipping, deliver to store, COD													▬	

▬▬▬ **A/W (Fall) collection**
▬▬▬ **S/S collection**

Figure 9.3 Marketing Timeline - shows how to integrate your marketing plan with your manufacture and distribution schedule. Working back from your delivery in August, the barchart chart shows when you need to start and finish all the sales and marketing activities. (This barchart chart is a segment of Figure 14.3, Fashion Design Project).

"Our latest collection will be available…….do ring for an appointment."

"Place your orders now for Spring."

"See Citron's exciting new line of accessories to compliment our clothing….do visit our showroom….view our collection online"

"Vogue Magazine will be featuring our latest collection in their March issue…you may wish to check that you have our merchandise in store."

Inform your customers of your latest collection's launch dates, product news and press releases.
Illustrator: Ella Tjader

It is vital that you spread the news about your brand wherever you can, where and when appropriate. You can do this by word of mouth but also:
- *Join groups were you will be able to network and market your products.*
- *Attend appropriate events, even help sponsor events by putting on a fashion show or exhibiting your products. This could be at charity events, or fairs/fêtes, gigs, clubs, etc.*
- *Partner with like minded bands and supply them with your fashions that they could wear when performing on stage.*

Control Sheet: As your customer list grows you need to develop your control sheet to track who you have contacted and to prompt you as to who you need to contact, as well as any important points and queries (see the *Networking* chapter). A simple spreadsheet created in Excel will help you to structure your data. As your business and contacts grow, you may prefer to use a specific software for small business management.

Control Data Base						
Company	Name	Tel	Email	Address	Date Contacted	Notes

Customer Service: Your strategy for customer service should endeavour to handle customers' questions and queries effectively, in order to keep your customers and grow your business (see the *Sales and Negotiation* chapter). For retail customers this could also involve making alterations to garments, or offering a consultation service in regard to personal image.

Exercises:

1. Discuss your marketing strategy.
2. Discuss the marketing tools you will need for your business.
3. Write a press release for your latest products.
4. Discuss how you will action your marketing and branding campaign.

Illustrator: Maria Cardelli

10

Sales and Negotiation

Generating sales is the reality test of your business - will people actually buy your products? Convincing your potential customers that your business and products will satisfy their needs and are better than those of your competition is the key to your success. Ultimately, you are the best person to communicate with your customers and persuade them to buy your products because no-one will be more passionate, more motivated or understand your products better than you.

The **Sales and Negotiation** process follows your market research (product development), marketing and branding (see Figure 10.1). This chapter will discuss the sales function; where to sell, how to present your products to your potential customer, and how to close the sale. This chapter completes the sales and marketing process and is the final link in the supply chain.

Figure 10.1 Sales and Marketing Flow Chart - shows Sales and Negotiation as the last link in the Sales and Marketing flow chart.

> **Definition: Sales and Negotiation** can be defined as, *identifying the channels and opportunities companies use to sell their products (where and to whom), creating an interest in their products, generating the sales, and closing the deal and, in the process of which, confirming the price, delivery, distribution and specific terms of the order.*

Although it might appear more prestigious and glamorous to sell through high-end fashion retailers and big department stores; Harvey Nichols, Browns (UK), or Barneys, Neiman Marcus (US), statistically fashion entrepreneurs start and grow their businesses by selling to independent stores and frequently directly to the public through designer/flea markets and even through their friends and family.

Your market research discussed ways to identify your customers and determine what they want to buy, when and where. The products or services that you have and the extent of vertical integration in your business; where to sell and when, depends on where you are on the supply chain (see *Opportunities in the Fashion and Creative Industries* chapter).

Sales and Negotiation Strategy

Your sales and negotiation strategy outlines how you plan to achieve your sales objectives. The key steps are as follows:

Step 1: Sales Brief - initiate and outline your sales and negotiation process.

Step 2: Customer List - where and who to sell to.

Step 3: Preparing to Sell - product knowledge checklist.

Step 4: Contacting Your Potential Customers - introduce your products.

Step 5: Selling Your Products - product knowledge, unique selling point (USP).

Step 6: Negotiating and Closing the Deal - terms and conditions of trade.

Step 7: After Sales - contacting customers, follow up.

You - the fashion entrepreneur!

Figure 10.2 Sales and Negotiation Strategy Flow Chart - shows the seven steps in the Sales and Negotiation Strategy.

Step 1: Sales Brief

Your sales brief initiates the sales process and determines your sales targets based on your sales history and market conditions. It identifies who is responsible for the sales (you or a sales rep), your sales budget and the timing of your sales (timing will integrate with your marketing and production schedule, together with any key dates such as, the fashion seasons, the fashion calendar, and the production schedule).

Step 2: Customer List

Your sales and negotiation approach should reflect the needs of your customers - this will change depending on where you sit in the supply chain and whether your customer is another business or the end user (see Figure 10.3). This section will identify customer types as:

- **Business to Customer (B to C)** - direct sales to the end consumer, individuals that could buy your products.
- **Business to Business (B to B)** - sales to businesses; independent retailers, large retail stores, fashion and textile companies (manufacturers, wholesalers).

Some retailers may place small orders constantly throughout the year, or buy large quantities just a few times a year. But the key is to make sure you contact them, to remind them that you are in business and any new products you may have.

Potential Customers

Business to Customer
- Private Clients
- Designer Markets
- Shopping Events
- Party Plans
- Catalogues, Mail Order, Media
- Your Own Retail Store
- Websites and Online Sales

Business to Business
- Selling to Small Retailers
- Selling to Large Retailers
- Sales Reps and Showrooms
- Fashion Shows
- Trade Shows
- Alternative Shows

Figure 10.3 Potential Customers Breakdown Structure - shows the list of potential B to C, and B to B customers.

Sales and Control Spreadsheet: Developing a control sheet will help you to pull together the components of your sales strategy into one summary document. Figure 10.4 - the first column lists existing and potential customers (those who have shown interest in buying or using your products or services, leads from your marketing campaign and your network of contacts). The other columns set out your strategy and allow you to note what you have actioned and what needs to be actioned (see the *Networking* and *Marketing and Branding* chapters).

Sales and Control Spreadsheet				
Customer Name, Position	Contact Details	Date Contacted	Follow Up	Notes
Steve Leeke, Buyer, Route 66	Tel, email		Date need to contact again	Will be placing order in Feb

Figure 10.4 Sales and Control Spreadsheet - shows an example of how to set up your list of existing and potential customers/clients to help you keep control of your sales process. As you develop your list you might wish to add more fields/columns.

Business to Customers (B to C)

B to C - Direct Sales to the Customer: Many fashion design entrepreneurs focus on selling directly to the end consumer, and this is the strength and success of their business. Your key **advantages** of B to C are:

• There is no middleman, therefore, your profit margin increases.

• With more control of your market you are essentially 'hands on' and closer to your customer. You can test the market and you will understand more about what customers want and what sells best (colours, fabrics, styles and sizes).

• Customers are always keen to meet the fashion designer who has created their garment - if they like you and your products they will buy more (brand loyalty) and even spread the news by word-of-mouth (more sales).

• Your cashflow should improve as you will be paid as soon as you make the sale as opposed to B to B where invoices might be paid 30 to 90 days or, in some cases, 120 days later. Sufficient cashflow is important, especially if you have started your business with limited funds and seed money.

The **disadvantage** of B to C is that it is very time consuming as you split your time between sales, design, marketing and production, and try to manage everything.

Working in a niche market, bridalwear for private clients - the final fitting!

Luxury Designer Label: KlûK & CGDT

Private Clients: Many fashion designers start their businesses by making and selling garments to family and friends who are happy to support them - this is often the trigger that encourages them to set up their own business in the first place. To be prepared for your clients, you will need your portfolio of designs, sketchbook, fabric samples and your order book always at the ready. In addition to making original, made-to-measure pieces you could design a small range of garments each season that your clients select from and you reproduce to their specific measurements.

To maintain continuity of work and a sustainable income you will need a sufficient number of private clients, and this number will depend on the type of garment and its selling price. Obviously, the more personal the service and time involved in the design and make of individual garments, and the better the quality of fabric used, means the cost of the garments would be at the top end of the scale. When an order is placed the terms of payment must be agreed. Typically, the client would pay you a percentage of the cost up front to cover the materials and, when the garment is finished, the client immediately pays the balance - this means you bear less financial risk.

Designer Markets: Most cities have designer markets (designer emporiums, retail spaces) where fashion entrepreneurs can sell their products directly to the public: London's Fashion Market in Spitalfields, New York's Young Designer Market (Mulberry Street) - just check out your nearest designer market.

At these venues you will find a growing number of groups of like-minded indie designers and artisans starting a business and *testing* the market before selling to retail stores. Customers at these venues are looking for something different, something original, and are prepared to pay more for a product's uniqueness and designer status. These markets are becoming so prestigious that it is not unusual to find celebrities and trend spotters amongst the crowd.

The merchandise sold at these designer markets includes: the latest fashion clothing and accessories, vintage and antique original pieces, once loved designer pieces, even ends of ranges and samples.

Fashion Markets have a reputation for producing designers with edgy, gritty products and are a hotbed of cutting-edge artistic talent. They are excellent venues for emerging fashion entrepreneurs to sell their products. With a low barrier to entry they can start small and at least get their 'foot' in the market.

Top: The Backyard Market, Truman Brewery, Brick Lane

Above: Katie Ruensumran, fashion designer at Spitalfields

Below: The Marais Market, Paris

Shopping Events: Fashion shopping events, (shows, exhibitions) include popular events like the Clothes Show Live in Birmingham (UK) and the LA Fashion Co-Op (US). Shows like these have become popular in many cities and are held seasonally or during special holidays. They are one-stop shopping experiences for the customer, where upcoming, emerging fashion designers, fashion graduates, high street and independent labels can display their merchandise, along with top commercial brands, and amongst celebrities and model scouts. There is a charge to rent space, prices will vary, and certain products sell better than others depending on the type of show and the customers they attract, so you will need to confirm that this type of event is really the appropriate venue for your business.

Party Plan: Party plans originated from the Tupperware concept and have proved successful for many fashion businesses; selling luxury fashion, lingerie, jewellery, accessories, beauty products and gifts – you name it, there is a party for it! The party holder (you or one of your network of contacts) invites friends and friends of friends to get together. The party organiser (you) would then present the products to the group, and take orders. Parties like this can create a good response and as one party leads to another, you could develop a thriving business. Overhead costs are low as you do not pay for the venue and, based on the sales at the party, the party holder will be given products typically to the value of 5% to 10% in return for hosting the party and collecting all the money for the goods. This percentage can be included in your retail price so that your actual profit is not affected. If the merchandise is not readily available at the party you will then need to organize the delivery of stock to the host/hostess once he/she has collected all the money.

Catalogues, Mail Order, Media: Selling your products through catalogues, mail order and the media (local or national, newspapers, magazines, radio and television) is expensive and, if you do not receive sufficient orders, will be a financial disaster. Until you have tested the market with your products, established fairly comprehensive sales figures, and really understand who is buying your products and which type of media could work best for you, it is advisable not to go this route. Alternatively, having your products in someone else's catalogue, or reviews and interviews which you do not have to pay for, will work in your favour (see the *Marketing and Branding* chapter).

Comfortable chairs and a comfortable space - this is especially important for the bored husbands and partners who hate shopping and need somewhere to observe from - this could actually increase sales - think about it!

Luxury Designer Label: 'KlûK & CGDT' - Malcolm Klûk and Christiaan Gabriel Du Toit

Visual Merchandising - not only the window display but how you present your merchandise in store (or in your retail space) is important. Consider; how you position the clothes rails, how you fold your garments, how the clothes are merchandised together with the right accessories, having mannequins displaying the 'total look' to show the customers how to wear the garments.

Designer Label: Marni's impressive retail space within a store.

Your retail store or space should be complemented with all the little extras that make shopping a pleasure and a 'shopping experience' for your type of customer.

Luxury Designer Label: 'KlûK & CGDT' - Malcolm Klûk and Christiaan Gabriel Du Toit

Your Own Retail Store: The main advantage of having your own retail store is that you have more control of how you select, visually merchandise and sell your products. For many customers shopping is their retail therapy, therefore the design and ambience of your store and the way they are treated is very important if you want to encourage them to browse, buy and come back again. The main disadvantage of having a retail store is that it can impact negatively on your budget and your time, so you will need to weigh up the pros and cons to decide if it is a cost effective proposition. You will need to sell a substantial amount of merchandise just to cover your fixed overhead costs and will need to plan your selling strategy carefully. Consider the following:

- **Location:** Passing traffic and your 'shop window' are key to attracting customers and creating sales. Most successful 'indie' designer stores are in trendy retail clusters which include other independent stores, galleries, cafes, and restaurants attracting customers looking for unique fashion from upcoming designers.

- **Costs:** You will need to budget for rent, services, equipment and perhaps decor and fitting out (see the *Starting Your Own Business* chapter). Collaborating and sharing space with other designers with complementary products means you could split these costs and, at the same time, attract a wider circle of customers. If space allows, you might even consider setting up a studio workroom behind your retail store.

- **Staff:** Staff are a fixed cost, independent of sales - they need to be paid salaries plus associated employment costs (medical, holidays). Additional staff might be needed to run things while you concentrate on new designs, production, seeing suppliers, dealing with sales and distribution.

- **Total Look:** When customers come to your store you should sell them not only one garment but present them with the whole look, the accessories and all the little extras. These additional items can often carry a bigger mark-up, and boost your profits. You could also stock other designer labels to complement your merchandise.

- **Promotions:** To attract customers into your store during quiet periods which happen depending on; the day of the week (before pay days), the weather, etc., you could introduce in store promotions, loyalty cards, free gift with a purchase, two items for one, as well as the obvious price cuts during sale periods.

- **Store Design:** This should match the type of customer you are trying to attract and relate to the way they live or would like to live: sophisticated and exclusive, cool and extreme, club type environment etc.

- **Visual Merchandising:** How you display your merchandise is important, consider; how you position the clothes rails, folding garments, clothes merchandised with the right accessories, mannequins displaying the 'total look' and showing the customer how to wear the garments.

- **Music:** Carefully selected music will create the right ambience to entice the customer to browse and spend. Some stores even have in-house DJs who start the morning with slow, relaxing music, progressing to more uplifting music by mid morning and lunch time (funky house, psychedelic trance) and sexier music by evening - this is called the feel good arousal theory aimed to enhance customer spending.

If your retail store is a womenswear or menswear store you could complement your clothing with shoes, accessories, jewellery and fragrances etc.

Websites and Online Sales: (See the *Marketing and Branding* chapter).
Statistically only certain fashion products sell online - accessories (belts, bags)
hats (caps) and jewellery are easier to sell online compared to clothing. If you
plan to sell online you will need a well designed, navigable website with a
shopping cart, but also need to consider the following:

- **Web designer, E-expert:** You will probably need to have a web designer to
create, and even monitor and manage your site. An online business will be very
time consuming, answering emails, dealing with questions and keeping the site
up to date.

- **Traffic:** Search engine optimization (SEO) is vital to your business so that
potential customers can find your site easily – no traffic means no sales. You could
even use Google's ad words so that your site has more chance of being found
when certain keywords are searched for - this service works well but can be
expensive for the small business.

- **Payment:** You will need to accept payment by credit card which must be set
up correctly. You could use PayPal which is an Internet business, account-based
system, which performs payment processing for e-commerce vendors. PayPal
would take the orders for you and then send your revenue directly to your bank
account, taking a small percentage of every order you receive, but is a more
convenient method than having to apply for a business license, rent out the
equipment and handle all the orders yourself.

- **Customer Satisfaction and Returns:** Most customers prefer to try clothing on
before they purchase, therefore, to successfully sell online the design of clothing
needs to meet certain criteria. It needs to be simple in design, sizing, colour and
fabric to provide customer satisfaction and few returns. This means:
  - Simple garments - unstructured garments, easy fits, regular fits, loose fits.
  - Specific sizes and measurements must be clearly indicated - chest, bust, waist,
    hip, centre back length to waist or hem, sleeve length, leg length.
  - Regular fabrics - cotton, knit, stretch fabrics, easy care fabrics are ideal.
  - Colours - the most popular being white, black, creams, khakis and brights.

- **Images and Descriptions:** You will need clear photographs, flats/technical
sketches and detailed descriptions of your products for customers to understand
very clearly what they are buying.

- **Retail Stores:** If you are also selling to retail stores, their buyers will probably
demand they receive the merchandise before you start to sell it online or you
could kill their market.

Case study: Exquisites London, www.exquisiteslondon.com. Fashion Entrepreneur
Hanna Han explains how she developed her five star website, *'I spent about two months
to design the site. Many features on the Exquisites London website are implemented to
ease the shopping experience of the visitor. For example, the customer has three levels of
view for a product: an in-page view integrated with product description, a larger view in a
separate window, and a user-friendly zoom view that allows every grain and wrinkle of the
product to be inspected in detail by the customer.*

This is how the Good Web Guide *think about* exquisiteslondon.com: *'Exquisites London is
a gorgeous website offering high fashion from a group of hand-picked Asian designers. As
an online boutique, Google's Adwords is our main marketing channel. It works very well for
us since it brings in international orders, i.e. we don't have to limit ourselves to the UK.'*

*To successfully sell online the design of
clothing needs to meet certain criteria. The
above design by Nicholas Huxley meets
that criteria - a luxury, quality garment,
easy relaxed fit, great colours.*

Illustrator: Nicholas Huxley

Top: *Fashion Design Entrepreneurs with retail stores may also have an space behind the store where they can see their buyers and customers.*

Luxury Designer Label: KlûK & CGDT

Above: *Selling your own merchandise is an excellent method for understanding more about your market and customer.*

Sally Moinet *in her studio office at home where she sells her luxury label direct to buyers and customers.*

Business to Business – B to B

B to B sales and negotiation involves selling to other businesses and retail stores (wholesale) – boutiques, independent stores, department stores, chain stores. This is where you have to strike a balance between larger orders than B to C, but with lower margins. Selling to the trade will require a more formal approach along with professional management skills to create the sales and assure the buyers that you can deliver the goods - no retailer wants to place orders with someone who might seem unprofessional and might not deliver. Fashion retail buyers have always supported creative and innovative designers and are constantly looking out for new designers and fashion entrepreneurs who can sell them the next great product range and the latest trends.

Selling to Small Retailers: Small business entrepreneurs tend to do well when they focus on a niche market, leaving the global saturation of the main market to the 'big boys', the larger fashion companies. Many fashion design entrepreneurs have built very successful businesses by dealing with a number of small fashion retailers season after season. Smaller retailers (boutiques, independents) tend to be more flexible when purchasing new designer labels and will typically place a small order to see how the range sells for them.

If they buy from you and your products sell well you can expect bigger orders to follow. Small retailers can be easier to work with on a personal level in regard to delivery, returns and terms. However, there is a danger that they could go out of business 'overnight', therefore, you must make sure that you have checked their credit worthiness before you finalise an order.

Selling to Large Retailers: The larger retailers (department stores, chain stores) are often only interested in you if you have had great press coverage, won various high profile design awards, been noted as the top graduate from one of the more prestigious fashion schools, and/or have a following of several celebrity clients. They might also require evidence that you have been in business a few seasons, which will assure them that your label is consistent before they purchase your collection.

Many department stores have concessions where designer labels are presented as a 'shop within a shop'. Essentially, these established brands rent an area and run the space as they would their own retail store supplying everything from the shop fittings to the sales staff. Obviously, this may not be feasible for the start up business fashion entrepreneur, but department store buyers might still buy from emerging labels and display the merchandise alongside other designer labels.

Sales Representative and Showrooms: Selling your own merchandise is an excellent method for understanding more about your market and customer, but not everyone will be able to 'sell' successfully and might find it best to have a sales representative. Sales reps take over the sales and negotiation, and can help you grow your business by creating a broader customer base including exporting. This would give you more time to concentrate on your passion of designing and producing your collections, while still managing the production side of the business.

You would need a rep who represents similar or complementary merchandise and who can do a better job than you as you will be having to pay the rep a commission. Certain buyers prefer to work through reps rather than individual designers and manufacturers, as the reps understand what merchandise they require and can advise accordingly. The rep might also receive more honest feedback on your range compared to the feedback you would receive if the buyer were to deal directly with you.

Fashion Shows: Fashion shows provide an excellent platform for presenting fashion designers' latest merchandise. If you are considering having a fashion show you need to weigh up the expense with the sales potential uptake. Sponsored shows, charity fashion shows or sharing the costs with other fashion designers could be an alternative to get your label known.

Tradeshows: Tradeshows attract hundreds of interested buyers from all over the world. The advantage for emerging fashion entrepreneurs is that they can set up appointments to see many of the buyers under one roof - and this is particularly beneficial as this is the time when buyers are looking for emerging talent with the latest ideas and merchandise.

Before committing to the expense of a tradeshow you should visit the show to confirm it is the right venue to sell through - some tradeshows encourage new young designers/emerging fashion entrepreneurs. Points to consider if you wish to exhibit at a tradeshow include; the cost of the stand, its size, its position and the props required. You might find direct selling to buyers is more profitable.

Alternative Shows: Many emerging fashion entrepreneurs cannot afford the expense of the large, commercial trade fairs or they might prefer to show at alternative venues during fashion week. These shows are often held at; galleries, marquees, clubs, even railway stations, and are marketed as unconventional shows attracting buyers who are looking for fresh products from emerging, innovative designers. The negative side can be that buyers attend the main shows and run out of time to visit the alternative venues.

Many fashion entrepreneurs, once they have established a loyal customer list, will rent a hotel room where they can comfortably display their merchandise and arrange for all their customers to come to them during the course of a few days and take their orders.

Step 3: Preparing to Sell (B to B)

Pre-Appointment Checklist: Before you contact your list of potential customers and buyers to make appointments, you need to prepare your sales pitch:

- **Product Range:** Your product range needs to look totally professional and well presented - concise, cohesive, co-ordinated, labelled and costed, together with fabric and colour swatches, brochures, business cards.
- **Product Knowledge:** You need to be knowledgeable about your product. This includes; the features, fabric properties, sizes available, minimum order, prices, promotions, terms and conditions of trade (discount and how many days before payment is due, delivery dates, returns policy, markdowns).
- **Appearance:** Think about the way you will present yourself at your appointment - you should represent your brand and dress appropriately; even better would be to wear your own designs. Statistical studies prove that 80% of the message we convey is communicated by how we dress and our body language.

Product Range: Your garments need to look professional and well presented labelled and costed, together with fabric and colour swatches, brochures, business cards. You need to be knowledgeable about your product - the features, fabric properties, sizes available, minimum order, prices, promotions, terms and conditions of trade.

Illustrator: Nicholas Huxley

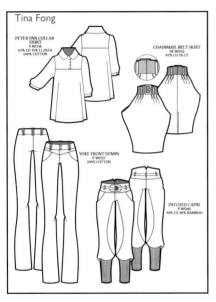

Top: Cold Calling: *All successful fashion entrepreneurs cold call to develop their extensive network of clients. Cold calling is your key to developing a comprehensive data base of potential contacts/buyers who could become your customers, because, if you do not contact them they will never know about your products.*

Illustrator: Maria Cardelli

Above: *Line Sheet of styles in the collection.*

Fashion Designer: Tina Fong

Step 4: Contacting Your Potential Customers

Contacting the Buyer: With a potential list of stores selling your particular type of merchandise the next challenge is to find the names of the buyers who would order your products. With an independent store it will most probably be the owner, but larger retail outlets are more likely to have several buyers for the various product areas.

Once you have the names of buyers you should send them a brief email, introducing your products and a few images that best represent your range. The bottom line is that you have to give potential buyers sufficient information to create an interest and recognize your products are suitable for their stores, but not overload them with too much information.

When you are ready to telephone buyers for the first time you are essentially 'cold calling'. Before contacting them you need to develop your selling strategy, otherwise you will not only waste your valuable time, but also their valuable time. You must know exactly what you are going to say because you will only have a few seconds to gain their interest. If you have emailed them beforehand you should refer to this, then get straight to the point with your name, company name, brief product description and how it will benefit them and benefit their customers. If you have press reviews, this will be of commercial value to the buyers and add to their interest.

Never start with *"I am sorry to bother you"*. It may be polite but it is weak and not a good image to start the sales pitch. Be enthusiastic about your product and how it is an ideal collection for their customers; perhaps you have already had successful sales that you can mention.

Step 5: Selling Your Products

In preparation for your appointments, it is a good idea to visit the stores beforehand to give you an awareness of their branding and merchandising then, when you meet the buyers, this shows you have a greater interest and understanding of their products, needs and their customers.

Appointment: Making presentations to the buyers is your opportunity to showcase your products. It is essential that you keep your presentations fairly short but focussed to get the point across clearly so the buyers understand your product's potential, how it meets their needs and how it will increase their sales. Consider the following selling process:

• Present your product samples and sales material and relate your products to the market and to the latest fashion trends.
• Show how your product's features will benefit and solve their problems (features refer to your product's great selling points, while the benefits refer to the characteristics of the product to attract customers).
• Discuss how they can order your products; direct or through distributors.
• Listen to the buyers feedback, good or bad. Buyers have to focus on what their customers want; their key to success is selling merchandise in store. Merchandise must sell or it will reflect badly on them and badly on you. If they place just a small order, find out how that could grow next time. If they do not place an order at all, ask what you have to do to get your collection in store - it may be something simple. Remember that every fashion entrepreneur, including top fashion designers who have made it, have had endless rejections.

For effective, long term sales, you will need to build a business relationship with your buyers which might take many meetings to gain their trust and confidence in both you and your company.

Step 6: Negotiating and Closing the Deal

The final step in the sales process is to negotiate and confirm the order in writing. The following lists techniques and considerations for closing the deal:

- **Consignment:** To lower the risk to the buyers you could offer your range on consignment. This means they only pay for the products when they sell them and can return unsold stock (be aware that if they return the stock you must be able to on sell it).

- **Quotation:** Larger companies may require a formal quotation which has to be signed off by senior managers (the buyers recommend your merchandise to someone higher up who has the signing power).

- **Terms:** This includes prices, discounts and delivery terms. Credit terms might be 30, 60 or 90 days (30 days ROG means payment in 30 days after receipt of goods). Delivery terms might stipulate that; they might collect the goods, or you have to transport to a forwarder, or you are expected to take care of the shipping (this will affect your costings).

- **Large Volumes:** Substantial orders from a large retailer will give you economy of scale (fabric minimums become less of a problem, the production unit costs reduce), but you might need extra money to finance the order. You will need to be extra vigilant and check the terms regarding delivery and returns. Department stores, especially, can be ruthless, and if merchandise is not performing you might find it being returned to you. You need to ensure you do not have a success-disaster (see the *Project Management Skills* chapter).

- **Exclusive Rights:** Exclusive rights means that buyers request exclusivity to your styles. This could mean that you cannot supply the same styles to another retailer in the same locality - the same town, shopping mall, or within a certain radius; it could also relate to timing - the retailer receives the merchandise several weeks before the other retailers. This could work well if the orders are substantial and if they were helping to launch your label with promotions in store, targeted visual merchandising (window display, front of the store). As you build up a business relationship with your buyers you might even produce styles specifically for their stores.

   If a customer wants exclusivity, it is accepted practise that they pay approximately 50 % when the order is placed (obviously you would negotiate). This is security for you as you would not want to be left with goods that are difficult to on sell, for example, if they were to try to cancel the order at a critical time during your production.

- **Delivery Dates:** This links with your production and distribution schedule. Buyers might require split deliveries, for example, tops and skirts in the beginning of the season, the jackets and heavier weight garments to follow; or they might want the whole story to be delivered as one; or request the order is delivered as one consignment to one location, or split and delivered to other locations (this will have distribution and storage implications).

- **Late Delivery:** Fashion seasons are short so deliveries need to meet deadlines. Buyers might specify a date and time when they can accept your goods in store. You need to confirm to avoid a potential problem with the store refusing to take delivery of your order, and you having to reschedule another date or, the worst scenario, they cancel the order completely.

- **Special Requests:** If these are not realistic, try to negotiate. Never promise what you cannot deliver - your reputation and business would be at stake.

Not all entrepreneurs can 'sell' successfully themselves and will choose to use a sales representative. Sales reps take over the sales and negotiation, and can help you grow your business by creating a broader customer base including exporting.

Showroom: *Ready for buyers to buy though the sales representative.*

Lock Leong, Visual Merchandiser uses his creative talents and entrepreneurial skills as he works and networks with some of the top companies; Versace, Richard Avedon, Gucci, Donna Karen, Valentino, Gianni Versace, Gianfranco Ferre etc.

ORDER CONFIRMATION				Purchase Order	
Date					
Bill To:				Ship To:	
Name				Name	
Address				Address	
Phone				Phone	
Mob/Cell				Mob/Cell	
Email				Email	
Buyer	Store	Dept	Start Date	Complete Date	
Terms		Shipping Specification		Packaging	
Special Instructions					
Style	Description	Sizes		Colour	
		XS	S	M	L		
Authorised By		Title		Date	

Above: *An example of an Order Confirmation form* (see Appendices for full and exploded view).

Lead Times: Some (bigger) companies have longer buying processes so an order might not be booked immediately with the buyer. You need to know your production and delivery lead times and how these could be impacted upon depending on when the eventual order is placed. For example, if using Italian components, you need to be aware Italy shuts down almost completely during August, if sourcing in China, all textile factories shut down for 4 weeks over Chinese New Year, etc.

Writing the Wholesale Order: Confirm everything in writing. Trying to remember specific details or terms is impossible, and you would have no legal standing if there was a problem with your goods. When writing the order make sure you have the following points covered: Order number, date, customer, store, department, contact details, shipping address, billing address, style number, style description, quantity ordered, price (wholesale price and retail price if applicable), sizes, colour, fabric, delivery date, cancellation date, any specific terms of the sale (consignment stock). The merchandise might also need to be hung on special hangers, covered in plastic, folded, require special packaging or special labels - all this needs to be documented (see the *Appendices*).

Step 7: After Sales

After sales contact and customer service for both B to C and B to B is an important part of your business to keep customers happy, as well as to comply with statutory requirements. Consider the following:

• Although it may not be your responsibility as the sales person to check the garments have been delivered, by contacting your clients it shows you care and gives you the opportunity to network and introduce your forthcoming range.

• It is easier to keep a customer satisfied than to go out looking for new customers. Repeat business through word of mouth recommendations and referrals to new customers are not only the most effective form of marketing but are five times cheaper than creating new business. The 80/20 analysis helps you identify who are your best clients - this means 80% of your business comes from 20% of your clients.

• Handling complaints effectively can turn a dissatisfied customer into a loyal customer. Customers who have received good service may well recommend your company to others, but customers who feel badly treated are likely to complain about your company instead.

• As a small business entrepreneur, you will not have national advertising campaigns to boost your image, therefore, you need to make sure that word-of-mouth publicity is positive, particularly if you rely heavily on local business.

• Once your products are in the store, that should not be the end of your input. Merchandise typically sells best in the first few weeks of being on the shop floor. If you live locally you can call into the store, or telephone to see how your merchandise is selling. Depending on the store's procedures you might be sent a regular report of sales of your merchandise.

• If feasible, you should pay a courtesy call to your customers' stores as part of your follow-up. By meeting and talking to the sales staff you will receive invaluable feedback, see how your garments are being merchandised, even make some suggestions, and talk through ways of creating more sales.

Returns and Surplus Stock: Every business has returns and surplus stock and needs to deal with it to avoid eating into the profits. Returns may be due to:

• Rejects (badly made, fabric damage), production over runs.

• The garments not selling in the store - consignment stock.

• Late delivery – this should be avoided at all costs by managing your production and distribution schedule.

Where possible you need to try to fix problems immediately. If you accept the merchandise back you might offer to replace it or offer the client a credit (for the next season if possible).

Alexander McQueen
Greenwich Village

Stunning visual merchandising displaying Alexander McQueen's creation entices customers into the store window.

Selfridges, London

Surplus stock needs to be sold as soon as possible to avoid it sitting on the 'shop floor' taking up valuable space and losing you money. Your options are;
• Sell the merchandise through the designers markets, shopping events, private parties, flea markets, etc.
• Contact your retailers - they might take merchandise on a sale or return.
• Sell off as job lots - certain businesses exist by buying merchandise as job lots at a good price to on sell; retailers T.K. Maxx (UK) and T.J. Maxx US) who offer top designer luxury labels.
• Advertise a 'Sale' of stock from your studio.

Export: Before you consider exporting you should establish your business first by learning all there is to learn locally or nationally. There are many additional issues you will have to consider when exporting. Apart from the fluctuating exchange rates impacting on your business, there will be; different prices, sizing, labelling, duties, terms, mark-ups, sales commissions, contracts; higher shipping costs and insurance; and you will need to allow much longer lead times. Going through a reputable agent or distributor could be easier, as they should understand the market, handle the orders, collect the payments and negotiate shipping. If you do start to sell offshore do so in one market first and that way you will ease into it slowly and can make an informed decision as to whether you will expand further.

You need to establish how you are going to handle returns. Returns may be due to faulty goods, late deliveries, or the garments have not sold at retail. You may set up an exchange policy, perhaps a money back guarantee, or if the returns are from a retailer who will buy from you the next season you may be able to carry over the credit.

Exercises:

1. Put yourself in your customer's shoes and become a customer for your type of product. Critically appraise the sales staff's performance.
2. Discuss your cold calling approach.
3. Discuss your selling technique.

TWILL CAP
A-W1012
98% COTTON 2% EL

TRENCH COAT
C-W1124
98% COTTON 2% EL
67% WO 29% PA 4% EA

CABLE PURSE
A-W1011
98% COTTON 2% EL

Illustrator and Fashion Designer: Tina Fong

11

Design and Production Cycle

As a fashion entrepreneur, the design and production cycle is an integral part of your business. It will need to be carefully planned and managed to ensure you achieve your business objectives and that your products comply with your quality standards and are delivered to your customers to meet their deadlines.

The design and production cycle outlines the steps you need to take to design, sell and manufacture your products. This cycle needs to be distinguished from the steps taken when starting a business (see the *Starting Your Own Business* chapter). Starting a business is a one-off process, whereas the design and production cycle is repeated with each new clothing or product range. This cycle is repeated at least twice a year with the fashion seasons, Spring/Summer and Autumn/Winter (Fall), but increases dramatically with *'fast fashion'*.

The design and production cycle steps are:

Step 1: Design and Production Brief

Step 2: Production Plan

Step 3: Research and Sourcing

Step 4: Design Development

Step 5: Sell Collection

Step 6: Pre-production

Step 7: Production

Step 8: Distribution

Fashion designer at Northumbria University developing her designs by working on the mannequin.

The Design and Production Cycle

The design and production cycle (Figure 11.1) presents the design and production process as a logical sequence of eight inter-related steps. Developing the steps progressively will enable you to manage the process and trade-offs between each area. For example, if your preferred fabric for your collection is not available in time to meet your production schedule, you would immediately have to source another fabric, otherwise this could have an impact on your delivery dates. Or, if the factory you want to outsource to has just received a large order and cannot meet your delivery dates, you will either have to find another factory or extend your delivery dates.

Step 1: Design and Production Brief
Initiates and outlines what you want your design and production process to achieve.

Step 8: Distribution
Packing and shipping to customers/retailers.

Step 2: Production Plan
Integrates the fashion design and manufacturing process with the fashion calendar to produce your production schedule.

Step 7. Production
Manufacture your products, quality control.

Step 3: Research and Sourcing
Includes; market and trend research, sourcing fabrics, trims and resources.

Step 6: Pre-production
Approve production patterns and production samples (seals), grade patterns, create markers, confirm fabrics and production details.

Step 4. Design Development
Design and make your collection, cost and finalise the collection and prepare to sell.

Step 5. Sell Collection
Market and sell your collection, collate the orders.

Figure 11.1 The Design and Production Cycle- shows where a change in one process in the cycle may impact on another. Developing the steps progressively will enable you to manage the trade-off between each process. By performing a number of iterations in the Design and Production Cycle you will progressively converge on your optimum plan to design and manufacture your collection.

Fashion Entrepreneur and Fashion Designer: Hannah Marshall (centre image)
Photographer: Victor de Mello

Step 1: Design and Production Brief

The design and production brief initiates the design and production cycle and outlines what you want to achieve; the scope of work, who is responsible, the budgets and key dates (start and completion dates). For example, you might design a high end, Spring/Summer womenswear collection, starting the design phase with the fabric selection in March, and making the first patterns and samples yourself with a budget of $5000. You already have two independent stores who want to buy your designs, and the orders will need to be delivered to their stores by end January.

Step 2: Production Plan

Your production plan integrates the design and manufacturing process with the fashion calendar to produce your production schedule. The plan enables you to co-ordinate the design and production cycle to ensure your collection is designed and manufactured to your quality standards, and to achieve your sales and production deadlines. The delivery completion dates are determined by the fashion calendar which establishes when your merchandise needs to be delivered to the stores.

To produce your production schedule you need to work backwards from when the products need to be delivered, allowing time for; shipping, production, pre-production, fabric deliveries, fabric sourcing etc. (See the *Fashion and Textile Calendar* in the *Fashion Entrepreneurs' Runway to Success* chapter, and *Fashion Design Project Barchart* in the *Project Management Skills* chapter.)

Creating a production plan by using a spreadsheet (Excel) will help you plan and control all stages of the production process. Initially you can estimate your key dates but you will soon need to firm up on your schedule by negotiating with your factories and suppliers.

Flexibility: Although many clothing factories are geared up for large production runs, some of them welcome small entrepreneurial businesses with smaller production runs. They are able to fit them in around larger orders, therefore making the best use of their resources. In this case, you need to be flexible with your production dates.

Lead Time: When planning your production schedule, you need to establish suppliers' lead times to ensure everything runs smoothly. Lead time is the time difference between when you order a particular product or service and when you expect to receive it. Unexpected problems and delays in your production process will inevitably occur and these need to be tightly monitored and controlled to reduce the risk of missing your key dates. For example, if you are using Italian components, you need to be aware that Italy shuts down almost completely during August, or if you are sourcing from China, all textile factories shut down for four weeks over Chinese New Year, etc.

Production Control: You will need to manage, monitor and control your production process to keep it on track and ensure the process runs smoothly. For example, you will constantly be working on several tasks at once, feeling a bit like a juggler - while your new collection's samples are being made you will be negotiating the costs and delivery times with the factory for your bulk production and, while you are in the middle of your sales, you could be sourcing new fabrics and trends for the next season.

Royal College of Art (RCA) and Manchester Metropolitan University (MMU) fashion designers in their design studios working on their next fashion collections.

Top: Fashion Designer: Amy Lappin

Above: Fashion Designer: Aina Hussain

These presentation boards show the design development of fashion collections - from the sourcing of the fabrics, the colours used in the collection and the inspiration fabrics create when designing the silhouettes and styles.

Step 3: Research and Sourcing

The research and sourcing process involves:

- Market and trend research (see the *Market Research* chapter).
- Sourcing and selecting fabrics and trims.
- Sourcing fashion technical experts (pattern makers, sample machinists, factories, CMTs and manufacturers) who will make your patterns, samples and production.

Part of your research and sourcing will be through your network of useful contacts, visiting the trade shows (fabric, clothing, accessories, footwear etc.), trade publications and the Internet (see *Internet Resources)*. For example, MAGIC (Las Vegas) is the premier trade event in North America with exhibitors that include manufacturers, fabric and textile mills, trim & components, textile/print design studios and supply chain service providers. Established companies and designers frequently use international sourcing agents or offices in China, India etc. which take care of the sourcing process, such as, sourcing fabrics, factories and dealing with the shipping. But, until you become more established and can afford such services, you will have to apply your entrepreneurial networking and negotiating skills to find the answers for your particular venture.

Fabric Sourcing

The fabric you use in your collections is an exciting part of the design process and can stimulate your design ideas for your whole collection. But it can also be the most challenging as you trade-off sourcing, budgets and minimums. Fabrics and trims can be sourced and purchased typically through several different avenues depending on your type of business:

- Textile and Fabric Trade Shows
- Textile Mills
- Textile Converters
- Fabric Representatives/ Agents
- Fabric Wholesalers
- Fabric Jobbers

Textile and Fabric Trade Shows: Textile and fabric shows are held all over the world at set times during the year (see *Fashion and Textiles Calendar)*. This is where textile mills, manufacturers and agents come together to show their fabric ranges and their latest fabric qualities, colours and trends, often a year in advance of when the fabrics will actually be seen as garments in store. Première Vision (Paris) is one of the biggest fabric fairs. There are many fabric fairs throughout the world; the Turkish Fabric Fair, Texworld (USA), etc. Even if you do not order fabrics from these shows, they are excellent sources of research, inspiration and to see the future and forecasted trend directions.

Textile Mills: Textile mills produce the fabrics and tend to specialise in specific fabrics. They sell direct to manufacturers and wholesalers or have agents to represent them.

Textile Converters: Textile converters buy unfinished (greige goods) and dye, print and treat the fabric themselves. They work closely with manufacturers and designers.

Fabric Representatives/Agents: Fabric reps or agents tend to represent several fabric manufacturers. They do not carry stock but display fabric ranges in swatch form, as swatch cards and as fabric headers, and negotiate orders and deliveries for manufacturers and designers.

Fabric Wholesalers: Fabric wholesalers are suppliers of finished goods from mills and converters. They carry stock but once the fabric is sold they generally cannot offer the same fabric type or colour again.

Fabric Jobbers: Fabric jobbers purchase unsold and leftover stock fabrics from mills, manufacturers and designers. They resell the fabric to retail outlets, markets and small fashion businesses at a low cost and with immediate delivery.

Fabric Considerations

When sourcing and deciding what fabrics you will use for your collection you will need to consider the following:

Fabric Properties: You need to select the most suitable fabrics for your styles, this includes considering; quality, fibre content, drape, handle, durability, stretch, if it is dry clean only, washable, preshrunk, etc. You need to handle the fabrics so that you get a feel for the fabric and if the quality and drape is right for your styles; check out the colours available; and sample your preferred fabrics so that you can make your final collection in the correct fabrics.

Minimums: Most suppliers require minimums in order to cover their fabric setup and supply costs. Initially it might be difficult for you to meet their minimum meterage/yardage when ordering your sampling and production fabric, especially when starting your new business. But, as an entrepreneur, there are several ways to get around this potential barrier:

- **Sample Lengths** - you will pay more for sample lengths but if you are intending to produce small production runs, sample lengths of fabric might be all you require.
- **Stock Fabric** - many suppliers and mills will have stock fabrics you can purchase. You will need to confirm that, should you require more stock for your production, they will be able to supply you. If they cannot guarantee this, you might need to buy the fabric upfront (risky when you first start a business, unless you are buying a base fabric that you are sure of using in your next seasons' collections).
- **Greige Goods** - this is unfinished fabric which you or the supplier would need to dye up and treat. You could even make the garments in the greige goods, then dye and treat them (overdye, special treatment washes).
- **Fewer Fabrics** - if you are astute with your styling you might be able to use just one or two fabric qualities for your whole collection. This means that you might be able to reach the minimum fabric meterage/yardage requirements once your orders are collated.

You could make your garments in the greige goods, then dye and treat them (overdye, special treatment washes).

Courtesy: Nokia Fashion Week - Young Designers

Lead Times: You need to establish availability and the lead times for delivery for your production fabric, especially if it is not stock fabric and needs to be woven, printed, dyed or treated before being shipped.

Costs: You need to establish the costs of both the sample fabric and the bulk fabric as these prices will be different; you will also need to establish the costs and terms of payment for the fabric and shipment.

Above: *The pre-production process at Foschini (womenswear manufacturer and retailer); pattern making, marker making both manually and using CAD; making samples in the design studio.*

Sourcing Fashion Industry Experts/Factories/CMTs

If you have excellent pattern making and sewing skills you will probably make your first patterns and samples yourself, but you should be aware of your time and technical limitations and, if necessary, outsource all or some of the work (see the *Competitive Advantage* and *Business Plans* chapters). These experts include; pattern makers, sample machinists, fashion services/outworkers/contractors, factories, CMTs. In fact, the business that makes your samples may well carry out your production also.

When starting your new venture you will probably prefer to work with someone locally but, as your business grows, outsourcing offshore could be more attractive due to the cost benefits. This would mean your communication skills and follow up will need to be even more vigilant and well managed.

A good starting point to find your resources is through your network of useful contacts and referrals from within the fashion industry. Others include:

- Fashion schools and universities.
- Fashion services on the internet (see *Internet Resources*).
- Trade associations (often give recommendations and surety of quality).
- Trade publications; Drapers Record (UK), WWD, California Apparel News (US), Canadian Apparel (Can), (see *Internet Resources*).

Qualifying Technical Experts: With a potential list of resources (factories/technical experts) to make your patterns, samples and production runs you will need to evaluate what they have to offer and the costs involved before you give them your business. You will need to establish:

> Have they the appropriate expertise in your particular area of design - someone who is an expert at making exquisite lingerie might not be able to make tailored suits? Who have they worked for in the past, and who are they working for now?
>
> Have they appropriate equipment to do the job? What machinery will be used? Do they do everything manually and/or use computer systems? Do they make patterns and grade both manually and on the computer (CAD/CAM)?
>
> Will they create the first patterns and samples, right through to the production patterns and production samples, and create the specification sheets, cutting information, grading and markers?
>
> Is it a home based business, studio, CMT? Where will the work be manufactured?
>
> How will the work be carried out - by one person or a team of people?
>
> Who is responsible for what? Do you have to order the trims, zips, buttons, hangers or do they take care of this and include it as part of their service?
>
> Who will inspect and approve the production? What quality control is there?
>
> Where will the finished products be stored?
>
> How will delivery dates be met? What transport will be used to deliver the merchandise? Do they deliver the finished goods to you or to the retailer?

By visiting the premises you can see how the work is carried out and determine if it looks clean and professional, and if you will be able to work with each other satisfactorily. Offshore premises could be more difficult to visit, so you may have to rely on recommendations from others who have worked with the same offshore contractors or suppliers.

Minimums, Sample Costs, Production Costs

Minimums: Many factories/CMTs require minimums for their production runs to cover their production setup costs. If you cannot meet these minimums your entrepreneurial options are:

- Use your network of industry contacts to find another factory.
- You or your sample machinists could make them in house.
- Employ the same people who made your samples to make the smaller production runs (outworkers, freelancers, fashion services).
- Increase the production order to meet the minimums (but you would want to feel confident you could sell these extra units).
- Pay a higher price for the production and accept a smaller profit margin to stay in the market.

In addition, you may need to use separate services for; buttons and buttonholes, embroidery, pressing, packing and delivering the garments to the stores. Managing this process will be time consuming but it could be the solution to the problems associated with small production runs.

Costs: Through your research and network of fashion industry contacts you should have a rough guide as to what costs to expect for your patterns, samples and production units. The cost to produce individual samples is obviously substantially higher than the production price per unit which will be based on the quantity of the final order. You should always try to get two or three quotes so that you can establish the going rates, as well as giving you negotiating power. You also need to consider and establish the following:

Are the costs of making patterns and samples charged by the hour or cost per item/per piece?

Are there extra costs involved for alterations to the patterns or samples?

You might be able to negotiate a set price for the whole collection to include making the initial patterns and samples, and any alterations, as well as the production patterns, production samples and duplicate samples (if required).

As a rough guide a sample might cost two to three times the price of the production garment.

Production garments are usually costed on a minute rating and dependant on the quantity - the larger the production run the cheaper the unit cost (once your samples are made you will get a more accurate costing).

You might negotiate costs for the complete sample and production process including distribution and shipping.

CMTs cut the fabric, sew the garments and trim (press, tag, hang/fold and pack ready for shipping). You will probably have to cost separately for the production patterns (graded), production samples and markers to be made, and for the distribution costs.

Additional costs could include specialist skills such as, embroidery, pleating, appliqué, hand beading, printing - you will probably have to organize this separately and be the go-between (specialist and factory).

Working relationship: There will always be technical and design problems to discuss and work through between you and the factories but, once you build up a good working relationship and you have been in business for several seasons, the production process should get easier.

Above: *Embroidery, rosettes, appliqué and printing can all be outsourced to industry experts.*

Courtesy of Cape Town Nokia Fashion Week and Viyella

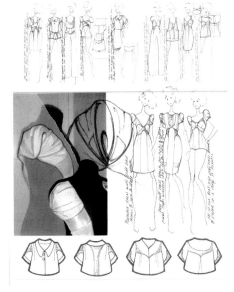

The design development process is where you use your market and trend research and integrate this with your creativity and innovation skills.

Fashion Designer: Cherona Blacksell

Step 4: Design Development

Designing and producing your collection: The design development process is where you use your market and trend research and integrate this with your creativity and innovation skills. When producing your collection you will find there are certain design trade-offs to consider between; fabrics (qualities and costs), production costs, lead times and minimums.

Fabrics: As you start the design process you should have at hand:
• Fabric swatches of your preferred fabrics (qualities and colours).
• Substitute fabrics to make your first samples/prototypes (calico, muslin etc., fabrics similar in weight and behaviour to the final material).
• Sample lengths of fabric to make your final collection (or at least ordered).
• Confirmation of fabric costs including delivery dates to meet your production deadlines.

Design Collection: With your selection of fabrics, and having researched the latest trends, silhouettes and styles for inspiration, you can now develop your collection. Once you select which designs to make up you should create specification sheets for the individual styles.

•**Specification Sheets**: Contain the technical drawing of the design, drawn to scale with construction lines and styling details, front and back views, specifications and key measurements, label positions, stitching details and any special requirements (embroidery, printing fabric treatment, etc.). These sheets are your primary source to communicate and liaise with the pattern makers, sample machinists and factories (see *Appendices*). A drawing package, such as, Illustrator is useful to draw up the final design for your specification sheets (see Burke, *Fashion Computing – Design Techniques and CAD)*.

First Patterns and Samples: You can now begin the pattern and sample making process. By making the designs in the substitute fabrics you can get a good idea of how the styles will look (fit, hang, drape) and make any necessary fitting or design alterations you need without wasting good fabric. Depending on who is costing your garments and carrying out your production, you might need to make up the samples in the final sample fabric before they do the initial costings.

Production Costs: Once your samples are made, you will need to confirm the fabric ratings and costings of each garment. The production experts (factories, CMTs) are often able to improve the unit costs of styles by achieving better fabric ratings or by improving the way the garments are made. Your negotiation skills will be advantageous when you discuss unit costs with factories but, to negotiate keener prices, it may take several production runs to establish yourself as a valued customer with regular and increasing units.

Finalise Collection: Based on your design brief and your budget, you will have established how many pieces you need in your collection (say 15 styles out of perhaps 30 you have made). With the costings confirmed and within budget, you can decide which styles to keep in your collection and have them made in the correct fabrics. Once you have finished your collection you need to stand back and look at your collection with a critical eye and consider the following:

• **Concise:** Your collection should be focussed, well co-ordinated and cohesive. When you look at the overall collection you will need to be ruthless. Research has shown that if people have too many products to choose from they will be overwhelmed and have difficulty making a decision, therefore, it is important to reduce the buyers' choice.

• **Stand Alone:** Can the collection stand on its own? Have you got the right combination of styles? Do you need another top or bottom piece to balance the collection?

• **Price:** Are all the garments within the correct price range for your target customer? Do they look the price? You might need to go over your costings again with the factory.

• **Fit:** Your collection needs to establish your professionalism and quality - well made, a good fit, look clean, labelled.

• **Extra Samples:** Duplicate sets of samples may be needed particularly if you have agents selling your range at the same time as you or if press samples are required. You might also need styles made up in alternative fabrics or colours (although you should have colour and fabric cards, line sheets etc. made up to show the design options).

Style Control Sheet: Figure 11.2 presents a typical *Style Control Sheet*, created as an Excel spreadsheet, showing the tasks involved in the design and pre-production phase of a collection. The example shows Linda Logan is responsible for the design; Ewa Liddington is responsible for the fabric, making of the patterns and samples, and the costings; Maria Leeke is responsible for marketing and sales of the collection.

The Design Board presents the final collection, the flats (technical designs) and the fashion illustrations to show how the garments are to be worn.

Fashion Designer: Cherona Blacksell

Style ID: 01S/S12		**Style Control Sheet**				
Style Desc: Dress						
Task	Description		Date Required	Responsibility	Date Complete	Date Approved
1	Style Created			Linda Logan		
2	Design Details Complete			Linda Logan		
3	Fabric Details Complete			Ewa Liddington		
4	Sample Fabric Available			Ewa Liddington		
5	Trims Costing Complete			Ewa Liddington		
6	Allocated to Pattern Maker			Ewa Liddington		
7	Patterns Complete			Ewa Liddington		
8	Fabric Ratings Complete			Ewa Liddington		
9	Allocated to Machinist			Ewa Liddington		
10	Sample Sewn			Ewa Liddington		
11	CMT/Factory Costed			Ewa Liddington		
12	Cost Card Complete			Ewa Liddington		
13	Sample Change 1			Linda Logan		
14	Sample Change 2			Linda Logan		
15	Sample Approved			Linda Logan		
16	Sample Finalised for Collection			Linda Logan		
17	Marketing and Sales			Maria Leeke		

Figure 11.2 Style Control Sheet - shows the tasks involved in the design and pre-production phase of a collection, who is responsible and dates involved. Note: It is often necessary to make sample changes (modifications) after the initial costing has been made so that the design fits the correct price point.

Part of a 60s inspired, psychedelic collection.

Fashion Designer: Emily Crump

Step 5: Sell Collection

You need to market your collection to create the interest and make your appointments to show your range to the buyers. This is covered in detail in the *Marketing and Branding*, and *Sales and Negotiation* chapters.

During, the first days of selling your collection you will receive essential feedback from your customers and, as the orders are taken, you will get a better idea of how the range is being accepted. Typically your sales figures will have an 80/20 profile where 80 % of your sales will come from 20% of your styles. By analysing your initial sales figures you should be able to identify the best selling items. You probably have a few options available to improve your sales if you need to, but you would need to act quickly:

- **'Hot' Item:** Perhaps there is a 'hot' item, or even a basic item which is missing from your collection which you can include.
- **Keep the Slower Selling Item:** If there is a style that looks like it is not going to achieve the production minimums and, if you are able to produce small runs by making in them in your workroom or make them using freelance sewers (outworkers), then you could continue selling the item.
- **Withdraw the Slower Selling Item:** If the slower selling item is diluting the sales of the other styles you may as well take it out of the collection so that the orders of the other styles improve.

Step 6: Pre-Production

As you receive your orders and prepare for production you will need to action the following:

- Capture all orders on a spreadsheet to establish your production quantities.
- Confirm that the required production fabrics and trims will be delivered to meet the production deadlines.
- Confirm the quantities and delivery of all labels; garment labels, size labels, wash and care labels (each fabric quality may need a different label), swing tickets etc.
- Confirm the quantities and delivery of packaging; bags, boxes, hangers etc.
- Make and approve the production patterns and production samples (seals), and update the specification sheets.
- Grade patterns - grading is the process of mathematically adjusting the production pattern to meet the required size range.
- Make markers for cutting the production fabric - marking determines the best layout for the pattern pieces (over the graded sizes) when cutting the bulk fabric and, therefore, decreases the amount of waste.
- Wrap up and finalise the orders

Extra Stock and Overruns: You may wish to add a small percentage of extra stock to your production run in case of rejects and to ensure that your customers' orders can be fulfilled. In practise, it is not good business sense to have too much extra stock unless you have a good outlet for selling remaining stock at the end of the season. If you need to make extra stock for customers who might reorder their 'best sellers', do so with caution until you have built up a good customer relationship and understand what the market wants. Sometimes being able to say the stock has 'sold out' can work to your advantage – it shows other people want your product, and people always want what they cannot have!

Documentation and Contracts (see *Appendices*)

You should confirm with those carrying out your production (factories/CMTs) what documentation they require before they commence. It is essential you confirm your order in writing, confirm your final production costs and supply documents to outline the scope of work, quantities, quality standards, shipping and delivery dates:

- **Final Cost Sheets:** Confirm the ratings and final costs of your garments, with all relevant details.
- **Cutting Orders** (Dockets/Sheets/Tickets)**:** Confirm that the production order contains all relevant details to avoid problems in the production process; style numbers, quantity to be cut and the sizes, delivery date, technical drawings, fabric and trim details, fabric swatches, sewing, cutting, finishing and packaging instructions and any special requirements.

Line sheets/design sheet present the styles in a collection - these are drawn as technical flats and could include a fashion illustration as well as the fabrics and colours in the range.

Fashion Designer: Tina Fong

OPEN COLLAR SHIRT
S-W1129
100% COTTON

NAPOLEON DENIM
P-W1125
70% COTTON 30% BAMBOO

Step 7: Production

As part of the production process you should ensure the following details have been covered:

- Orders collated and finalised.
- Fabric and trims, labels, packaging delivered.
- Fabric checked for any flaws.
- Production patterns graded.
- Production samples approved (sealed sample).
- Production documentation in place and signed off.
- Contracts signed - terms and conditions established.
- Packaging, hanging and shipping details clarified.

Once everything is in place the production process can begin.

Quality Control: Although the factory doing your production should take care of the process you should be ready to follow up and answer any questions and sort out any unforeseen problems that may arise (potential late deliveries, soiled or badly constructed garments). The factory should have a quality controller checking that garments are produced according to your approved (sealed) production sample and the order, but it is important that you also inspect some of the production process and garments as they come off the line. If you cannot feasibly get to the factory, ask them to send you one of the first garments from the production line for you to approve. The key is to ensure that your products meet your quality standards and will be delivered to your customers to meet their deadlines.

Production Control Sheet: Figure 11.3 presents a typical Production Control Sheet, created as a spreadsheet, showing the tasks involved in the production process.

Style ID: 01S/S12		Production Control Sheet			
Style Desc: Dress					
Task	Description	Date Required	Responsibility	Date Complete	Date Approved
1	Style Approved		Linda Logan		
2	Bulk Fabric Delivered		Ewa Liddington		
3	Bulk Trims Delivered		Ewa Liddington		
4	Production Patterns Finalized		Ewa Liddington		
5	Production Samples Finalized		Linda Logan		
6	Labels, Packaging Delivered		Ewa Liddington		
7	Graded Patterns (sizes)		Ewa Liddington		
8	Markers Made		Ewa Liddington		
9	Production Commences		Ewa Liddington		
10	Quality Control Check 1		Linda Logan		
11	Production Complete		Ewa Liddington		
12	Quality Control Check 2		Ewa Liddington		
13	Pack and Ship		Ewa Liddington		

Figure 11.3 Production Control Sheet - shows the tasks involved in the production process and who is responsible. Completion dates and approval dates will also need to be confirmed.

Left: Eveningwear design - 'red carpet' design

Fashion Illustrator: Naomi Austin

Opposite: Fashion Shoot for a magazine.

Stylist: Lucy Laucht

Step 8: Distribution

Once your production is complete the garments can be hung, packaged or boxed according to the order, and then shipped to the customer.

The packaging and shipping of goods might be done by you, your team or by the factory. If you do this process yourself at least it means that you will be able to do a final check to ensure that your products have achieved the correct quality standards before shipping them to your customers.

Exercises:

1. Write a design brief for your product.
2. Develop a design and production cycle for your product highlighting some of the key features within each step.
3. Show how your production schedule is influenced by outside stakeholders.

Models - courtesy of ADAGE at the Custard Factory   *Photography - Jamie Kelly*
Location - Sela Sweet shop at National Trust   *Stylist - Lucy Laucht*

LUCY LAUCHT
STYLIST · ILLUSTRATOR · PERSONAL SHOPPER

Illustrator: Montana Forbes

12

Sources of Finance

Ready cash and seed money are the life-blood for starting your own business. Without sufficient funds your new venture's success will be self-limited because there simply will not be sufficient resources available to develop, manufacture, distribute, market and sell your fashion products. Calculating how much money you need to start your business often mirrors how much money you can raise. By being realistic you can converge on an optimum starting amount. But, at some point, you should formalize your thinking with a coherent financial plan (see the *Business Plans* chapter). The financial requirements can be subdivided into the following areas, depending on your type of business:

• **Startup Capital:** This is the finance required for your **setup costs** - the costs to set up your company and get yourself ready to do business. The startup capital needs to be sufficient to; register the business, buy or rent premises, buy or lease equipment, purchase consumables (materials, stationary), hire labour and office staff, along with the marketing and advertising costs to promote the products.

Startup capital is often referred to as 'Sunk costs' and 'Seed money'. Sunk costs are the costs that cannot be recovered (rent, labour costs), and seed money is the money which stimulates the growth of the business (marketing and advertising).

• **Development Capital and Production Costs:** This money is required to design, develop, manufacture and distribute the products (garments, samples) and includes market research, flying to fashion shows and trade shows.

• **Stocking Capital** is required to build up stock of the products. This particularly applies to retailers that incur stocking costs (stock/inventory and storage).

• **Working Capital** is required for the 'Running Costs' and 'Overheads' - capital required to run your business on a day-to-day basis. This includes the fixed overhead costs that your company will incur whether you sell/make any products or not, for example, rent, salaries (management), services (telephones, water, rates) and maintenance.

This chapter will use the structure set out in Figure 12.1 to discuss the different types of finance.

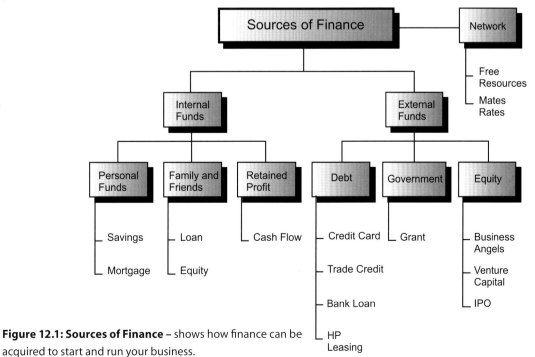

Figure 12.1: Sources of Finance – shows how finance can be acquired to start and run your business.

Gavin Rajah Couture's *niche market is in designing and making high end couture fashion.*
Fashion Designer: Gavin Rajah
Photo: Courtesy of Nokia Fashion Week

1. Networking

Although networking is not a source of finance per se, it is through your network of contacts that you might be able to borrow or acquire some of the resources you need to start your own business, either costing you nothing or at greatly reduced prices or rates. This may sound unprofessional and verging on 'cheap', but this is actually a classic entrepreneurial approach to obtaining the use of resources to get started, for example:

- Borrowing patterns, a sewing machine, use of a design studio.
- Buying up end of lines or materials at an extra special 'knock-down' price.

2. Personal Funds

Personal funds are the most common source of startup capital. You are always going to have to reach into your own pocket first, even if it is only to show potential investors you are totally committed.

The main advantage of using personal finance is that it is the least expensive source of finance to obtain, it also gives you the greatest level of control with the least amount of outside interference, as well as the maximum level of profit. The disadvantage is that it means you carry all the financial risk.

If banks and private equity were to consider investing in your new venture they would want evidence that you were financially committed to your enterprise before they invested. So, if the going got tough, you would be more likely to be highly motivated to work through the problems and not admit defeat at the first obstacle.

3. Family and Friends

Acquiring startup capital from family and friends are the third and fourth most common sources of finance when starting a new venture. From a business management point of view this might appear amateurish, but research clearly indicates that few new companies are able to source startup capital from banks and other institutions during their startup phase.

A loan from family and friends means they are backing you personally and, therefore, they do not usually need convincing with a formal business plan and cash flow statement. This means they can be approached in the early stages of setting up your business.

4. Credit Card

Credit card finance is one of the easiest sources of finance to obtain and is a very practical way of providing **short term** funds to cover the payment for goods and materials. Credit cards offer between 30 to 60 days of free credit before a payment is required. Credit card interest rates are very high, so they should definitely not be used as a long term source of finance.

5. Trade Credit

Trade credit is really a cash flow loan where you negotiate with a supplier to give you credit for 30, 60 or 90 days before they require payments for their goods and services. This is essentially an interest free, short-term loan. Trade credit is the most easily accessible external source of short-term finance and the simplest to negotiate. Trade credit can be used as an opportunity to help get you started - you obtain the materials to produce your products and receive payment from your clients before paying your suppliers. This is 'living life on the edge', but if it gives you a 'kick-start' and puts money in the bank, then this is a route you could consider.

Giving extended credit to clients, distributors and retailers can impact negatively on your cash flow - this is trade credit in reverse. In this situation you pay for the manufacture and supply of your products before receiving payment from your clients. This is obviously not to be encouraged. Giving extended credit and 'consignment stock' can lead to a vicious circle of chasing debts and fending off your suppliers because you cannot afford to pay them.

6. Retained Profit

Retained profit means you put your profits back into your business to achieve sustainable, organic growth. For example, most entrepreneurs draw very little money from their fledgling businesses - they are more focussed on growing their businesses than income.

7. Banks

The commercial high street banks are a logical source of short and long term finance for entrepreneurial ventures. Banks do not like to take risks so a formal business plan would be required before they would consider investing in a new business. A business plan enables the bank manager to assess the risk of the proposal (see the *Business Plans* chapter).

Short term finance in the form of an **overdraft** is useful to have in place as working capital to cover negative cash flow - negative cash flow could happen at any time during your business cycle. As a growing business, you must anticipate the possibility of this as you try to control uncertain cash flow projections.

The availability of a loan can be influenced by your relationship with your bank, therefore, your bank manager should be considered as a key stakeholder in your venture and part of your network of useful contacts.

Leasing (hire purchase) is a popular method of financing capital equipment acquisition (sewing machines, overlockers) because the repayments are spread over a few years. These payments could be tax deductible when the equipment is used to produce an income. Leasing capital equipment (rather than buying up front) will have a positive short-term effect on your cash flow which will give you some breathing space to get your venture established.

8. Business Angels

Business Angels are usually wealthy private investors who are willing to provide small amounts of their own capital to seed entrepreneurial ventures. Business Angels not only bring an injection of funds into a new venture, but also a wealth of entrepreneurial experience and a network of contacts, which can be invaluable for a fledgling startup (Dragons' Den). They are able to mentor the entrepreneur, help them develop their business plans and advise them how to apply for government grants. Business Angels understand the entrepreneurial process having made their fortunes through their own entrepreneurial endeavours.

9. Venture Capital

Venture capitalists invest other people's money. They professionally manage a pool of 'equity capital' which is obtained from the investments of wealthy partners, pension funds, endowment funds, large corporations and other institutions. Venture capital would be of more interest to you later, once you have established your business and need a substantial injection of funds to grow.

Hannah Marshall focuses on the classic 'Little Black Dress' for her collection, and incorporated tactile Braille messages into her designs.

Fashion Designer: Hannah Marshall

Photographer: Victor de Mello

I'll invest more in the person than the idea. Whoever I back has to be passionate about their market. James Caan, Dragons' Den.

Mannequins, fashion and business!

Fashion Designer and Illustrator: Frances Howie, Central Saint Martins

Frances' entrepreneurial talent and skills helped her acquire a prestigious position as a fashion designer at Lanvin, Paris.

Case Study: International Herald Tribune, By Suzy Menkes

'The Boudicca show, which was designed by Broach and her partner, Brian Kirkby, is this season's rag trade-to-riches story. After struggling to make their aesthetic understood, let alone finding the money to make up the clothes, the design duo has found a fairy godmother. American Express decided to back them, as it had previously supported Alexander McQueen and watched its seedling protégé grow into an international brand with the Gucci group.'

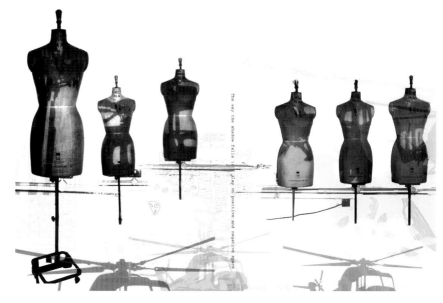

10. Debt or Equity Financing

There are two basic ways for fashion entrepreneurs to acquire finance:
- **Debt:** A loan which must be repaid.
- **Equity:** Share capital which gives the investor part ownership.

Selecting the type of finance or the balance of the two is a *risk management assessment*.

Debt finance (borrowing funds) requires the loan to be repaid in full, plus interest, irrespective of whether the borrower has made any money from sales or profits. The lender will require collateral (security such as a house or land) to reduce their exposure to any risk. Although the borrower (entrepreneur) appears to be carrying all the risk, the advantage is that if the new venture does really well, the borrower will keep all the profits. However, if the company collapses, all the money borrowed will still have to be repaid in full.

Equity finance is where an outside investor takes some form of equity or ownership (share holding) in the entrepreneur's new venture. The investor does not require collateral or interest payments from the entrepreneur, but does require a share of the profit and, conversely, will accept a share of the loss - this is done on a pro rata basis. This has the advantage of limiting the risk, but the disadvantage for the entrepreneur is having to share the profits (and maybe control of the company). However, if the entrepreneur's company goes under the entrepreneur does not need to repay the investor's equity.

Table 12.1: Debt – Equity Finance (matrix) – shows a comparison of the different sources of finance plotted against the cost to borrow, the level of control of the company, the profits and the risks.

	Cost to Borrow	Level of Control	Profits	Risk
Networking	Low	High	High	Low
Personal Funds	Low	High	High	High
Family and Friends	Medium	High	High	High
Credit Card	Low (if repay within credit period)	High	High	High
Trade Credit	Low	High	High	High
Retained Profit	Low	High	High	High
Banks	Low	Medium	High	High
Business Angels	Low	Medium	Shared	Shared
Venture Capital	Low	Low	Shared	Shared
IPO	Low	Low	Shared	Shared

11. Lifecycle Finance

The availability and attractiveness of the different sources of finance change through the businesses' lifecycle. The list below, Figure 12.2 , aligns well with the availability of funds for fledgling startup companies. For example, a new venture without a track record is unlikely to attract venture capital investment and, conversely, an established company is unlikely to ask family and friends for a major injection of cash.

Concept Phase	Startup Phase	Survival Phase	Growth Phase	Maturity Phase	Declining Phase
Networking					
Personal Savings					
Family					
Friends					
Credit Card					
	Trade Credit				
		Retained Profit			
	Banks (Overdraft / Loans)				
			Business Angels		
			Venture Capital		
			IPO (Initial Public Offering)		

Figure 12.2 Lifecycle Finance - graphically outlines the typical sources of finance as the company progresses through the business lifecycle. This will help entrepreneurs focus on the types of finance they should be pursuing as they progress through the different phases. In the initial phases entrepreneurs should focus on networking, personal funds, family and friends, as they are unlikely to attract venture capital. In the rapid growth and maturity phases, entrepreneurs should focus on venture capital, because an established company is unlikely to ask family and friends for finance. The IPO is outside the scope of this book but fashion entrepreneurs should be aware of it as a future source of finance.

Rock Chics.

Fashion Entrepreneur: Scott O'Byrne, is a *fashion stylist, illustrator and co-owner of fashion label,* Any Broken Nerd.

Exercises:

1. Discuss how you might network to borrow equipment or obtain a better deal on fabrics or other materials needed to produce your products.
2. Discuss how you could use a credit card or trade credit for short term funds.
3. Discuss your preference for debt or equity finance.

AUTUMN/WINTER
Kiss me deadly

Fashion Designer: Amy Lappin

13

Small Business Accounts

If you want your business to become successful and expand you will need more than the 'shoebox under the bed' accounting system that you probably started with! Accurate accounting records are essential for keeping your finger on the financial pulse of your company and also to comply with tax and other statutory reporting requirements.

You are in business to make a profit, so monitoring financial performance is important. However, as your skills probably lie in design and fashion, and not in accounting, you should seek some assistance. Accountants and business mentors will help you formalise and quantify your own estimates of the start up costs of your business, assist you in applications for initial funding, monitor your financial progress, educate you in business systems and advise you on ways to grow.

That is not to say they will do all the work for you! You will need to have a solid accounting system in place, one which satisfies the basic objectives of: recording and analysing your business transactions; calculating goods and service taxes; enabling you to monitor your cashflow at any given point by reconciling the cashflows to the balance on the bank statement; forming the building blocks for the financial statements and providing an audit trail.

Each phase of the life of your business requires different sets of financial statements. At the start up stage, you will need budgets for the cost of physically setting up the business and marketing it. You will also have to produce a production budget using estimates of the selling price of your products and your total projected turnover (i.e. the projected selling price multiplied by the number of items you expect to sell) together with your estimated costs. The selling price is typically made up of the actual costs of producing the item (direct and indirect) plus a margin which will cover a percentage of the overheads and provide you, the entrepreneur, with a profit. Later you will have management reports showing you how profitable and stable the business is and cashflow reports which monitor the actual cashflows. Annual Financial Statements at the end of each financial/tax year are mandatory.

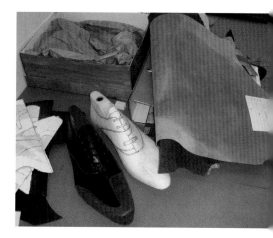

If you want your business to become successful and expand you will need more than the 'shoebox under the bed' accounting system that you probably started with!

Footwear Designer: Northampton University

Top: *Designer creating her textiles on CAD at the University of Plymouth Colleges Somerset*

Above: *Design Studio Office*

As a small business entrepreneur you can start by using Excel for your accounts but, as your business grows, you could use specific computer accounting software, such as, QuickBooks Accounting Software, Simply Accounting Accounting Software, Microsoft Office Small Business Accounting. Check out the reviews on the Internet and through your network of contacts to see what they use and what could work best for you.

1. Estimating the Setup Budget

When starting a new business you will typically have three types of budgets to estimate and assign:

- Setup budget
- Production budget
- Overhead budget.

Accurate estimating of the costs to establish these three budgets is essential, because these costs underpin the whole financial viability of your new venture and help you avoid spending more than you realistically need, to setup your business.

> **Definition:** A **Budget** may be defined as, *the funds allocated to pay for the estimated costs of making the product, or incurred to carry out the work. These costs are then compared with the funds available to establish a realistic budget.*

When estimating the three budgets there are many types of costs to consider, but for the purpose of this chapter the **three** main types will be introduced as; direct costs, indirect costs and labour costs:

Setup budget	Production budget	Overhead budget
Direct Costs	Direct Costs	Direct Costs
Indirect Costs	Indirect Costs	Indirect Costs
Labour Costs	Labour Costs	Labour Costs

Direct Costs: Direct costs, as the term implies, are costs which can be specifically identified and assigned to a job. This means the costs can be individually budgeted for and controlled.

- Direct management costs refer to you, the entrepreneur, and other managers working on the new venture (project manager, production manager).
- Direct labour costs refer to people working on an activity (pattern cutter).
- Direct material costs refer to material used to complete an activity (fabrics).
- Direct equipment costs refer to the cost of acquiring machinery and plant to complete an activity (hiring of sewing machines, pressing equipment).
- Direct bought-in expenses refer to the costs associated with services used directly to complete an activity (CMT).

Direct costs are also known as **variable costs** as they fluctuate, with the level of production.

Indirect Costs: Indirect costs are **overhead-type costs** which cannot be directly attributed to any particular job, but are required to keep the company functioning and need to be included for accurate estimating. Indirect costs are usually financed by an overhead recovery charge, which is generally included in the labour rate. Consider the following:

- Indirect management costs refer to head office staff.
- Indirect labour costs refer to reception, maintenance and security functions required to keep the company running.
- Indirect material costs refer to stationery, cleaning materials, maintenance parts, etc.
- Indirect equipment costs include costs associated with computers, printers.
- Other indirect costs include training, insurance, etc.

Some indirect costs are also called **fixed costs** because they are incurred whether you do any work or not.

Labour Costs: Labour costs are a key component of most jobs and are generally expressed as a rate per hour ($/hr). The labour rate, or charge out rate, is what the customer pays. As a general rule, the labour rate can be calculated from the employee's wages which are known:

1/3	Wages	$30
1/3	Overheads	$30
1/3	Profit	$30
	Labour Rate	$90

For example, if you pay your workers $30 per hour, your contribution to overheads would be $30, your company profit would be $30, therefore your labour rate would be $90 per hour.

An even easier way is to see what other companies are charging! You will have to do this anyway to ensure that your rates are competitive.

Setup Costs: These are the funds required to setup your company and get yourself ready to do business.

Production Costs: These relate to the design, manufacture and distribution of your fashion range. These are **variable costs** as they relate directly to the number of garments produced.

Overhead Costs: These relate to the activities and costs required to run your business on a day-to-day basis. For example, rent, staff salaries, and services - some of these costs are **fixed costs** as they are incurred irrespective of the number of garments produced.

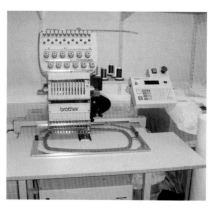

Top: Many textile designers start their businesses selling their textiles designs as ready made garments and accessories.

Textile designer at work, University College Northampton

Above: The equipment you buy is a setup cost. If you hire your equipment, short term, to do a specific job, this is a variable cost.

Embroidery machine, University of Plymouth Colleges Somerset.

It is sometimes difficult to separate setup costs from production costs and overhead costs as there is a certain amount of overlap and interpretation between the three. But it is important to understand the difference as you need to separate these costs to calculate your breakeven analysis (P. 136).

The setup, production costs and overhead costs can be identified as:

Setup Costs - Seed Money	Production Costs - Variable Costs	Overheads Costs - Fixed Costs
Market research	Market research	Staff salaries
Product development	Designing and making the products	Utilities - power, water, telephone
Registering a business	Maintaining a sewing machine	Admin
Company logo design, branding	Buying fabric for your product	
Buying equipment, a sewing machine etc.	Manufacturing	
Buying stock fabric	Warehousing and distribution	
A deposit to rent premises		Monthly rent
Buying office equipment, shop fittings, company stationery		Servicing office equipment and replacing company stationery
Marketing and advertising		

It is important to understand the basics of small business accounting but you might also use an accountant or bookkeeper to handle the big issues such as taxes, wages (payroll) and the end-of-year financial statements.

You need a solid accounting system which at the very least enables you to keep track of your income and expenditure, to calculate and pay your goods and taxes on time and reconcile the total income and expenditure to balance the bank statement. Ideally it will also incorporate features that allow you to quantify your debtors (people who owe you money) and your creditors (people you owe money) thus creating a structured database from which the financial statements draw their raw data.

2. Cash Book Accounting Method

The cash book accounting method captures all the financial transactions for the period and logs them in a structured data base - it is from this data base that other accounting documents draw their raw data (for example, the cashflow forecast, breakeven point analysis, balance sheet etc.). A computerized accounting package will enable you to produce all the financial statements without the manual effort.

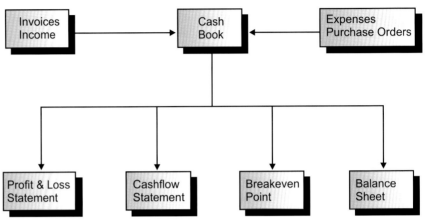

Figure 13.1 Cash Book Accounting Method - shows the income and expense information, and a number of the standard reports which can be drawn from the information.

Cash Book Expenses (Purchase Ledger)

Date	Purchase Order	Supplier	Description	Amount Payable	Date Paid
1 June Yr	P1008	The Hire Shop	Equipment	$1000	1 July Yr
2 June Yr	P1009	The Fabric Store	Material	$5000	2 July Yr
3 June Yr	P1010	Best Make	CMT (labour)	$2000	1 July Yr

Figure 13.2 Cash Book Expenses (Purchase Ledger) - shows the format for expense information under six key headings, under which all relevant details are listed in fields (columns).

The cash book expense headings are set out to summarise and control the payments of expenses. The headings in Figure 13.2 are typical of a simple cash book format. The headings are shown here as a guide to help you understand the cash book concept and indicate where more fields (columns) can be added for more information and control, such as, local taxes.

Date: The date field states the date the purchase order is raised. This enables the expenses to be sorted in date order.

Purchase Order: The purchase order number field links the purchase order (or transaction number / cheque number) to the company's budget, the supplier's quotation and the supplier's invoice. When you receive an invoice you need to check that the invoice amount is the same as the original quotation. One way of achieving this is to add additional fields (columns) such as, 'budget', 'quotations' and 'invoices', and flag any variance between the amounts.

Supplier: The supplier field identifies the company that supplied the goods, and enables the goods to be sorted by supplier. When dealing with a supplier it is useful to be able to quickly list all their deliveries.

Entrepreneurs that are skilled at textile design could start a business offering a textile design service.

Textile Designer at work, University College Northampton.

Description: The description of the goods or service field helps to identify the expenses. The description field also enables all the goods of the same description to be grouped together. This could be useful if you have used a number of different suppliers.

Amount Paid: The amount paid field enables a comparison between the amount paid with the purchase order, the quotation and the budget. Another field can be added to show the sales tax which is an essential component of bookkeeping. It is important to have an easy method to ensure the payment is not greater than the invoice.

Date Paid: The date invoice paid field enables you to confirm the payment has been made.

Cash Book Income (Sales Ledger)

Date	Invoice Number	Customer	Invoice Amount	Amount Received	Date Received
1 June Yr	07-1001	Barneys	10,000	$10,000	25 June Yr
1 June Yr	07-1002	Whistles	$2,000	$2,000	2 July Yr
1 June Yr	07-1003	Citron	$5,000	$4,000	10 Oct Yr

Figure 13.3 Cash Book Income (Sales Ledger) - shows the format for income information.

The cash book income headings are set out to summarise and control your clients' payments. The headings in figure 13.3 are shown as a guide to demonstrate the cash book concept, and indicate where more fields can be added.

Date: The date of invoice field sorts the invoices into date order. This field is required to structure the 30, 60 and 90 day statements, and identify any late payments which require further action.

Invoice Number: Your invoice number field links the invoice to the work (job number), the company's budget and the clients' purchase order.

Customer: The customer field identifies the customer and enables you to sort by customer. By grouping all the invoices per customer, this will enable further analysis. For example, if a customer is late paying an invoice you might want to investigate to see if they were late paying any previous invoices.

Invoice Amount: The invoice amount field shows the amount of the invoice. Another field can be added to show the sales tax (VAT) which is an essential component of bookkeeping.

Amount Received: The amount received field confirms the invoice has been paid in full.

Date Received: The date received field shows the date the invoice was paid. Adding another field for the time to pay the invoice (Invoice Due Date) will enable you to quickly identify any customers who consistently pay their invoices late.

Variance: A variance is the difference between two numbers. As mentioned above, additional fields can be added to measure the variance between key figures - this is referred to as a management by exception (MBE) approach. For example, if two key fields differed by more than 5%, or say $1000, this could automatically be brought to your attention.

Fashion Entrepreneur, Melanie Casper, 'Munko': *I do have a very good computerized system in my office so if customers have not paid their account after 30 days I know immediately, then I will email or phone and follow up. I also have a bookkeeper who writes up the cash book every day keeping a check of all the money I pay out and money in, and keeps an eye on the Internet banking.*

All that glows is gold in this sleek, slick and sophisticated statement.

Your expenses could include fashion magazines and fashion forecasting services that you purchase every month, these would be indirect costs (overhead costs), however, if you only purchased them when you performed a certain job (a new collection) they would be direct costs.

Accrual Method: The profit and loss statement uses the accrual method which records income when the sales occurs or when an item is ordered. You do not wait until the product or service is delivered, or when the customer actually pays you. Likewise, the expenses are recorded when the goods or services are ordered, even though you might pay for them later.

3. Profit and Loss Statement

The profit and loss statement and the cashflow statement offer two different ways of presenting future accounts. The profit and loss statement uses an accrual method, while the cashflow statement uses a cash method (see side columns for explanation).

Profit and Loss Statement: The fashion project example below (Figure 13.4) shows the future cashflows using the accrual method of incurred income and incurred expenses. It presents a typical cashflow situation that you might experience as you set up your own business selling to independent stores. The fashion design, manufacturing and distribution cycle is repeated twice a year as you sell your Autumn/Winter (Fall, US) and Spring/Summer collections.

	Jan	Feb	Mar	Apr	May	Jun	Jul	Aug	Sep	Oct	Nov	Dec	Jan	Feb
Brought Forward ($/£)	Seed 10,000	8,500	7,500	7,000	6,000	5,000	3,000	-2,000	500	4,500	10,500	14,500	16,500	17,500
Income ($/£)	0	0	0	0	0	0	0	3,000	4,000	6,000	4,000	2,000	1,000	3,000
Funds Available ($/£)	10,000	8,500	7,500	7,000	6,000	5,000	3,000	1,000	4,500	10,500	14,500	16,500	17,500	20,500
Expenses														
Setup your business	1,000 Setup													
Source fabric, design and make collection	500 A/W	1,000 A/W	500 A/W				S/S	S/S	S/S					
Sales and marketing				1,000 A/W						S/S				
Production					1,000 A/W	2,000 A/W	5,000 A/W				S/S	S/S	S/S	
Deliver to Store								500 A/W						S/S
Total Expenses ($/£)	1,500	1,000	500	1,000	1,000	2,000	5,000	500						
Closing Statement ($/£)	8,500	7,500	7,000	6,000	5,000	3,000	-2,000	500	4,500	10,500	14,500	16,500	17,500	20,500

Figure 13.4: Fashion Project Profit and Loss Statement – shows the profit and loss statement using the accrual method of incurred income and incurred expenses (see exercise at the end of the chapter).

Explanation Figure 13.4: Starting with seed money of $10,000 in January, it takes one month to setup your company (register premises etc.) and costs $1,000. The next step is design development which starts with sourcing fabrics and trends, designing the collection and making the patterns and samples from January to March, and costs $500, $1,000 and $500.

In April you do your sales and marketing, costing $1,000. Once your sales are finished you collate the orders and finalize the fabrics and trims, approve the production patterns and samples, and then production can begin - this takes from May through to July and costs $1,000, $2,000 and $5,000.

Delivery to the retail stores is carried out in August and costs $500. The sales income of $3,000, starts in August, builds up, then trails off towards the end of the season when the January sales period begins.

The bottom lines shows the closing statement which is the difference between the income and the expenses. In July the cashflow is negative ($2,000), this will obviously need to be financed by an overdraft. Excluding the Spring/Summer, the Autumn/Winter (Fall) ends with a positive cashflow of $20,500.

The prospect of negative cashflow should bring out your entrepreneurial traits to find ways to overcome it, for example, by negotiating with your clients to speed up their payments, and with your suppliers to delay expense payments. If a short fall of funds still exists you might need to negotiate an overdraft facility from your bank.

4. Cashflow Statement

The cashflow statement (forecast) gives a monthly snapshot of the actual amount of money coming in and going out of your company's bank account. Because of the differential timings of the costs and incomes this will paint a different picture to the accrual method (profit and loss statement). Most importantly the cashflow forecast gives an indication of the amount of working capital required (if any), when, and how much. This will enable you to plan ahead.

Cash Method: The cashflow statement uses the cash method of accounting which only records income when you receive the cash from your customers and, likewise, only records expenses when you pay a supplier. Most individuals use the cash method for their personal finances because it is the simplest and the least time-consuming.

The cashflow statement below uses the cash method of recording income when it is received and recording expenses when they are paid. Figure 13.5 shows the cashflow income and expenses incurred in March.

	Timing	Jan	Feb	Mar	Apr	May	Jun
Opening balance							
Income	1 month credit				14,000		
Funds available							
Cost of Sales (expenses)							
Rent	1 month up front		1000				
Heating, light, water	1 month credit				200		
Telephone, Internet	1 month credit				100		
Professional fees	2 months credit					100	
Bank charges	1 month credit				100		
Wages	Paid in the month work is carried out			5000			
Material	1 month credit				2000		
Equipment	2 months up front	300					
Transport	1 month up front		200				
Total Costs							
Closing balance							

Figure 13.5: Cashflow Statement – shows when you receive the income for sales made in March, and when you pay expenses incurred in March.

Explanation Figure 13.5: The opening balance for each month is the brought forward amount from the previous month's closing balance. In this case it has been left blank.

- Depending on the type of business, the income you receive from sales could be an up front payment with the purchase, or one, two or three months after a sale is made - here you receive $14,000 in April, one month after the sale.
- Office rent of $1,000 is one month in advance.
- Heating, lighting and water authorities charge $200 and give one month credit.
- Telephone, Internet and communication charge $100 and give you one month credit.
- Professional fees charge $100 and give you two months credit.
- Bank charges are $100 and give you one month credit.

- Wages and salaries of $5,000 are paid in the same month the work is carried out.
- Material costs of $2,000 (could include a range of terms); in this case they give you one month credit.
- Equipment costs of $300 (could include a range of terms); in this case they require payment two months upfront.
- Transport costs of $200 (could include a range of terms); in this case they require payment one month upfront.

Capital equipment and machinery purchases can have a big impact on the cashflow, particularly if they are purchased as a lump sum. For this reason, capital equipment is often leased and paid for monthly, or financed separately from an investment account.

Exercise:

If Figure 13.5 was a profit and loss statement, what would be the profit (see end of chapter for solution).

5. Breakeven Analysis

The breakeven point analysis is an important financial calculation which will give you a feel for your venture's exposure to risk and uncertainty. The breakeven point analysis calculates the number of units your company must sell to cover the setup costs or fixed costs. These figures are particularly important for products that initially consume a large amount of resources before you make a profit (Figure 13.6).

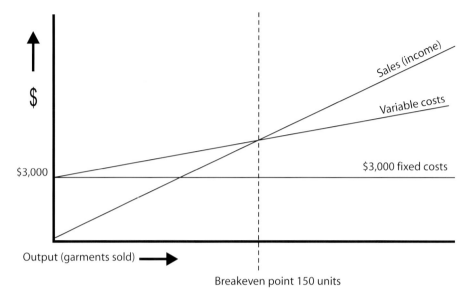

Figure 13.6 Breakeven Point Analysis - shows the breakeven point at the intersection of the sales (income) and the combined value of the fixed costs and the variable costs.

As a fashion entrepreneur you might start a business in textile design and printing.

Digital printer, University of Plymouth Colleges Somerset.

The breakeven point analysis calculates the breakeven point by subdividing your expenses into 'fixed costs', 'variable costs' and 'contribution per unit sale' where:

- **Fixed costs** are comprised of setup and overhead-type costs (design, samples, machinery, office rent, salaries, marketing etc.), and would typically be one off costs to develop your products or samples (see section on indirect costs). By their nature, fixed costs are incurred whether any products are manufactured or not. Fixed costs are shown as a horizontal line in Figure 13.6.
- **Variable costs** are the costs of actually making the product. The costs are variable in the sense that they increase with the number of units manufactured, and are only incurred when the product is manufactured. This would obviously include direct labour, direct materials and variable overheads (electricity and heating). Assuming the cost of making each unit can be averaged out to be the same, the 'variable costs' can be represented by a diagonal line as shown in Figure 13.6. Note this calculation has not considered any economy of scale - in practice you would expect the unit cost to reduce as the production run increases.
- **Income** is from the sales turnover and increases with sales.
- **Contribution** is the **contribution per unit sale** - the amount available to repay the fixed costs after the variable costs have been deducted from the income - as follows:

Contribution per unit sales = Income per unit sales - variable costs

The breakeven point is calculated by dividing the *'contribution per unit sales'* into the *'fixed costs'* - as follows:

Breakeven point = <u>Fixed Costs</u>
  Contribution per unit sales

You can now see why you need to calculate separately the *'fixed costs'*, *'variable costs'* and *'contribution per unit sale'*.

Breakeven Example 1: Using the profit and loss statement, Figure 13.4, calculate the breakeven point for the A/W fashion range. From the cashflow statement the production fixed costs include the design, sales and marketing costs and are [$3,000]. Note the cost to setup the business [$1,000] is not included as this is not part of your production cycle. The dresses sell for $30 each. The variable cost to make the dress is $10 per unit; this covers the direct labour, direct material and the direct overhead costs to make the dress, leaving $20 per unit as a contribution towards the fixed costs (costs you incur whether you make any garments or not). The breakeven point is reached when the contribution per unit sale equals the fixed costs.

Breakeven point = <u>Fixed Costs</u>
  Contribution per unit sale

= <u>$3000</u> = 150 units
  $20

The breakeven point is 150 units, this is when the sales income [150 units x $30 = $4,500]) equals the total cost of labour and material x sales units + fixed costs [$10 x 150 + $3000 = $4500].

If the company sells less than 150 garments they will make a loss, while if they sell more than 150 garments they will make a profit.

Textile design for Moontide.

Textile Designer: Alissa Stytsenko - Creative Director FLY 'N' SHOOTER

6. Balance Sheet

The balance sheet is a snapshot of the balance between the company's assets and the company's liabilities on any particular day. For management purposes the balance sheet can be presented as a two column format of assets and liabilities (Figure 13.7), or as a one column format with the figures from previous years to show any trends (Figure 13.8).

ASSETS		LIABILITIES	
1. Fixed Assets		**3. Capital**	
Property	$500,000	Shareholders' Capital	$600,000
Plant, Machinery, Vehicles	$500,000	Retained Earnings (Profit)	$200,000
TOTAL FIXED ASSETS	$1,000,000	TOTAL CAPITAL	$800,000
		4. Term Liabilities	
		Loans	$100,000
2. Current Assets		**5. Current Liabilities**	
Cash in Hand (Bank)	$50,000	Bank Overdraft	$0
Stock	$100,000	Tax Payable	$60,000
Debtors	$50,000	Creditors	$240,000
TOTAL CURRENT ASSETS	$200,000	TOTAL LIABILITIES	$300,000
TOTAL ASSETS	**$1,200,000**	**TOTAL CAPITAL & LIABILITIES**	**$1,200,000**

Figure 13.7 Balance Sheet - shows a two column format balancing assets and liabilities.

	Year	One Year Prior	Two Years Prior
1. Fixed Assets			
Property	$500,000		
Plant, Machinery, Vehicles	$500,000		
TOTAL FIXED ASSETS	$1,000,000		
2. Current Assets			
Bank Accounts	$50,000		
Stock	$100,000		
Debtors	$50,000		
TOTAL CURRENT ASSETS	$200,000		
TOTAL ASSETS	**$1,200,000**		
3. Capital			
Shareholders' Capital	$600,000		
Retained Earnings	$200,000		
TOTAL CAPITAL	$800,000		
4. Term Liabilities			
Loans	$100,000		
5. Current Liabilities			
Bank Overdraft	$0		
Tax Payable	$60,000		
Creditors	$240,000		
TOTAL LIABILITIES	$300,000		
TOTAL CAPITAL & LIABILITIES	**$1,200,000**		

Figure 13.8 Balance Sheet - shows additional columns to input historical information.

The income you make from the sales of your collection is entered in your sales ledger.

Fashion Illustrator: Eric Hagen

Explanation of Figure 13.7 and 13.8:

1. Fixed Assets: Fixed assets are items of a permanent nature that will be part of your business for a long period of time. Fixed assets include all the capital items in your business, even items which have not yet been paid for (unpaid amounts will be included in liabilities under creditors).

2. Current Assets: A balance sheet is based on actual figures at the reported date. This includes actual cash in hand (bank account), actual amounts owed to you (debtors), and actual stock in hand even if the stock has not yet been paid for (unpaid stock will appear as a liability under creditors).

3. Capital: Any money you have invested in your business is entered as shareholders' capital. The profit for the period, brought out in the Profit and Loss statement, is shown as retained earnings. A loss is represented by brackets ( ) as a deduction from your capital.

4. Term Liabilities: Term liabilities are loans which are not due to be repaid within the current year.

5. Current Liabilities: Include bank overdrafts, tax payable (sales tax) and trade creditors.

Bottom Line: The bottom line of the balance sheet must balance - the total liabilities must equal the total assets. If there is a difference check your figures to ensure all balances have been included.

Historical Analysis: With the one column balance sheet (Figure 13.8) you can show figures from the previous years. The historical figures enable you to identify trends which may be more important than the actual numbers.

Exercises:

1. Develop a setup budget showing the costs subdivided into; setup costs, production costs and overhead costs, for a new venture, either:
- A new fashion Spring/Summer collection,
- A new fashion retail store, or
- A fashion design service making bespoke clothing for private clients.

2. Draw the profit and loss cashflow for exercise (Figure 13.4) - Start the next production cycle, Spring/Summer, in July using the same costs and income as Autumn/Winter (see solution in the Appendices).

3. Figure 13.5: Solution $5000.

Once your business starts making you a profit it is like the cherry on the top.... or the olive in the martini, in this case!

Illustrator: Sarah Beetson

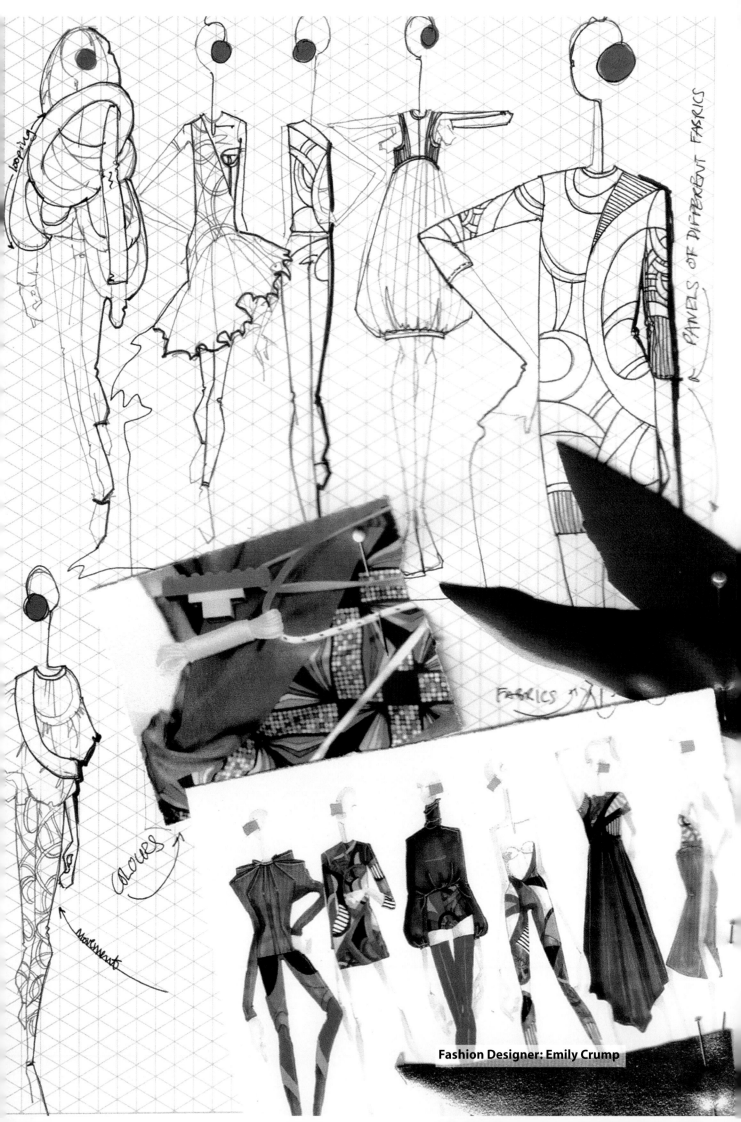

looping

PANELS OF DIFFERENT FABRICS

FABRICS

COLOURS

movement

Fashion Designer: Emily Crump

Project Management Skills

Project management is being recognised as a key skill within the fashion entrepreneur's portfolio of technical, small business management, leadership and team building skills. This is because so many of the fashion tasks, jobs and events have all the characteristics of a project - they must be completed on time and within budget; for example:

- Starting your own business.
- Designing new products.
- Putting on a fashion show or fashion exhibition (trade show).
- Marketing and promoting a new fashion range.
- Manufacturing and distributing a new fashion range.

In project management speak these project characteristics can be listed as project goals and objectives:

Completion deadlines	Fashion ranges must be completed by a certain date, perfectly timed to coincide with a specific design and manufacturing cycle.	
One off tasks	Non-repetitive tasks (bespoke tailoring, millinery, special embroidery) that require a higher level of work definition will need to be communicated to the design team.	
Tight budget	To improve the level of estimating and budget control a fashion project may need to be subdivided into sub-tasks - fashion ranges, fashion events to ensure they do not exceed allocated budgets.	
Work in temporary teams	Temporary design and production teams brought together for a fashion project will need to quickly learn how to work together.	
Co-ordinating	The input from suppliers, manufacturers, contractors and freelancers will need to be organized and co-ordinated.	
Leadership	Leading, co-ordinating and motivating your innovative team.	

Project Strategy

To achieve a fashion project's goals and objectives there are a number of key project management tools and techniques that, as a fashion entrepreneur, you should consider using. These are set out in the following steps:

Step 1: Project Brief - the project brief initiates the project and identifies what you need to achieve.

Step 2: Project Planning and Project Control - uses the barchart to schedule, monitor and control the work.

Step 3: Growth Phases - include the concept phase, the start up phase, the survival phase and the growth phase of new ventures.

Behind the scenes at the Klûk & CGdT fashion show - designers and owners of the luxury womenswear label, Malcolm and Christiaan prepare for their show.
Top: Malcolm Klûk
Above: Christiaan Gabriel du Toit

Above and Opposite: *The project design brief initiates the fashion project and outlines what you want to achieve. Emily crump, fashion designer set out to achieve a cohesive collection inspired by music, sound, notes and a kaleidoscope of colourful imagery.*

Fashion Designer: Emily Crump

Step 1: Project Brief

The project design brief initiates the fashion project and outlines what you want to achieve, who is responsible, the budget and a completion date. For example, a fashion project for an emerging fashion design entrepreneur may be expressed as; design a luxury womenswear collection; Linda Logan is responsible for leading the design team; the design budget (research, fabric sampling, samples) is $9,000 and the schedule is as follows (see Figure 14.3);

- The collection must be finalised by end January.
- The collection will be presented at during Fashion Week in February.
- The sales and marketing will begin in February and finish by end March.
- Pre-production samples and patterns will be approved by end March.
- Production will begin 1st April and finish end July.
- Shipment and distribution will be complete by end August.
- Cash on delivery (COD) will begin in August and continue into the next month depending on the terms of payment agreed.

Project Plan: The project plan develops a strategy and a scope of work for achieving the fashion project's goals and objectives. The scope of work can be broken down into a number of manageable tasks by using the work breakdown structure (WBS) technique (Figure 14.1).

Work Breakdown Structure (WBS): The WBS technique is used to subdivide the scope of work into a checklist of manageable units of jobs or work packages. This will not only improve the accuracy of your estimating, but forms the backbone of the project. Consider the fashion design project to design, manufacture and distribute the collection.

Market Research	Design Garments	Sales and Marketing	Production
Interviews	Source fabrics, buy sampling	Brochures	Order bulk material
Trend research	Design collection	Product Launch	Manufacture
	Make patterns and samples	Fashion Show	Distribution

Figure 14.1 Fashion Design Project Work Breakdown Structure – shows a fashion project broken down into its component work packages, and each component broken down into its main activities.

Work Packages: At the work package level there should be sufficient detail to carry out the work; for example, a job description, a technical specification sheet, the time allocated, the materials required, the budget and quality control details.

Project Control Sheet: The starting point for all fashion projects is to quantify and communicate your goals and objectives. This can be set up on a control sheet matrix format on a spreadsheet where the left hand column uses the work breakdown structure (WBS) to list the scope of work, and the other columns outline the required condition (what you want those involved to achieve/the activities to achieve) with respect to the project's goals and objectives (Figure 14.2).

WBS	Responsibility	Time	Budget	Procurement	Resources	Quality	Risk
Market/trend/ fabric research	Linda Logan	4 months	$1,000		Interviews, fashion and forecasting publications		Medium
Design, make, finalise collection	Linda Logan	3 months end Jan	$8,000	Sampling fabric	Pattern cutters and sample machinists	Defined by sample	Medium
Sales and Marketing	Maria Leeke	2 months end March	$1,000	Brochures and website	Sales and marketing team		Medium
Production	Ewa Liddington	3 months end July	$12,000	Fabrics and trims	Production team - manager, machinists	Production sample	High

Figure 14.2 Project Control Sheet – shows the project's goals and objectives in a matrix format. In practice these fields would be subdivided into 'planned' and 'actual' so that performance can be monitored and controlled.

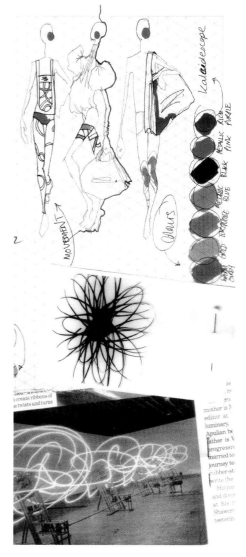

Responsibility: The responsibility column identifies who is **responsible** for the work, together with who should be **consulted** and who should be **informed**. If you have a design team this would be an effective way of indicating who does what. By transferring this information to the barchart you will be able to check resource loadings (how many people are needed per day to complete a task) over the duration of the project.

Time: The time column outlines the sequence of work, the hours allocated to do the work and the duration of the task (activity). The time column also includes any key dates (milestones); for example, the date the bulk fabric needs to be ordered and the start date for production.

Budget: The budget column outlines the budget for each task (activity). By assigning a budget at the work activity level, this will greatly increase your level of monitoring and control.

Procurement: The procurement column identifies all the bought-in items (fabrics and trims). These can be transferred on to the barchart to find the required delivery date. By working back you can calculate when the items need to be ordered. You are particularly looking for long lead items which could delay your project; for example, if your bulk fabric is being specially dyed or printed.

Resources: The resource column outlines what resources (people and equipment) are required for each task . These can be transferred onto the barchart as resource required per day. The loadings can then be compared with the resources available.

Quality: The quality column outlines the required condition and the methods of inspection and quality control (the approved production samples would confirm the style, design details and quality, together with the approved specification sheets).

Risk: The risk column enables you to identify areas of high and low risk. This enables you to focus on high risk activities where potential problems could occur and that need to be monitored more closely. It also allows you to put in place response contingencies specifically developed for these potential problems. For example, if one of your pattern cutters was ill, you might need to find a replacement or, if the bulk fabric for your production arrives damaged, you would need to quickly have it replaced or find a substitute fabric.

Step 2: Project Planning and Project Control

The barchart (Figure 14.3) is an excellent technique to use, to plan and control small fashion projects by communicating information and instructions to the project team. The barchart visually shows the scope of work [1] against a time scale along the top of the diagram [2]; the sequence of the work; the timing of the work (start and finish dates [3] and [4]); the diamonds represent milestones or keydates/deadline [5]; who is responsible for the individual tasks [6]; the procurement, the resources, the budgets – all on one document. And further, when the project starts, it can be used to show the progress, and be used to control the project.

▬▬▬ A/W (Fall) collection

▬▬▬ S/S collection

◆ Milestones (keydates/deadlines)

Scope of Work	Aug	Sep	Oct	Nov	Dec	Jan	Feb	Mar	Apr	May	Jun	July	Aug	Sep	Oct	Nov	Res
Market and trend research	A/W Fashion Cycle						S/S Fashion Cycle										Linda
Source and sample fabrics	[3] ▬▬		[4]				▬▬										Linda
Designs, patterns and samples		▬▬▬▬						▬▬▬▬									Linda
Review and finalise collection					▬▬					▬▬							Linda
Marketing Kit, website					▬▬					▬▬							Maria
Fashion show, fashion week						[5]◆								◆			Maria
Sales and marketing						▬▬▬							▬▬				Maria
Confirm fabric and production								▬▬					▬▬				Ewa
Collate orders, fabrics delivered								▬▬▬					▬▬				Ewa
Pre-Production samples, patterns									▬▬								Ewa
Production										▬▬▬▬				▬▬			Ewa
Shipping, deliver to store, COD													▬▬				Ewa
Collect Payments														▬▬			Maria

Figure 14.3 Barchart - Fashion Design Project – shows how the barchart can be used to plan a fashion design collection from design, sales, manufacture to distribution.

Linda [6] starts the Autumn/Winter fashion design cycle in August with market/trend research, sampling fabric, designing and making the samples. The collection is finalised in January, along with the sales and marketing material (brochures, line sheets, look books and website).

In February, the collection is launched at a fashion show during 'Fashion Week' [5]. Sales orders are taken in February and finish end March when they are collated. During March the orders for the raw materials are confirmed, along with the confirmation of the production schedule with the CMTs. By the end of April all fabrics and trims for production are delivered.

During April the pre-production patterns and samples are approved. Production takes three months from 1st May to end July. The goods are shipped/distributed to the stores during August. Payments are collected as COD, and during the month of September.

While the Autumn/Winter design and manufacturing cycle is in progress so the next season, Spring/Summer's fashion cycle begins, and so the design cycles are repeated.

This cycle could be repeated several times a year depending on the type of fashion business (fast fashion etc.) and how many collections, or projects are being carried out.

Expediting: Even well planned projects can fail to meet the objectives if the instructions are not followed up. This is where the expediting function is used to check that everyone (team members, suppliers and contractors) has received their instructions, they understand the instructions, they have ordered all the resources they need, they do not have any problems carrying out the work, and they will be able to complete the work as planned.

Project Control: The project control function monitors the performance of each activity with respect to:

Monitor Scope	Are there any design changes? For example, the specified buttons may not be available so they need to be substituted with another style.
Monitor Progress	Confirm the work has started on time, measure the progress either as percentage complete or remaining duration, confirm the work will be finished as planned.
Monitor Procurement	Confirm the materials have been ordered, whether they will arrive on time and whether storage space is available (rolls of fabric for production).
Monitor Resources	Check resource loading (how many people are required to do the work on a per day basis), and confirm sufficient resources are available.
Monitor Budgets	Check the planned expenditure versus the actual expenditure and note any variance (the work/project is within budget), compare the cost-to-complete the work/project with the funds remaining.
Monitor Quality	Note any quality issues.

Progress Meetings: Progress reports are usually produced to coincide with the weekly progress meeting attended by the project participants.

The fashion design and production cycle starts with market and trend research, sampling fabric, designing and making the samples. This presentation shows fashion designer, Jessica Whitehead, in the design stage of planning her collection; the fabrics, colours, inspirational photographs and sketches of her garments together with sketches of the finer details involved.

Fashion Designer: Jessica Whitehead

Delivering a successful fashion show involves excellent project management skills to present the event on time, within budget, and to the quality expected by the punters.

KlûK & CGDT fashion show success!

Courtesy: KlûK & CGDT

Step 3: Growth Phases

All small businesses pass through a number of distinct phases or stages as they grow and develop. Each distinct phase involves different types of work and requires a different style of management and leadership. Presenting new fashion projects as a lifecycle enables the fashion entrepreneur to plan and control each phase. Figure 14.4 subdivides company growth into six phases.

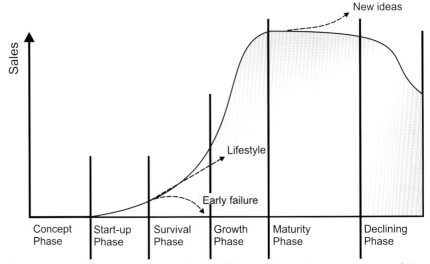

Andy Penaluna, "Designers are like 'cultural compost' - like a plant, they soak up what is going on around them and in consequence, grow in their understanding and ambition. They follow trends, watch the latest TV shows, pick up magazines (cultural compost) and are always hungry for more inspiration and ideas to feed them (the roots). They mix all this information together into new and exciting forms, looking for enlightenment, discarding worn out concepts and developing new ones to replace them (leaves?). Nothing is ever fixed and just like the plant they are constantly evolving and changing, reaching down with their roots for that extra bit of cultural compost to guide them and to help them to develop as designers. They are continuously growing taller and broader as their knowledge and experience accumulates."

Figure 14.4 Fashion Entrepreneur Growth Phases – shows the company growth in six phases.

Concept Phase: Considers ideas and opportunities – this is where the design feasibility study is carried out. Many entrepreneurs wait on the starting blocks for a **trigger** to kick-start their new venture – this could be an award of a large order for a fashion collection or approval of finance to start the business.

Start Up Phase: The start up phase sets up the business and begins to offer the products or services to the market. There will be high excitement and enthusiasm fuelled by finally getting the business off the ground - the thrill of the first customer. But, as the reality of the business kicks in, having learnt what is involved, the entrepreneur must develop business skills to be able to respond to customer needs, expectations and reactions.

Survival Phase: The survival phase is the viability test - is the venture going to develop sufficient income to pay the bills before the seed money runs out? Is the company attracting sufficient customers - particularly repeat business? Is the cash flow generating positive working capital - is income greater than expenditure? And are the products making a trading profit - is the selling price greater than the manufacturing costs?

Growth Phase: As new ventures make it through the start up and survival phases this confirms they have established a niche market, formed a solid customer base and built a sound reputation for their products. This also implies the company is trading profitably and the venture is now in a position to consider its future direction – possible expansion and growth. There are many reasons why entrepreneurs might want to grow their businesses or, in some cases, have growth thrust upon them:

- Expand to meet growing demand for the product.
- Restrict competition (perhaps the most important reason) because, if entrepreneurs cannot meet the demand, they are simply inviting competitors into the market they have established.
- Expand the production facilities to achieve economies of scale - with bigger production runs entrepreneurs should be able to reduce the unit cost.

Growing Pains: Rapid growth usually requires some major changes in the entrepreneur's leadership style and the company's management systems so that they can plan and control larger volumes of the product. Otherwise there might be some unpleasant surprises, not least the contradictory sounding **success-disaster** scenario.

A success-disaster can happen when the sales and marketing team hits the sweet spot and demand for the product suddenly takes off. The entrepreneur's reaction is usually to try and gear up production to meet the demand. But if the management systems are not in place this will lead to poor communication, shortages of materials, stressed out workers, producing poor quality, late deliveries, and negative cash flows and, in the worst case scenario, liquidation.

The product shortages will cause the entrepreneur's help desk to get swamped with enquiries from angry customers. The effect of the inability to deliver will result in the company developing a bad reputation with its customers, which might allow its competitors into the very market the entrepreneur has personally pioneered and developed.

In the attempt to meet demand, the employees will be over worked and be getting increasingly frustrated which could result in some key people actually leaving the company. These people will be replaced by new workers who will not understand the business - this has the potential of creating a vicious spiral.

The financial side could be even worse as the company builds up stock and has to wait for the inflow of income. Without financial support, the upfront costs will create negative cash flow which could drive the company into liquidation.

The tragedy of this scenario is that it usually does end in disaster - the company simply spirals out of control. The best way to survive the success-disaster is to try to prevent it happening in the first place by being prepared to manage growth with effective small business management skills, leadership skills and production controls.

Maturity Phase: Company growth often expands into bureaucracy and red tape which stifles the very innovation that underpinned the company's original growth. Management begins to replace business leadership, as they prefer to keep tried and tested products rather than risk investment in new product development.

Declining Phase: Failure to respond to new technology leaves the company with obsolete products and declining sales. The company is seriously in need of entrepreneurial shock treatment, or it will end up as a candidate for takeover or closure.

Happy Birthday, your company has survived the six growth phases and is now two years old! Make sure you have your management systems in place to avoid a success-disaster scenario.

Illustrator: Sarah Beetson

Can you measure up to the job? Can you measure the growth of your business?
This tape measure is, not only, a measuring tool but acts as a marketing tool with the name of the brand clearly printed on the end of the tape.
Courtesy: Stafford College

© Fashion Entrepreneur - Sandra Burke

4. Small Business Management

Entrepreneurs and small business managers are often thought of as being one and the same. But, in practice, entrepreneurship is the management of change, particularly when starting a new venture or introducing a new product or service. Whereas, small business management is the management of the company on a day-to-day basis - particularly with respect to repetitive jobs. Some of the key small business management functions include:

- Marketing the company and the products.
- Accounts, budgets, book-keeping and cash flow.
- Paying wages, invoices and debtors.
- Complying with rules, regulations and taxes.
- Buying or renting premises.
- Buying, leasing or hiring plant and equipment.
- Procurement of material and services.
- Warehousing and stock control (JIT).
- Distribution.
- Labour relations, recruitment and hiring.
- Supervision and leadership.
- Manufacturing the product (technical), and scheduling the workflow.
- Quality control.
- Customer service.

Entrepreneurship and small business management obviously go together. Small businesses swing in and out of periods of entrepreneurial change as the business introduces new products, then consolidates its gains, before repeating the cycle at the next opportunity. For example, entrepreneurial change would include the starting of the business, the development of new products, the introduction of new management systems and the penetration of new markets. But, after each entrepreneurial change, the small business would need to consolidate the change and continue at the new level until there is a need or opportunity to change again.

In practice the true entrepreneur would get bored running a small business that did not continually challenge the status quo. These topics will be covered in detail in Burke, Rory, *Small Business Entrepreneur*.

Producing a fashion collection, producing a fashion show and putting on a wedding are all projects and involve expert planning to be within budget and delivered on time!

Courtesy: KlùK & CGDT

The Design Team! - *The entrepreneur is the driving force - leading, coordinating, managing and organizing the input of suppliers, contractors and design team members.*

Fashion Designer: Amy Lappin

5. Teamwork and Leadership

The entrepreneur is the driving force behind a new venture - leading, co-ordinating, managing and organising the input of suppliers, contractors and team members. This requires:

- Leadership skills to communicate the vision.
- Inspiration to motivate the team to work towards a common goal.
- Influence and power to make the work happen.

New ventures, by their very nature, require that extra push to overcome a minefield of obstacles and challenges associated with changing the status quo. Entrepreneurs need to build management teams for a number of reasons:

- To increase the number of people available to match the workload as outlined in the resource plan.
- The nature of the work may require a range of complementary skills which any one person is unlikely to have.
- To solve problems - interactive team work and brainstorming encourages cross-fertilisation and synergy, where the team generates more and better ideas than people acting on their own.
- To make decisions - gain collective commitment and resources from the team members.
- To enhance motivation - team cohesiveness will motivate team members to give 110% and not let the side down.
- Risk taking - management teams generally make riskier decisions than an individual would because there is a feeling of mutual support and sharing of implications.

The entrepreneur, as team leader, is responsible for building an effective team that has the technical skills required to do the work, together with a balance of appropriate human personalities and behaviours so that the team members can work together effectively. Team building incorporates a range of functions that the entrepreneur is responsible for:

- Team design - to establish a resource profile of complementary skills.
- Team selection - psychometric testing to achieve a balance of human personalities and behaviours.
- Team building - to integrate the team to work effectively together.
- Team coaching and mentoring - guiding and encouraging each team member's performance.
- Succession planning and handover as players leave and new members join the team.

Exercises:

1. Develop a project control sheet for your fashion project.
2. Develop a barchart for your fashion project.
3. Discuss the growth phases for your new business.
4. List items of your work which have the characteristics of a project.

Hannah Marshall®

Photographer: Victor de Mello

Fashion Entrepreneurs' Case Studies

Hannah Marshall Designer and Owner of Womenswear Label 'Hannah Marshall'

Hannah Marshall is a young fashion entrepreneur who has established herself through education, networking, fashion shows, hard work and passion. Hannah is an excellent role model for young fashion designers who want to start their own fashion business. Her refined designs and talent attracted the attentions of the first ever Creative Pioneer Programme to come from NESTA (The National Endowment for Science, Technology and the Arts). At the age of just twenty-one, Hannah was the youngest of 30 young entrepreneurs, to receive personal and business training to help transform their ideas into a business.

How did you gain your fashion skills?
I received a First Class degree from Colchester School of Art & Design and gained work experience with several leading London and New York fashion designers.

How have you showcased your work?
I have been recognised in the UK by the BBC, The Princes Trust, Channel 4, and 'New Generation' which is sponsored by Topshop, and received sponsorship to show at London Fashion Week. (New Generation is an internationally recognised organization whose support has helped launch the careers of some of Britain's top designers, including the likes of Alexander McQueen, Matthew Williamson and Julien Macdonald and more recently, Christopher Kane and Marios Schwab.)

How do you describe your business and your niche market?
My womenswear label, Hannah Marshall, endeavours to push the boundaries of sophistication, encapsulating a range of luxury contemporary classics. Initially, I designed it with the professional and socialite woman in mind, and my label soon developed into something unique with the increasing desire for my capsule wardrobe. Each collection is based upon one philosophy – addressing clothing in a socially inclusive context, combined with the idea of defying the seasonal trends that fashion so regularly dictates.

What motivated you to start your own business?
The main motivation for starting my own business was to be in control of my own career. I am a very ambitious individual with many goals that I hope to achieve and only by working for myself could I find this rewarding experience. But, it was only when I realised there was a niche in the market that I was able to design for, and that it was really worth pursuing my ideas, that I then decided to set up a business.

Where did you find help with setting up your business?
For my business to be successful I knew it could not solely survive with creativity, and I needed to be able to back up my ideas and plans with sound business knowledge and planning. Through business training programmes; NESTA, the Portobello Business Centre, Business Link and the NCGE Flying Start Programme, I have developed a strong business sense and the understanding of the importance of innovation. Mentoring with key industry figures such as Helen Storey and Caroline Coates has proved to be an incredibly useful method of pushing my ideas forward, and by receiving honest, critical advice from inspirational individuals with a wealth of experience in the fashion industry.

What are the highlights of running your own business?
The main highlight of running a creative business operating in the creative industries, has to be the versatility of the way my business can operate. The most rewarding aspects are seeing my entire collection come together, and my collection hit the catwalk during London Fashion Week.

What aspects of setting up and running your own business have you found particularly challenging?
Financing my business start up has been a huge issue, and is something that cannot be ignored. Dealing with all the financial goings on – like cash flow forecasts and VAT returns. It's boring and time consuming but absolutely essential. This is a challenge that I am currently facing and, by constructing a sound business plan, I am making applications to creative funding bodies such as NESTA. I am looking for investment alongside ongoing support to nurture my business, to ensure it is sustainable and has a strong growth strategy.

Sally Moinet Designer and Owner of Womenswear Label 'Sally Moinet'

Fashion entrepreneur Sally Moinet has built up an extremely successful fashion business over the last ten years, which she runs from her stunning home by the sea and her office in the city. She specializes in high end fashion with a classic, sophisticated twist. Her designs appeal to women who want to be seen in stylish designs but not too highly trend driven. She has built up a loyal customer base of private clients and independent stores with whom she deals directly. Her understanding of what her customers want is exceptional, so much so, that when she brings out her new collections twice a year, she can predict her forthcoming sales and how many garments to put into production almost before she shows her range.

What motivated you to start your own business?

It might sound a cliché but it was a real passion for fashion and a love of the fashion business. I was working for someone else and I kept thinking, *'Why don't I do this for myself instead?'*

What training did you have?

I started my career in advertising in media and communication liaising with the press, but left to do a three year degree in fashion design, as I realized fashion was what motivated me.

How did you choose your company name?

My surname is French and it seemed obvious that I should use it - it just sounded right for my label. It has also turned out to be a great way of self marketing – people know my name and, therefore, remember it and associate my name with my products.

How did you break into the fashion industry?

I started by designing my first range using a Czech damask tablecloth fabric for the main range and a beautiful lightweight satin for the tops. Once the range was complete, I phoned all the local fashion stores and made appointments to see them, then went store to store carrying piles of clothing. My first retail buyer gave me a sizeable order, my lucky break, which set me on the road and I never looked back. Now the retailers come to me!

What skills have you developed in your business?

I started with very basic fashion and business skills and have gradually mastered the art of managing the whole scope within my business. I am very close to my customer and everything in the business and have developed an intuition and a 'gut feel'. I don't really have any major issues but I do monitor absolutely everything constantly. I have developed good management skills, but it is also absolutely vital to have the right people working for me - I might have to pay a little more for them but it is worth it.

What are the highlights of running your own business?

Without doubt when I am selling my range and it is selling well, and I can see satisfied customers. And, of course, reaping the rewards from my sales. Because I deal personally with my customers I receive direct feedback.

Do you lead or manage a design team?

I use freelance experts - pattern makers and graders, but I do employ several sample machinists and an ironer - I have a lot of my own equipment now. I also use a quality controller – a key person. She is very experienced and also specializes in clothing for export. I definitely have to be a good project manager.

What aspects are particularly challenging?

Staff! That is the hardest! Finding good staff to work with, and who have the technical skills, is by far the most challenging.

What entrepreneurial traits make your business a success?

Passion, determination, networking and negotiating - these are important as every day presents some kind of problem. I am a perfectionist so I persist until the problem is solved. For instance, if the fit of a jacket is wrong I will keep going back to the pattern maker, four or five times in a day until it is right. I will not let go until it fits perfectly.

What has been the key to your success?

Selling direct to my end customer. This has kept me afloat because, with a small business and small units, the margins are really not sufficient to deal only with retailers. If I only sold to stores I would not survive.

Do you ever feel like giving up when business gets hard?

Initially, working on my own I was not sure if what I was doing was right, but now my business has grown I have no time to worry, it is like being on a roundabout and you have to keep going – there is no time to jump off!

Have you advice for those setting up their own business?

This is hard as there is so much advice I could give - you learn so much in the fashion business. But the main thing is *'Never ever give up, be persistent and determined and passionate always!'*

coming soon

SALLY MOINET

Ricki Wolman Designer, Manufacturer and Retailer of Womenswear and Menswear Label 'Citron'

CITRON was created in 1992 in Santa Monica, California, the brainchild of Ricki Wolman. Ricki was born and raised in Cape Town, South Africa, where his initial experience in retail and manufacturing was acquired. Ricki has spent the ensuing years travelling throughout the world, studying and gathering elements and techniques that form the basis of his unique design esthetics. The influence of many different cultures, as well as past and present eras, is Ricki's inspiration for the original textiles that distinguish every Citron creation. He currently supplies many of the key fashion retailers all over the US including his own store.

How did your entrepreneurial skills get you started in Cape Town and help you establish your US fashion company?

I started the business more out of a **need** to **prove** to my dad that I wasn't just a 'lazy bum' who studied for the sake of being a student. With a Degree in Psychology and Literature I had no idea what I would do with it. My dad was closing his shop in Station Road, Wynberg (a back street in an out of the way area frequented by working class people next to a railway station). He asked me to help him to get rid of the old stock in the process of winding down the business. I suddenly found myself **challenged** and **inspired** by his incredible, antique inventory. Some of the classic men's shirts, for example, were made from the highest quality white cotton, with detachable collars and a shirt tail, and had become yellowed and stained with age.

I took these shirts home and dyed them in my bathtub with dye that I bought at the local supermarket. Although I could only get hold of primary colors the cotton took beautifully to the dye and the shirts were radiant after the process.

This started a huge trend and I became the first in Cape Town to initiate garment over-dyeing! The shop became a 'trendy destination' - it was so out of the way and in a low class, less desirable area, but this seemed to encourage the intrigue and fascination associated with the desire to visit the shop. We were so packed on Saturdays that we had to have a guard at the door. Out of towners would visit and buy 20 to 30 garments at a time.

The store was called 'Sell Out', not intentionally but, because I wanted to create the image of having a sale, I asked a window dresser to make a poster with the words 'sell - out' to hang in the window. The shop soon came to be known as Sell Out so I **registered** the name.

The business really developed out of **necessity** rather than a desire to create, but I enjoyed the results and felt creative in the process and I was very well rewarded by the sales.

I pretty much recycled all the inventory in the store using my 'bathtub' dyeing method along with other wash techniques - the store became known as a destination for unique but inexpensive, laundered look, vintage inspired clothing made from natural fibres.

I approached local fashion manufacturers and started buying their 'dead', flawed even stained end of season stock which I re-dyed, sandwashed or stonewashed (now at a

professional dyehouse) and sold at much lower prices than any other retailer could. This was a blessing in the beginning but turned against me as the manufacturers of these garments received complaints from the retail stores who were selling the brands at full price; even though I had altered the appearance of the garments, there were still sufficient complaints so that several of my sources could no longer supply me.

It occurred to me that these same manufacturers had large inventories of fabrics that they would be prepared to sell at substantially lower prices. Having **negotiated** this with them, I would select the fabrics, submit the designs, and they would cut and sew the garments and also oversee the garment dye or other treatments. I created my own label for this purpose, *Zoe Utility,* which then became a well known brand.

I had no formal representatives or showroom, and would **sell** to other retailers nationwide **over the phone**, sight unseen, and **payment in advance**, and I never had a single return! This was a most unique situation! Most of my customers heard about my product by **'word of mouth'** - there seemed to be some kind of intrigue and mystique due to the lack of commercial formality and the unconventional style of the garments.

My inspiration came from magazines and visiting Europe, in particular, Paris and London. I also visited the European design manufacturers - Marithé & François Girbaud, Naf Naf, Biscote, Replay. And, this is when I started to **import** offprice fashions from France and Italy. They were only too happy to supply me as South Africa was far away from their markets which meant I would not interfere with their image in any way by discounting their products.

I had always wanted to live in the States so with several years of experience in running my own successful business, and a good contact in the US, I felt I was ready to make the move - and I have never looked back!

Ceci n'est pas un Citron.

CITR⬢N

Melanie Casper Designer, Retailer and Owner of Kidswear Label 'Munko'

'Munko' is a unique brand of baby and children's clothing started by Melanie Casper in 1996. Melanie comes from a clothing background and after several years as a fashion designer in the industry she identified a gap in the market for fun, fashionable and creative clothing for kids. And so Munko was born!

What motivated you to start your own business?

Several things - having worked in the fashion industry as a childrenswear designer, and loved it, and having been a fashion designer working with the chain stores I was starting to feel that with all my experience I wanted something else, more flexibility and I wanted to be my own boss. It was about this time that I saw a gap in the market to set up a business designing childrenswear.

How did you start your business?

I started selling my kidswear range in a 'designer emporium' alongside other designers selling their collections. After a couple of years, I started to sell some of my merchandise on consignment to a couple of small retailers and, was doing so well, I decided it was time to leave the emporium and develop the manufacturing side and sell direct to the retailers.

As my sales grew, I saw the potential to expand and have my own kids shop as well. When one became available in the right location I decided to go for it. It has been very good for business but it is not easy - managing a store, the hours you have to work (you have to keep the store open at set times to comply with the shopping malls regulations), and especially finding good staff – all this while trying to design and manufacture the clothes as well – it is quite stressful.

How do you get inspiration for new designs and products?

I research on the Internet and check out what other brands are doing. I look at my sales figures and work with the best sellers – maybe redesign, recolour a design that worked well and adapt it for the next season. I also travel to the States and Europe and look for new ideas and inspiration. Sometimes it can be a simple trip to a local shopping area that suddenly triggers off an idea for a whole collection!

I am always looking at ways to improve my collection and am currently looking for new products. I already offer booties and beanies but will probably start offering shoes and more accessories. As I work closely with my customers, I am getting feedback that this is what they want – the whole look.

I produce two collections a year and I might have 50 or 70 styles. Once I start selling I then can judge whether to leave a particular style in or not. Once I collate my orders if a certain style has not sold the minimums I require I will not put it into production, then I have to contact the customers and offer them something else. I will make a minimum of 30 garments per style no less. When consolidating my production run I will round the figures up over the various sizes so that I can get the best use out of the fabric lay, and I will also add about 10% for rejects.

What are the highlights of running your own business?

Seeing my brand being worn – seeing kids in my designs.

What aspects of setting up and running your own business have you found particularly challenging?

FINANCE! This is really the most challenging. I was fortunate that I was able to start my business with a small amount of cotton fabric and managed to get terms on the fabric and the trims, which meant that I did not have to pay for the materials up front.

Most of my customers are very good at paying but I sometimes have to chase the money. I have an excellent computerized system in my office so, if customers have not paid their account after 30 days, I know immediately and will follow up. I have an assistant who does the invoicing and we write up the cashbook every day keeping a check of all the money I paid out and money in, and keep an eye on the Internet banking.

What advice would you give to others?

It is really important to gain as much experience as you can first. Get a design job, get some practical, design and factory experience for a couple of years – learn as much as you can of the industry - learn the ropes first. If you work in the industry you will start to build up a great network of contacts to help you get started.

Melanie *designs all the* Munko *garments herself and uses CMTs to make the samples and the production garments. She has established a very successful business selling to retail and selling directly to customers in own retail store.*

Lynnette Murphy Design Consultant, Designer and Owner of Accessories Label 'Cloakroom Bags'

Lynnette Murphy, a London based Design Consultant (fashion illustration, fashion design and fashion education), has worked with numerous influential fashion companies and brands within the fashion industry and also runs courses on fashion entrepreneurship, *'How to Start Your Own Fashion Business'* at Central Saint Martins. She is finding a growing interest from students, graduates and those already working in industry who are keen to start their own fashion businesses.

Lynnette is currently in the process of starting an additional new business, 'Cloakroom Bags', specialising in a unique concept designing various types of bags.

What has inspired you to start your new business, *'Cloakroom Bags'*. What was the opportunity you identified - your unique selling point (USP)?

I was inspired both by my MA Design research and by my own experience with the difficulties of carrying heavy bags. I identified a common problem and a need to redesign bags and the way we wear them, so I decided to design a range of bags that would balance the weight distribution and take the weight off of one shoulder, and also be more practical. I feel certain styles of bags need to be updated for modern day life - we all have so much more we need to carry these days; new gadgets, mobiles and iPods - all these need specialised pockets.

What stage are you at with your new business?

I am at the prototype stage and plan to redesign bags for men and women who need bags for various activities. I have included a City life range, a Sports range and a Country range. The fabrics I am using are tough and waterproof - some leather versions have already been made.

Once I have finished the prototypes, planned for this summer, I will continue my market research by using focus groups and questionnaires.

How will you market and sell your products?

The future plans are dependant on the research. I may have a Website or I may show at a Trade Show for active Sportswear and sell to sports outlets - I am exploring all options.

When will you write your Business Plan?

Before you start a business plan it helps to know what your product will be. I had an idea of what I wanted to do but needed to do market research first. This establishes that; a) I have a product that people want, b) I have looked at the competition, c) that I know my price structure, d) I know where to manufacture small/med and large orders, e) I know who my customer will be, their lifestyle and the way they prefer to shop (their buying behaviour) and, f) how much I will need to start up.

Once all this research has been done I will know what to put in my business plan.

What advice would you give those thinking of setting up their own fashion business?

Do thorough research and planning, think of all the positives and negatives, be realistic. How will you support yourself for two or three years without an income? Are you willing to work harder than you have ever done before? Is your partner/family going to be supportive? And then finally start small and just go for it!!!

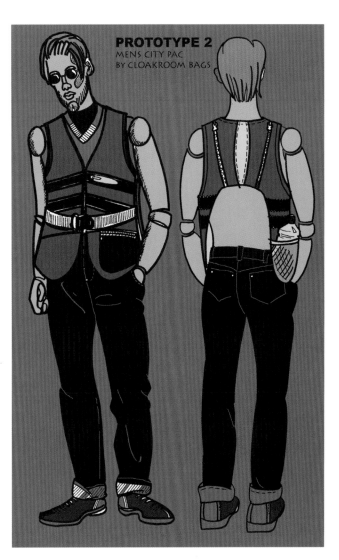

PROTOTYPE 3
Walking Pac
CLOAKROOM BAGS

Above: *The Walk Sac is for men and women to wear as an alternative to a rucksack. It ties around the hips or the waist, or can be worn on the shoulders as it is formed by two sleeves joined together by a reversible bag.*

Right: *This garment is to be worn over or under clothing. It is an alternative to a Courier or Man Bag. It is similar to a waistcoat but can detach into two halves and become two shoulder bags. It is rainproof and reversible.*

Fashion Designer: Aina Hussain

Appendices

The Appendices present the solution to exercise 13.4 and several key fashion industry/business documents which you can use as examples to develop your own specific documents. These are:

1. Profit and Loss Statement Solution

2. Design Style Sheet/Specification Sheet

3. Costing Sheet

4. Range/Line Sheets (Brochures, Catalogues)

5. Order Confirmation Form

Design Ideas:
Aina Hussain

1. Profit and Loss Statement Solution to Exercise 2 (Figure 13.4): Draw the profit and loss cash flow for exercise (Figure 13.4) - Start the next production cycle, Spring/Summer, in July using the same costs and income as Autumn/Winter.

	Jan	Feb	Mar	Apr	May	Jun	Jul	Aug	Sep	Oct	Nov	Dec	Jan	Feb
Brought Forward ($/£)	Seed 10,000	8,500	7,500	7,000	6,000	5,000	3,000	-2,500	-1,000	2,500	7,500	10,500	10,500	6,500
Income ($/£)	0	0	0	0	0	0	0	3,000	4,000	6,000	4,000	2,000	1,000	3,000
Funds Available ($/£)	10,000	8,500	7,500	7,000	6,000	5,000	3,000	500	3,000	8,500	11,500	12,500	11,500	9,500
Expenses														
Set up your business	1,000 Set Up													
Source fabric, design and make collection	500 A/W	1,000 A/W	500 A/W				500 S/S	1,000 S/S	500 S/S					
Sales and marketing				1,000 A/W							1,000 S/S			
Production					1,000 A/W	2,000 A/W	5,000 A/W				1,000 S/S	2,000 S/S	5,000 S/S	
Deliver to Store								500 A/W						500 S/S
Total Expenses ($/£)	1,500	1,000	500	1,000	1,000	2,000	5,500	1,500	500	1,000	1,000	2,000	5,000	500
Closing Statement ($/£)	8,500	7,500	7,000	6,000	5,000	3,000	-2,500	-1,000	2,500	7,500	10,500	10,500	6,500	9,000

Solution to Exercise 3 Figure 13.4: Fashion Project Profit and Loss Statement - shows the profit and loss using the Accrual Method over the full A/W fashion design and production cycle and the S/S design and production cycle up to the delivery of garments to the stores. Unplanned negative cashflow is a trap that will put a company out of business. Although the profit and loss calculations for the A/W (Fall) and S/S collections are both going to make a profit, they will both incur negative cashflow and the overlap, in the middle of the year, will compound the size of the negative cashflow.

2. Design Style Sheets/Specification Sheets: These documents are used extensively in the fashion industry to present information about the garments/products to ensure they are made to the required specifications and include; the technical drawing, fabrics, measurement, colour, etc.

DESIGN STYLE SHEET/SPECIFICATION SHEET

Style No	Designer	Customer/Buyer	CMT/Factory
Season: S/S Yr	Pattern Maker	Department	Sample Size
Commitment No	Machinist	Delivery	Created
		Colour	Modified
		Units	Approved
			To Grade

FABRIC DETAILS		GARMENT DESCRIPTION		
Fabric Swatch	**Description**			
	Design	**GENERAL NOTES/TRIMS**		**NOTES CONT'D**
	Type	Fusing Info		
	Order No	Binding Details		
	Composition	Zip		
	Quality	Seams		
	Weight	Seams		
	Width	Hems		
	Open/Tubular	Wash		
	Sub Sampling	Label Position		
	Check Repeat	Buttons (type, size, quantity)		
	Bulk Del. Due	Thread		
	Sample Fabric	Swing Ticket		
	Design	Wash		
		RATING		

FRONT DESIGN	PATTERN MAKER NOTES
	(Specific measurements - lengths, widths etc.)
	CUTTER NOTES
	(Specific cutting instructions)
	MACHINIST NOTES
	(Specific sewing instructions)
	BACK DESIGN

3. Costing Sheets: Cost sheets list all the required information to calculate the total costs to manufacture the garments or products, and establish the required selling prices (wholesale and/or retail) and includes; the material/trims ratings and costs, processes, time costs, and all relevant information as shown in the example below.

COSTING SHEET

Style No		Buyer		Delivery Date			Units	

Commit No		Dept		Style Description				

FABRICS

Fabric Description	Colour	Order No	Width	Rating	Rate + 7%	EST Cost	ACT Cost	Value
					0			0
					0			0
					0			0
					0			0
						FABRIC TOTAL		

TRIMS / RATING

Supplier	Description	Size/Type	Order No	Reference No	Mtrs/Yds	Quantity	Price		Value
	Hanger	Dress 10							
	Brand Label	Woven				1			
	Fabric Label					1			
	Wash Care	Dry Clean				1			
	Swing Ticket	Embossed				1			
	Polybag								
	Cut Bias	25 mm				0.88			
	H/ Tape	Branded							
							TRIMS TOTAL		

GARMENT SKETCH

Fabric + Trims	
Waste	
CMT	
Grand Total	
Mark Up	
Selling Price	
Gross Profit	
Retail Selling Price	
Sold to Buyer	
Actual RSP	
Actual Profit %	

4. Range/Line Sheets: These are a catalogue of all the styles available in a product range and are used to market the collection to the retail buyers. They include; flats/working drawings of the range, the fabrics and colours available, prices, and perhaps photographs of the products.

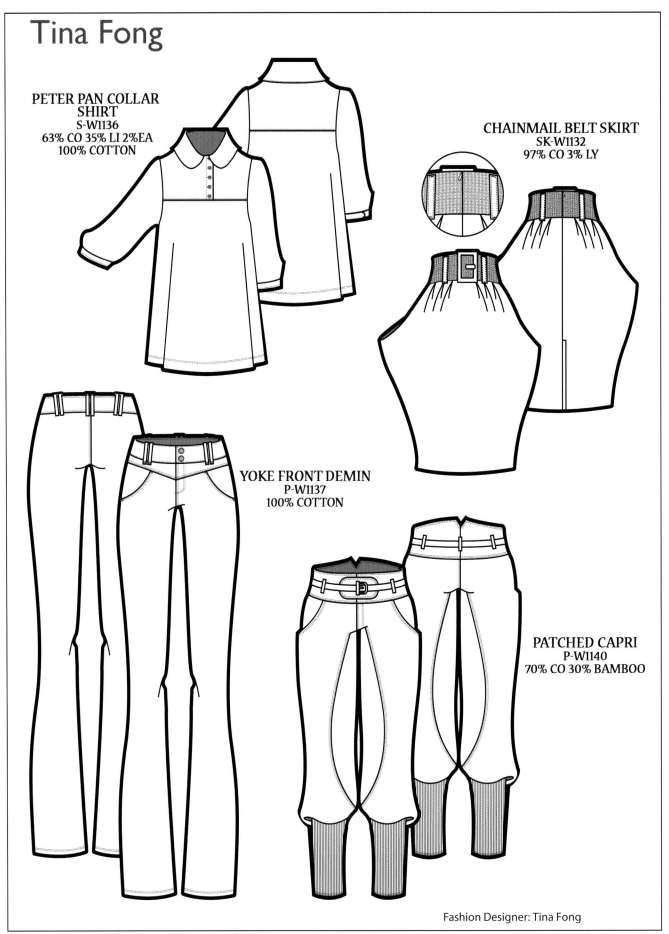

Tina Fong

PETER PAN COLLAR SHIRT
S-W1136
63% CO 35% LI 2%EA
100% COTTON

CHAINMAIL BELT SKIRT
SK-W1132
97% CO 3% LY

YOKE FRONT DEMIN
P-W1137
100% COTTON

PATCHED CAPRI
P-W1140
70% CO 30% BAMBOO

Fashion Designer: Tina Fong

5. Order Confirmation Forms/Documents: These forms are written out by the sales person and list all the necessary information with regard to the customers' orders. This information is required to produce, ship and bill the customer for the products.

ORDER CONFIRMATION				Purchase Order No				
Date								
Bill To:				**Ship To:**				
Name				**Name**				
Address				**Address**				
Phone				**Phone**				
Mob/Cell				**Mob/Cell**				
Email				**Email**				

Buyer	Store	Dept	Start Date	Complete Date	Cancel Date	In Store By	Sales Rep
Terms		**Shipping Specification**		**Packaging**			
Special Instructions							

Style	Description	Sizes				Colour	Quantity	Unit Price	Total
		XS	S	M	L				
							ORDER TOTAL		
							GRAND TOTAL		
Authorised By		**Title**		**Date**				

Glossary

Inspired by fabric!
Illustration: Courtesy of Eric Hagen, UTS.

Accounts: The financial records of the business including the cashflow statement, the profit and loss statement, and the balance sheet.

Assets: An asset is anything of worth that a person or business owns.

B2B (Business-to-Business): Trade between businesses.

Balance Sheet: Is a financial 'snapshot' of your business at a given time (usually at the end of the financial year). It lists your assets, your liabilities and the difference between the two, which are your equity or net worth. Where assets = liabilities + owner's equity.

Bespoke (Clothing/Tailoring [a bespoke tailor]): Custom-made garments, specifically individual, made-to-measure tailoring for men's suits.

Brainstorming: A group method of generating a flood of creative ideas and novel solutions.

Branding: The process a company uses to identify and communicate its product or services and provide customers with assurances of a level of quality and consistency of standard.

Breakeven Point: The number of products the company needs to sell to cover the setup costs - after this point the company starts to make a profit.

Business Angels: Private investors who invest their own capital to seed entrepreneurial ventures and offer support and guidance (mentoring) to help entrepreneurs establish their new businesses.

Business Plan: An all encompassing document which outlines how the company will produce the product and confirm the new venture is feasible.

Cash Book: Collates and documents all the business transactions into a cash book (manual and/or computerized).

Cashflow: The money that flows in and out of the business each day - typically presented as a monthly snap shot.

Cluster: See Fashion Cluster.

Company (Limited): A legal entity that is separate from its owner/s. Companies are registered and must operate in accordance with company laws. Liability of each shareholder is restricted to the amount of their actual investment in the business.

Competitive Advantage: The strategies, skills, knowledge, resources and competencies that differentiate a business from its competitors - this may be by offering a product which customers find is more attractive than the competitors'.

Competitor: A business that provides the same or similar products and operates in the same market or location.

Compliance Costs: The cost of complying with government rules and regulations (red tape).

Consignment: A shipment of goods with the provision that payment is expected only on sales of the goods and that unsold items may be returned.

Cool Hunters : A person who investigates and predicts cutting-edge trends, fashions, and ideas and sells them as market research to companies so they can incorporate them into their latest products.

Creditor: A person or company to whom money is owed. (Someone who gives you credit. Someone you owe money to.)

Debtor: A person who owes money. (Someone who owes a debt. Someone who owes you money.)

Decision-Making: Decision-making focuses on gaining the collective support of the team members to commit company resources to implement an agreed course of action.

Depreciation: A decrease in value through age, wear or deterioration. Depreciation is accepted as a normal business expense.

Diffusion Lines/Label: A line of clothing that is secondary or lower in price, and a simplified version of a designer brand - but is still associated with the brand as a label of desire and good design.

Distribution: The process of moving a product within the supply chain.

Dragons' Den: A television programme that originated in Japan. The format, which now airs internationally, consists of entrepreneurs pitching their ideas to secure investment finance from business experts/venture capitalists/business angels.

Enterprise: A bold undertaking or business activity which shows initiative and foresight - characterized by innovation, creative thinking, dynamism, and risk.

Entrepreneur: A person who identifies an opportunity or new idea and exploits and develops it into a new venture or project.

Equity: The value of a business owned by the shareholders after all the debts and liabilities have been taken into account. A financial investment in a business. An **equity investment** carries with it a share of ownership of the business, a stake in the profits and a say in how it is managed.

Equity Investor: Funds provided for company growth in exchange for a shareholding in the venture.

Estimating: Uses estimating techniques to predict future costs, incomes and durations.

Fashion: A succession of ever changing trends, fads and concepts.

Fashion Cluster: Clusters develop when a number of companies operating in similar businesses set up in the same location. This facilitates the cross flow of ideas and sharing of resources.

Feasibility Study: An investigation into a proposed venture to confirm it will work, confirm there is a market, and ensure it is making the best use of the entrepreneur's resources.

Focus Group: A form of qualitative research where people are brought together to openly discuss their thoughts on a particular product, service, concept, the price, the packaging, advertising etc.

Franchise: An agreement enabling the franchisee to sell or provide a product or service owned by the manufacturer or supplier (franchisor). The franchise is regulated by a franchise agreement that specifies the terms and conditions of the franchise. The franchise fee usually includes management systems, equipment, training and support.

Franchisee: The person who buys the rights from the franchisor to operate the franchise business.

Franchisor: The person who sells the rights to the franchisee to operate the franchise business.

Funding: Money required to set up and run a business.

Grading: The process of mathematically adjusting a pattern to meet a range of specific sizes.

Growth Phase: Small businesses pass through a number of recognisable phases, beginning with the set up phase and the survival phase, followed by the growth phase where the company rapidly grows as the demand for the product increases.

Guerilla Marketing: Marketing tactics available to every small firm to compete with bigger firms by carving out narrow but profitable niches.

Hypnagogia: A state of deeply relaxed consciousness, between sleep and waking-up, during which flashes of inspiration and creative insight often appear. Researchers have found these transition periods to be quite short, seldom more than ten minutes.

Incubator: A business centre which helps to develop fledgling start up businesses until they can operate successfully on their own. The incubator provides access to shared facilities, support and networking.

Indie Designers: Include independent designers, artists and crafts people who design and make a wide array of products without being part of large, industrialized businesses.

Innovation: Is more than a flash of inspiration, it is the systematic development and implementation of creative ideas.

Intrapreneur: A person acting as an entrepreneur within a company environment.

Inventory: All stocked goods/merchandise - fabric, trims, garments, finished goods which a company has available to sell.

IPO: Initial Public Offering is the sale of company equity through the stock market.

Jobbers: A trader who acts as a middleman and buys inventory (surplus stock/fabric) from manufacturers or wholesalers and resells the goods to fashion designers and fashion businesses who do not require large quantities of cloth or cannot afford the minimum wholesale lengths.

Just-in-Time (JIT): JIT Manufacturing or JIT inventory - manufacturing and stock-control system where goods are produced and delivered just-in-time in response to consumer demand. This eliminates waste and avoids the need for large inventories.

Liability: Is something owed (a debt), or a claim a creditor has against the company's assets.

Market Research: The study and questioning of groups of people to help determine the target market, determine what products they want, and determine the competition, to ensure a product has competitive advantage and the best chance of success.

Marketing: The co-ordinated process to promote and inform potential customers and existing customers of the company's products or services and create an interest.

Marketing Strategy/Plan: A document outlining marketing objectives, strategies and activities, usually part of the business plan.

Marking: The process used to determine the best layout when cutting each pattern piece for a garment/style.

Mentor: An experienced business person (often previously an entrepreneur) who offers their advice (usually gratis) to start up companies.

Negotiation: The process of resolving differences between two or more parties, preferably using the win-win collaborative approach.

Networking: The ability to connect with a broad range of contacts for the purpose of sharing useful information and resources. The relationship is usually mutually advantageous and collaborative (win-win).

Niche Market: A non-mainstream market, usually small and requiring specialised skills.

Offshoring: Outsourcing work to an overseas company.

Opportunities: Business opportunities are ideas and changes which will give the entrepreneur competitive advantage over their competitors.

Organic Growth: Is the rate of business expansion through increasing output and sales as opposed to mergers and acquisitions. The focus is on internal actions taken to expand the company as opposed to external influences. Organic growth is a good indicator of how well management has used internal resources to expand profits.

Outsourcing: The term used when a product or service task which has previously been carried out within the company (an inside source), is now being purchased from another company (an outside source). It usually refers to non-core activities which can be performed cheaper by an outside company that specialises in that line of work. Outsourcing also reduces operational costs and capital expenditure on equipment.

Partnership: When two or more people set up a business together. Partnerships benefit from the interaction and complementary skills of the members. However, this needs to be balanced with the risk of each partner being liable for all the partnership debts and unpaid taxes.

Payback Period: The time it takes to reach the breakeven point, or the length of time it will take for an investor to recoup the set up costs.

Point of Difference (POD): See Unique Selling Point.

Portfolio of Skills (Body of Knowledge): The fashion entrepreneur's portfolio of skills is an inclusive term used to describe the sum of the knowledge of the industry; the skills, creativity, tools and techniques within the fashion profession.

Pre-Production: The processes necessary to produce the products/garments before production.

Primary Data: Data obtained through questionnaires, interviews and focus groups.

Problem Solving: Generating a number of technical solutions to solve a problem, which is then handed over to the decision-making function to select the solution which enjoys the widest support and commitment from the team members.

Production: The construction process by which products or garments are made – in the fashion industry this is the manufacture of garments or products which results from the orders collated after the sales of a collection.

Production Sample (Sealing/Sealed Sample): The approved sample that serves as the approved standard to which the production must be made.

Products: Goods or services the entrepreneur intends to manufacture and sell.

Profit and Loss Statement: Collates the incomes and expenses of a product, and calculates the bottom line; whether the product will make a profit or loss for the business.

Project Management: Management techniques used to plan and control change, particularly implementing a new venture.

Qualitative Research: Data based on a customer's attitudes, views and feelings.

Quantitative Research: Data based on numerical information (sales figures, people's sizes).

Ready-to-Wear: Clothing separates, apparel that is mass produced, also known as off-the-peg and prêt à porter.

Risk Management: Procedures to identify, quantify and respond to minimise the risks and uncertainties which could prevent the business operating efficiently.

Secondary Data: Data obtained through published information, government statistics, libraries, etc.

Shareholder: A person who owns equity in a company.

Small Business Management: The management of a small company on a day-to-day basis.

SME: Small Medium (sized) Enterprise - companies with 0-250 employees.

Sole Trader (Sole Proprietorship): A form of business ownership in which one person owns the entire business, earns all the profits and assumes all the risks and losses.

Stakeholder: Any company or person who has an interest in the venture.

Start Up Company: A company formed to implement/exploit an opportunity.

Sub-Brand: A product/service that has a persona and brand values that separate it from the parent brand. A product or service that has its own brand identity, which is proprietary and can be trademarked.

Success-Disaster: The situation that occurs when production cannot supply the increasing demand for the product, leading to manufacturing chaos and financial difficulties.

Supply Chain (Value Chain): The vertical integration of the key links in the supply chain from textiles to retail (sales to the customer). At each point on the supply chain there are potential business opportunities for the fashion entrepreneur.

Sustainable Growth: Using retained profits to consistently grow the business.

SWOT Analysis: Quantifies your present strengths and weaknesses, and your future opportunities and threats.

Triggers: In the entrepreneurial context, events and situations that encourage someone to start their own business or venture.

Unique Selling Point (USP) or Point of Difference (POD): A particular element that makes a product/service different from anything else on the market and gives competitive advantage.

Variance: The difference between two numbers. In financial accounting it is the difference between actual expenses and the budgeted amount.

Venture Capital: Funding provided by investment companies looking for high growth businesses.

Viral Marketing: To promote a product/service/brand, a message is passed from person to person using social networks (Facebook, YouTube, MySpace), and through viral promotions such as, video clips, interactive Flash games, e-books, and text messaging.

Warehousing: The facility used to store merchandise or other materials or equipment. Warehousing usually involves storing, stock control, inventory control and retrieval.

Wholesale: The selling of goods/merchandise from business to business (retail) - usually in bulk quantity and includes terms and conditions that might cover discounts and credits.

Zeitgeist: Reflect the spirit of the times.

Internet Resources

'The Cyber Information Runway to Success'. As an emerging fashion entrepreneur, you can travel on the Internet global information highway to search for information and advice to help you start and develop your new venture. This includes; small business startup topics, financial advice, small business management advice, tax rules and regulations; and fashion and textile industry topics including; the latest fashions and trends, trend forecasting agencies and publications, fashion and textile shows, fashion and textile suppliers, manufacturers, PR agencies, stylists, and wholesalers etc. All this in less time than it takes to pack a suit case and jump on a plane to a fashion show!

The Internet is your international fashion **Yellow Pages**, an A to Z for entrepreneurial, small business fashion ventures. Listed here are examples of the sites and the type of information available. You should do a **key word** search using a search engine such as Google to find the information you need pertaining to your specific location and country.

Fashion and Small Business Resources

www.bl.uk: The British Library - researching business information on the fashion industry (each country will have something similar).

www.businessandemployment.biz: Business plans and advice, AUS.

www.businesslink.gov.uk: Practical advice for business; starting up, grants, taxes, health and safety, regulations, licences, contacts, trading abroad and exporting.

www.businesslink4london.com: Specifically London

www.census.gov: Statistics and reports on population (age, sex, martial status), income, wholesale and retail trade (online sales, shopping centres), US.

www.cfda.com: Council of Fashion Designers of America - Non-profit trade organization for North-American designers of fashion and fashion accessories.

www.creativelondon.org.uk: Creative London, centre for fashion - offers support to emerging early stage London fashion start-ups.

www.design-online.net: Design online (Designer Forum) supports the business of fashion and textiles, UK.

www.fashion-enterprise.com: London's pioneering business incubator, supporting and nurturing emerging fashion design talent, CFE at London College of Fashion.

www.fashion-incubator.com: Interactive site on the fashion industry and lessons from the sustainable factory floor.

www.fashionontheedge.com: FOTEuk., website for independent fashion designers, events, exhibitions etc.

www.fitnyc.edu: Fashion Institute of Technology, New York, business classes and computer training.

www.fsb.org.uk: The Federation of Small Businesses.

www.lloydstsbbusiness.com: Small Business Guide Lloyds, TSB.

www.londonapparel.com: London Apparel Resource Centre (LARC) and Production Innovation Centre (PIC), services, support, courses and space for startup business.

www.londonfashionweek: Events, news, British Fashion Council link.

www.pbc.co.uk: Portobello Business Centre, non-profit organisation which aims to help start-up and existing businesses to grow and succeed.

www.princes-trust.org.uk: The Prince's Trust support for young people, for entrepreneurs, for start-up, money for business.

www.sba.gov: Small Business Administration, support, resources, tools for small businesses, US.

www.sbinfocanada.about.com: Small business info.

www.score.org: The Service Corp of Retired Executives (SCORE) mentoring, advice from successful business advisors, US.

www.smallbusinessbureau.org.uk: The Small Business Bureau, UK.

www.statistics.gov.uk: Access to data produced by the Office for National Statistics, government departments.

www.ukfashionexports.com: Export, sourcing, shows.

www.uspto.gov: US patent and trademark office.

www.womenintothenetwork.co.uk: Network support.

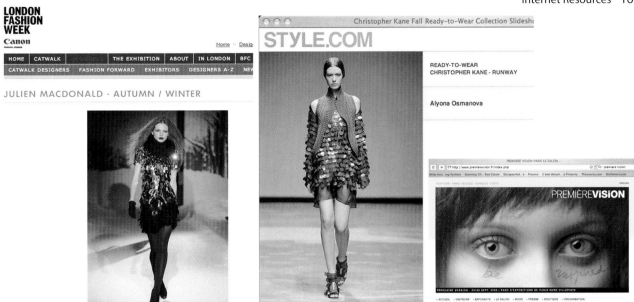

Trade Shows / Sourcing

www.apparelnews.net: Trade shows and more.

www.apparelsearch.com: Fashion industry news search for services, events, shopping globally, one of best sites for sourcing information.

www.cottoninc.com: Search for fabrics globally.

www.fashioncenter.com: Based in New York's Garment District - provides lists of factories, fabrics and services.

www.fashioncoop.com: Designer Market, details of events, US.

www.infomat.com: Fashion industry search engine - fashion calendar, manufacturers apparel, textile and accessories products, global.

www.premierevision.fr: Première Vision, the key fabric trade fair held in Paris.

Fashion Trends / Forecasting

www.fashion.net: Great research site, hypertext links short cuts to other sites, fashion magazines and general industry news.

www.fashionangel.com: Fashion designers and magazines on the Net - updated daily, linked with www. FUK.co.uk (fashion shows and more).

www.fashionguide.com: Info, sourcing, brands, shopping, and links to other fashion/clothing related sites.

www.fashionmall.com: An international fashion industry Yellow Pages list from A to Z, dedicated to fashion; update on collections, seasonal highlights and what to wear.

www.fashionwindows.com: Great site, listing fashion trends, runway shows and a calendar of events.

www.global-color.com: Forecasting company, information and inspiration for colours and trends.

www.infomat.com: Excellent information on services used by the fashion industry worldwide; from designers, publications to retail organisations.

www.londonfashionweek.co.uk: Great catwalk shows.

www.modaitalia.com: Fashion from Italy plus a lot more such as; textiles, beauty, fashion calendar.

www.promostyl.com: International design agency researching trends, selling their books and products online.

www.style.com: Excellent site linked with Vogue and W; video and slide coverage of the latest designer fashion shows; celebrity style, trend reports and breaking fashion news.

www.stylesight.com: Trend forecasting.

www.thetrendreport.com: Cool site! Fashion runways, editorial and consumer buying.

www.wgsn.com: WGSN, Worth Global Style Network, latest news and reviews of the developing fashions and trends around the world, and daily fashion news.

New Sites: The Internet is constantly developing as more companies make the transition to using and establishing their presence on the Internet. Key word searches are the only sure way of accessing the latest sites and information.

Further Reading

 This selection of books and periodicals will keep you informed about fashion business and entrepreneurship, fashion design, fashion illustration and future trends. With growing public interest in fashion, most countries now have their own fashion based publications. For more information do a keyword search on the Internet and visit the fashion bookshops and websites such as *Franks Bookshop*, London, **www.rdfranks.co.uk**, and *The Fashion Bookshop,* LA, **www.thefashionbookstore.com**.

Fashion Business

Bruce, Margaret, and **Hines**, Tony, *Fashion Marketing: Contemporary Issues,* Butterworth Heinemann

Easey, Mike, *Fashion Marketing,* Blackwell

Gehlar, Mary, *The Fashion Designer Survival Guide,* Dearborn

Goworek, Helen. (2006), *Careers in Fashion & Textiles,* Blackwell Publishing

Granger, Michele, and **Sterling**, Tina, *Fashion Entrepreneurship Retail Business Planning,* Fairchild

Harder, Frances, *Fashion for Profit,* Harder Publications

Jackson, Tim, and **Shaw**, David, *The Fashion Handbook,* Routledge

Raymond, Martin, *Tomorrow People,* Pearson

Entrepreneurship

Belbin, Meredith, *Management Teams,* Butterworh-Heinemann

Bolton, W.K. and **Thompson**, J.L. (2000), *Entrepreneurs - Talent, Temperament, Technique,* Butterworth Heinemann

Burke, Rory, *Entrepreneurs Toolkit,* Burke Publishing

Burke, Rory, *Introduction to Project Management,* Burke Publishing

Burke, Rory, *Project Management Leadership,* Burke Publishing

Burke, Rory, *Small Business Entrepreneur,* Burke Publishing

Burns, Paul. (2001), *Entrepreneurship and Small Business,* Palgrave Macmillan

Chell, E. *Entrepreneurship: Globalisation, Innovation and Development,* Thomson

Frederick, H. and **Kuratko**, D. (2006). *Australasian Entrepreneurship: Theory, Practice and Process,* Thomson Learning

Kirby, David. *Entrepreneurship,* McGraw-Hill

Lang, Jack. (2002), *The High-Tech Entrepreneur's Handbook,* FT.com

Legge, John, and **Hindle**, Kevin. (2004), *Entrepreneurship Context, Vision and Planning*, Palgrave Macmillan

Porter, Michael, *The Competitive Advantage of Nations*, MacMillan

Roddick, Anita. (2002), *Business As Unusual*, Thorsons

Williams, Sara. (2003), *Lloyds TSB Small Business Guide*, Penguin

Fashion Design and Illustration

Armstrong, Jeni, *From Pencil to Pen Tool,* Fairchild Books

Abling, Bina, *Fashion Sketchbook,* Fairchild

Borrelli, Laird, *Fashion Illustration by Fashion Designers,* Chronicle Books

Burke, Sandra, *Fashion Artist - Drawing Techniques to Portfolio Presentation,* second edition, Burke Publishing

Burke, Sandra, *Fashion Computing - Design Techniques and CAD,* Burke Publishing

Callan, Georgina O'Hara, *The Thames and Hudson Dictionary of Fashion and Fashion Designers,* Thames and Hudson

Dawber, Martin, *Big Book of Fashion Illustration,* Batsford

Jenkyn Jones, Sue, *Fashion Design,* second edition, Laurence King

Lazear, Susan, *Adobe Illustrator for Fashion Design,* Prentice Hall

McKelvey, Kathryn, *Fashion Source Book,* Blackwell Science

Morris, Bethan, *Fashion Illustrator,* Laurence King

Seivewright, Simon, *Research and Design,* AVA Publishing

Stipelman, Steven, *Illustrating Fashion: Concept to Creation,* Fairchild

Tain, Linda, *Portfolio Presentation For Fashion Designers,* Fairchild

Zaman, Zarida, *The Fashion Designer's Directory of Shape and Style,* Barrons

Trade Publications / Journals

California Apparel News (US)

Daily News Record (DNR) (Men's Fashions) (American)

Drapers Record (British)

Fashion Business International (World)

Fashion Forecast International

Fashion Theory: The Journal of Body, Dress and Culture

Gap Press

Journal of Fashion Marketing and Management

International Textiles (British)

Retail Week

Textile Report (Trend info for Fashion and Textiles)

Trends View on Colour (British)

View - Textile View Magazine (British)

WeAr (Collections, Stores, Market News - Global)

Woman's Wear Daily (WWD) (American)

Zoom on Fashion Trends

Trend / Fashion Forecast Services

Doneger Design Direction (American)

Faces Fashion Reports (British)

Fashion News (British)

Jill Lawrence Design (British, Fashion and Colour)

Lutz Keller (Colour)

Milou Ket (Trends, Colours - Netherlands)

Nelly Rodi (French, Colour and Global Lifestyles)

Pantone View Colour Planner

Pat Tunsky, Inc. (Trends, Forecast - American)

Perclers Paris

Promostyl USA (American)

Stylists Information Services (SIS) (American)

The Fashion Service (American)

The Wool Bureau (American)

Trend Union

Trends West (American, Trends and Textiles)

Trendzine (On-Line Forecast and Trends)

WGSN - Worth Global Style Network - www.wgsn.com

Periodicals

Another Magazine (British)

Collezioni (Italian): Trends, Sport and Street, Ready to Wear, Accessori, Bambini (children), Donna, Uomo (men)

Dazed and Confused (British)
Elle (American, Australian, British, French, German, Italian, SA, Spanish Publications)

Fashion Collections GAP (American)

Fashion Show (American)

Fruits (Japan)

GQ (Men)

Harpers and Queen (British)

Harper's Bazaar (American, Italian)

ID (British)

Joyce (Hong Kong)

L'Officiel da la Couture (French)

Marie Claire (American, Australian, British, French, German, Italian, SA, Spanish publications)

Oyster (Australian)

Pop (British)

Street (Japan)

Tank

This is a Magazine

Vogue (American, Australian, British, French, German, Italian, SA, Spanish publications): also **L'Uomo**, Bambini, Vogue Sposa Italia

W (American)

Wallpaper (British)

Online Magazines

Use search engines to look for online fashion magazines; Elle, Harpers Bazaar, Vogue, Marie Claire, etc.

www.elle.com: Excellent Street Style.

www.papermag: New York based, focusing on downtown New York, updated daily with cutting edge coverage on fashion, catwalk shows, trends.

www.vogue.com: Vogue guide to European shows.

Index

project management series

Introduction to Project Management
Rory Burke
ISBN: 978-0-9582733-3-6, 288 pages

This book is a broad based introduction to the field of Project Management which explains all the special planning and control techniques needed to manage projects successfully. This book is ideal for; managers entering project management, team members in the project management office (PMO), and undergraduate programmes.

Project Management Techniques
Rory Burke
ISBN: 978-0-9582733-4-3, 384 pages

This book presents the latest planning and control techniques, particularly those used by the project management software and the body of knowledge (APM bok and PMI's PMBOK). This book has established itself internationally as the standard text for Project Management programs.

Project Management Leadership - Building Creative Teams
Rory Burke and Steve Baron
ISBN: 978-0-9582733-5-0, 384 pages

This book is a comprehensive guide outlining the essential leadership skills to manage the human side of managing projects. Key topics include: leadership styles, delegation, motivation, negotiation, conflict resolution, and team building.

Entrepreneurs Toolkit
Rory Burke
ISBN: 978-0-9582391-4-1, 160 pages

Entrepreneurs Toolkit is a comprehensive guide outlining the essential entrepreneur skills to spot a marketable opportunity, the essential business skills to start a new venture and the essential management skills to make-it-happen.

Small Business Entrepreneur
Rory Burke
ISBN: 978-0-9582391-6-5, 160 pages

Small Business Entrepreneur is a comprehensive guide outlining the essential management skills to run a small business on a day-to-day basis. This includes developing a business plan and sources of finance.

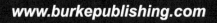

www.burkepublishing.com

bluewater cruising books

This *Bluewater Trilogy* includes a preparation guide, a travelogue and a checklist. Bluewater cruising has all the features of a complex project, requiring effective budgeting, procurement, scope management and time planning. Most importantly it requires effective risk management and disaster recovery for the safety of the crew and integrity of the yacht.

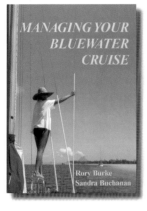

Managing Your Bluewater Cruise

Rory and Sandra Burke
ISBN: 978-0-473-03822-9

352 pages, 200+ photographs

This **preparation guide** discusses a range of pertinent issues from establishing budgets and buying equipment to preventative maintenance and heavy weather sailing. The text works closely with the ORC category 1 requirements and includes many comments from other cruisers who are *'out there doing it'*. This book also outlines what training courses to attend before leaving, what gear to take, provisioning strategy and, equally important, how to stow it all. So if you wish to bridge the gap between fantasy and reality then your bluewater cruise must be effectively managed.

Greenwich to the Dateline

Rory and Sandra Burke
ISBN: 978-0-620-16557-0

352 pages, 200+ photographs

This is a **travelogue** of our bluewater cruising adventure from the Greenwich Meridian to the International Dateline – sit back with a sundowner and be inspired to cruise to the Caribbean and Pacific islands. In this catalogue of rewarding experiences we describe how we converted our travelling dreams into a bluewater cruising reality.

Bluewater Checklist

Rory and Sandra Burke
ISBN: 978-0-9582391-0-3, 96 pages

Checklists provide an effective management tool to confirm everything is on board, and all tasks are completed. Why try to remember everything in your head when checklists never forget!!! This book provides a comprehensive portfolio of checklists covering every aspect of bluewater cruising. To ensure your bluewater cruise will be successful, it must be effectively managed. Checklists provide an excellent tool for this purpose - even NASA uses them!!!

www.burkepublishing.com

fashion design series

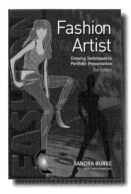

Fashion Artist - *Drawing Techniques to Portfolio Presentation, 2ed*
Sandra Burke, ISBN: 978-0-9582391-7-2, 176 pages

Fashion drawing is an essential part of the fashion designer's portfolio of skills, enabling the designer to develop creative ideas and visually communicate design concepts on paper. This book is set out as a self-learning programme on how to draw fashion figures and clothing/flats, render fabrics, create fashion illustrations and mood/story boards, and present them in a portfolio. The text is fully supported with self-explanatory drawings and artwork from international fashion illustrators and fashion designers.

Fashion Entrepreneur - *Starting Your Own Fashion Business*
Sandra Burke, ISBN: 978-0-9582733-0-5, 176 pages

This book outlines the entrepreneurial traits, creative and innovative techniques, and small business management skills you need to start, develop and operate a successful fashion business. The theory is presented in easy steps, enhanced with inspirational fashion illustrations, visuals, interviews and case studies from established fashion entrepreneurs in the fashion and creative industries.

Fashion Designer – *Design Techniques, Catwalk to Street*
Sandra Burke, ISBN: 978-0-9582391-2-7, 176 pages

This book will help you develop your portfolio of fashion design skills while guiding you through the fashion design process in today's fashion industry. It explains how to analyse and forecast fashion trends, interpret a design brief, choose fabrics and colour ways, develop designs, create design presentations and develop collections for specific target markets.

Fashion Computing – *Design Techniques and CAD*
Sandra Burke, ISBN: 978-0-9582391-3-4, 176 Pages

This book introduces you to the computer drawing and design skills used in the fashion industry. Through visuals and easy steps, you learn creative fashion computing design techniques. It includes, flats/working drawings, illustrations, fabrics, presentations and the digital fashion portfolio. Specific software includes: Photoshop, Illustrator, CorelDRAW, Freehand, PowerPoint, Gerber and Lectra Systems.

Sandra Burke, M.Des RCA (Master of Design, Royal College of Art), is a fashion designer, author, publisher, and visiting lecturer to universities in Britain, America, Canada, South Africa, Australia, New Zealand, Hong Kong and Singapore.

"In writing these books I have combined my career in fashion, education and publishing to produce a fashion design series. The result is a combination of the educational requirements of fashion programmes with the practical application of fashion skills used in the fashion industry."

www.fashionbooks.info